MARY OF THE KORAN

*A Meeting Point
Between Christianity And Islam*

Original Drawing by Rev. Jerry McDonald OFMC, on facing page.

The artist explains the symbolism of the work:
The focus of the picture is the child Jesus. The tree and spring of water form a protective frame, symbolizing the protective providence of God. The figure of Mary and the prayer rug form a triangle, symbolizing that Mary's life was completely oriented to God above, being founded on prayer. Thus she was deemed worthy by the grace of God to bear Christ within herself.

The idea is inspired by the Koran's Sura 19, 22-27:

The Angel, Gabriel, brought Mary the good news:

"Thereupon she conceived, and retired to a far-off place. And when she felt the throes of childbirth, she lay by the trunk of a palm-tree, crying...

"But a voice...cried out to her: 'Do not despair. Your Lord has provided a brook that runs at your feet, and if you shake the trunk of this palm-tree, it will drop fresh ripe dates in your lap. Therefore wipe your eyes, and rejoice. Eat and drink...' "

MARY
OF THE KORAN

A MEETING POINT BETWEEN CHRISTIANITY AND ISLAM

by

Rev. Nilo Geagea
Translated and edited by
Rev. Lawrence T. Fares

Philosophical Library
New York

Library of Congress Cataloging in Publication Data

Geagea, Nilo.
    Mary of the Koran.

    Includes bibliographical references.
    1. Mary, Blessed Virgin, Saint, in the Koran. I. Fares,
Lawrence T., 1925-   . II. Title. BP133.7.M35G413   297
.24 82-3804 ISBN 0-8022-2395-8   AACR2

Copyright 1984 by Philosophical Library, Inc.
200 West 57th Street, New York, N.Y. 10019

Manufactured in the United States of America

The Vatican II Council, in a gesture of pastoral concern, entreats Christians and Moslems to live at peace together the world over.

The belief in Allah — One, Creator and Remunerator — is not the only basic dogma they share in common. In the Marian sector also, Islam finds itself largely in accord with Christianity. In the Koran, for instance, Mary outranks in dignity any other woman in the universe. Singularly favored by Allah, she is the mother-virgin of Issa (Jesus), pure, holy, devout, and an eminent model of faith, piety and self-restraint.

Contrary to the gloomy previsions of Hanna Zakarias, Mary remains a luminous point where Moslems and Christians may converge in brotherhood. And, as has been remarked by Sheik Hamza Boubakeur, the Rector of Paris Moslem Institute, the Blessed Virgin and her son are at once of interest to both Christians and Moslems — though from different motives. And whenever the cause of the Virgin Mother is brought into discussion, "the Moslem feels hurt in his deep convictions, upset in his veneration for the Virgin." Again, Mary "is dear to the two largest inspired religions of the world, Christianity and Islam."

Our present research has practically no other aim than to offer a positive contribution to an auspicious collaboration among Christians and Moslems toward the assertion of the values of the spirit and the triumph of the cause of Allah, through Mary's fascinating and attractive personality.

INTRODUCTION

We live in an age when dialogue has become not only a significant way of life, but also a necessity of survival. Our lives are constantly challenged with new understandings, experiences, problems and are bombarded with all sorts of new data and possibilities. Unless we enter into dialogue with the whole range of these challenges, our potential for growth will atrophy.

For the Christian believer, besides the wide spectrum of daily challenges he encounters in everyday life, there is the ever present need to dialogue with other religious traditions and faiths.

In recent years, in ways that have not been true of past generations, we have come face to face with the religion of Islam. Political and economic conditions in the Middle East have brought before us the lived experience of this historic faith as it is professed by millions in every part of the world.

The Christian would like to enter into dialogue with Islam in order to know it better and to uncover points of contact in the realm of religious belief and practice. He feels that he does not know Islam well until he knows what that person believes about the things that matter most; what man is, what is his nature, duty and destiny, what is right and wrong, and what is the meaning of life and death. Whatever the answers, these questions of "ultimate meaning" are religious and they are central to what makes each of us the unique person that he is!

In the process of knowing another, there are several things that make dialogue difficult. Dean M. Kelley and Bernhard E. Olson have outlined the main contours of that difficulty:

1) So many of modern man's relationships are impersonal, manipulative, exploitative, even predatory, that it is not easy for him to come out from behind his habitual defenses and to be both gentle and direct, to risk knowing and being known by other persons. Even when he tries, he is apt to slip back into his accustomed postures of offense or defense and thus bring the dialogue to a close before it has fully begun.

2) More serious than modern man's impersonality is ancient man's vehemence and vindictiveness about religion — which we have far from outgrown. So central are some of our religious convictions to our whole outlook on life that we are easily offended, even scandalized, by differing views. So much of our emotional capital is invested in them that we feel threatened, anxious, defensive or depressed if these certainties are questioned by the mere expression of an opposite opinion.

3) It can be stimulating to explore the ideas of those with whom we disagree — for a while — if they do not lie "too close to home." Not only in religion, but in politics, economics and family life, we have a limited tolerance of dissent. After we have "patiently" explained the "correct" view for the seventh time, it may become more exasperating than stimulating to discover that it still is not accepted! We must be prepared to contemplate disagreements — not only temporary but permanent disagreements — and to see in them the precious reality of another person whose being and direction are marvelously independent of our own.

4) Conversation across religious lines is especially difficult when generations of conflict have left scars of bitterness and

resentment. Islam and Christianity have been separated by centuries of alienation. Are we able to surmount the memories of this history? These are not merely centuries but millennia of hostility to overcome.

The problem is compounded in the present effort to establish dialogue between Christianity and Islam. Dr. Riffat Hassan, Professor of Islamic Studies at the University of Louisville, pointed out these present obstacles:

1) Some Islamic scholars see this dialogue as a plot to drain Islam of its spiritual depth.

2) There is a great fear that this dialogue is only a subterfuge used to proselytize Islamic believers in countries where they are a minority.

3) There is really nothing to talk about. Islamic believers see their religious faith clearly. The Koran holds the key to all that must be believed and therefore one must take it or leave it. There is no need for dialogue.

On the other hand, Islam is living through a period of great development — one of the most important periods in its history. It is possible that dialogue can be of help in this world situation. The need for dialogue is further encouraged by the quest for peace, which requires that misunderstandings must be avoided. Many insights can be learned from Islam.

In view of these difficulties, how can we hope to lift the obstacles to dialogue? Were our human efforts the sole hope of reconciliation, then that hope would indeed be vain. Stubborn as man sometimes may be, the God of Mercy and Forgiveness has implanted in us the possibilities of becoming more like what He wanted us to be. We can clear away the obstacles that stand in His way, offer ourselves as channels of His will, and leave the outcome in His hands.

It is in this context that we welcome the translation by the

Reverend Lawrence T. Fares of the important study **Mary of the Koran** by the Reverend Nilo Geagea.

It is not just another study of the relationship between Christianity and Islam. It is the work of immense scholarly importance and is rooted soundly in the Koran itself. This is not a work written for the faint-hearted ecumenist or those who dabble in inter-religious dialogue.

Its perspective is to say to both Christianity and Islam alike that the Koran is extremely important as a source of revelation. We must take seriously its message of faith. In this serious study we will, according to the author, discover that Mary is indeed "a luminous point where Islam and Christianity converge."

I commend this work to those many Islamic and Christian believers who would like to know each other better, not just as fellow citizens and neighbors, but as persons of faith. We will discover a forgotten kinship in whose warmth the alienation of the past will vanish like a bad but fading dream.

Rev. Alex J. Brunett
President, National Association of Diocesan
Ecumenical Officers.

Vatican II's Declaration on the Relationship of the Church to Non-Christian Religions

"Upon the Moslems, too, the Church looks with esteem. They adore one God, living and enduring, merciful and all-powerful, Maker of heaven and earth and Speaker to men. They strive to submit wholeheartedly even to His inscrutable decrees, just as did Abraham, with whom the Islamic faith is pleased to associate itself. Though they do not acknowledge Jesus as God, they revere Him as a prophet. They also honor Mary, His virgin mother; at times they call on her, too, with devotion. In addition, they await the day of judgment when God will give each man his due after raising him up. Consequently, they prize the moral life, and give worship to God especially through prayer, almsgiving, and fasting.

"Although in the course of the centuries many quarrels and hostilities have arisen between Christians and Moslems, this most sacred Synod urges all to forget the past and to strive sincerely for mutual understanding. On behalf of all mankind, let them make common cause of safeguarding and fostering social justice, moral values, peace, and freedom."

CONTENTS

Introduction 9

A Word to the Reader 19

Foreword 25

Chapter One — Analysis 37

  I. The Sources 45

    Sura 19, Maryam 46
      Time 46
      Structure 51
    Sura 3, The Imrans 54
      Time 54
      Structure 57

  II. The Content 59

    Mary's Nativity 60
    Retreat into the Temple 68

The Annunciation 74
The Messenger 76
The Message 80
Psychological Reaction 83
The Childbirth 89
Defense against an Outrageous Calumny 94
Eschatological Events 97

A) Sura 23, 50 98

B) Sura 5, 17 106

Chapter Two — Synthesis 113

I. Singular Position 114

II. Eminent Position 119

Mary Ayat for the Universe 121
Mary's Predestination 125
Mary's Purification 127
Mary's Singular Maternity 139
Mary's Unity with Christ 150
Mary's Eminent Dignity 155
Cult by Veneration 160
Cult by Invocation 163
Cult by Imitation 168
Mary Mathal, a Model 169
First Premise: Islam "ante litteram" 169
Second Premise: The Rehabilitation of the Woman ... 181
Mary, the "Moslem" 183
Mary, the Model 186
Model of Faith 193
Model of Religiosity 197
Model of Self-restraint 205

Chapter Three — Conclusion 211

I. Historic Origins 211

General Solution 219
Jewish Solution.................................... 220
Christian Solution 228
Partial Solution 233
Mary's Nativity.................................... 238
Presentation in the Temple........................ 242
The Annunciation 245
The Birth of Jesus 248

II. Dogmatic Remark............................... 252

III. Ecumenical Remark 255

Bibliography 279

Index of Authors 291

Index of Arabic Words 295

Index 305

A WORD TO THE READER

Dear Reader,

Christians and Moslems living together in peace is not an impossibility, as one might think; nor is it a dreamer's utopia. If attitudes are motivated by good will, mutual respect and understanding, it indeed can become a "way of life."

Here are two examples from personal experience to illustrate the point:

Lebanon in the 30's enjoyed a sense of relief under the French Protectorate. Her people, emancipated from the Turks, were regaining confidence in one another. In and around the major cities and towns schools were flourishing — "l'on y parle du français!" Business was rapidly picking up, and for the average citizen life seemed easier and happier.

Not so was it for two Lebanese young men, victims of the Ottoman 1914-18 draft: Tannouse, an unwavering Roman Catholic Maronite, and Mahmoud, a staunch Moslem Sunnite.

While hunting for means to support their families, they separately heard of *Katelby* — a secluded farm unit in the North, nestling within the slopes of the Akkar Mountains, at the skirts of Kobayath, my home town. Hilly, charmingly scenic, and murmuring with waters, this corner of Swiss Alps was deprived of roads, electricity and telephone; all it afforded were primitive opportunities for hard living — such as breeding livestock, growing crops, and felling trees for fuel, pine tar or charcoal.

Each decided in his own heart to give it a try as the only alternative. Neither however knew of the other's plans until a concurrence of circumstances brought them one morning to the same landlord, begging for farming land on lease.

Skeptical, the stern man asked: "Can you two really make it?"

Their eyes met. A silent entente was formulated. Turning then to the landlord, they answered: "*Naam, Effendi!*" — "Yes, Sir!"

"On a one-year tenancy?"

"*Amrak, Effendi!*" — "As you say, Sir!"

"Deal!"

The one-year experiment went on for three happy years, during which the new settlers lived in peace like two brothers — helping each other, respecting each other, and, more important, each avoiding what displeased the other.

Surprisingly, not only the children got along, but the wives as well.

Aisha, Mahmoud's wife, for instance, often ran short of kitchen salt, flour, or baking yeast. She just called on her neighbor for supplies till shopping day. Next, it will be her neighbor's turn; Nejmeh, Tannouse's wife, only hollered for whatever she needed. Unassumingly, each lady took the other for granted.

Religion was never an argument. Tannouse spoke of Mohammad always with deference, never asking why he took himself several wives, or why he had founded a new religion. For him, the Arabian was a *rasùl*, Allah's messenger, and a prophet. True or not, *"let the learned worry about it!"* he decided.

Nor has Mahmoud, in turn, accused his neighbor of worshipping three gods, or of claiming Jesus to be God's son. Speaking of Jesus, he always called him *Sayidna Issa* — "Our Lord Jesus." Mary is *Settena* — "Our Lady." Her picture, holding Baby Jesus and near St. Joseph, was honored in his home. "She is virgin, holy, Allah's chosen one."

Holidays were a source of joy for both to share. On Christmas, Mahmoud and his family came over to wish their neighbors, *"Merry Christmas!"* "Jesus belongs to us all!" On Ramadan, Tannouse and his family went over to wish their neighbors, *"Blessed Ramadan!"* "Mohammad is a baptized Christian too!" they admitted.

This saga ended in 1932, to the heartbreak of both. Grown up now, the children were due for advanced schooling, available only in a distant town.

Thirty years later, Tannouse's son, then Fr. Lawrence, was assigned to the Carmelite-run Catholic Mission of Kuwait, Persian Gulf, recently declared a diocese of its own. Besides manpower, the new Bishop badly needed a site and funds to erect a Cathedral, a grant reserved to the sole owner of the land — the Emir.

"Let us approach the Emir, then!" came the suggestion.

"You must be kidding!" was the answer, following a pause.

The idea, however feasible, sounded indeed like a joke. Ironically it condoned a morality unacceptable to the petitioner by his Old Seminary standards of a few years before. Yet the culprit question forced its way through the mind:

"*Will, or can, a Moslem King contribute to the building of a house for worship for an infidel?* — *a Christian associator, who worships other gods besides Allah?*"

The answer was obvious. And understandably so.

Was it so also for the Emir?

His Highness, Abdullah As-Salim, As-Subbah (may God rest his soul!), the father of modern Kuwait, was known to be a convinced Moslem. Deeply religious, and above all, very "humane" and tolerant, the good Papa-like Monarch enjoyed friendly terms with the staff of the Mission. Upon request, he granted the interview.

On the appointed day, a gate opened to admit us through a thick enclosure, showing a two-story clay-brick-edifice — the palace. Not fancy, rather humble. Only it rose a little higher than the average home in the area. A flight of stairs led us up to a waiting room, and on into a modest hall — at the end of which an empty divan waited, and a guard stood at attention nearby.

His Highness entered — majesty and simplicity and grandeur following him — and the richly decorated hall seemed at once full of his oriental presence.

We bowed reverently, then were motioned to sit down.

Bishop Stella turned to me, signaling, "Go ahead!"

"*Your Highness, Allah save you,*" said I, interpreting, "*His Excellency requests a piece of land in your kingdom on which to build a Church to worship Allah and honor Our Lady, Maryam.*"

Time seemed to stand still as our unbelieving eyes noticed the Emir's head nodding consent. There were questions chasing answers, at the end of which His Highness graciously granted the location and 38,000 Dinars (roughly $134,000) as an interest-free loan payable in ten years.

Two years later, the Statue of Our Lady of Arabia landed in Kuwait Airport, coming from Rome. Carved there from the Cedar wood of Lebanon and blessed by Pope Paul VI, a triumphal procession brought it to the Cathedral of the Holy Family. There, in her own Shrine, the Mother of Jesus is a live testimonial to the Arab King's munificence, a tangible evidence of mutual acceptance of Christianity and Islam.

Now the compelling question:

What turned out so right for our two young men, that cannot be a norm of behavior for the average Christian and Moslem in today's world? Or for Emir Abdullah and the Catholic Mission, that Christianity and Islam cannot take as a guideline for mutual relationship at an official level?

The secret?

"*Common sense, and good will*," thought Tannouse in 1963, then 75 and with only a few months left to live. That much he knew. And he said a mouthful.

"*Faith in Allah*," guessed the Emir, unaware of how proverbially "humane" and "good-hearted" he was. Not a trinitarian faith, but theological, nonetheless. Like Abraham's, accepting Allah in His strict unity, but still open to recognize Him as He really is, should He so one day be revealed. "**Were Allah, the Merciful, to have a son, I would be the first to adore him.**" (43, 81)

"*Common sense, good will, and a little faith*." Elemental basics, granted. But the only ones likely to set the right tone and mood for both parties in order to approach, better know, respect and accept one another — with the lid, of course, on all proselytizing, nationalistic and political aims.

To promote these basics so earnestly stressed by the Vatican II Council, **MARY OF THE KORAN** is presented to you with pleasure. A vision in my mind since college days in the late forties, Fr. Geagea masterfully brought it to light in *"Maria Nel Messaggio Coranico."*

The compilation as to structure remains unchanged, except for a few necessary retouches: The Koranic Text was rendered from the original script; the concept of revelation, its mechanics, and the God-man two-way relationship, clarified; the psychological solidarity between Mary and Jesus, elucidated. A few explanatory notes were added, quotations updated, Koranic parallelisms restored — and the like.

For people of good will, of all careers and walks — whether average citizens or in care of souls; whether in professional responsibility or public office — the book is a rare chance to broaden knowledge and sharpen skills toward a better ecumenical world, namely with Ismael's descendants — Abraham's great grandchildren.

For Christians and Moslems, it is a cordial invitation to come together and face one another, not just like one faces another person — *but like people who already share basic values in common: our faith in the same Allah, our Creator and Rewarder, and our veneration for Maryam,* "Settena" — "Our Lady," *and her son,* "Sayidna Issa" — "Our Lord Jesus"; like people, I love to repeat, who in the image of the characters above, resort to *wisdom, goodwill, and who believe!*

Lawrence T. Fares

Detroit, October 11, 1982
the 20th anniversary of the opening
of the Vatican II council

FOREWORD

The theme, **Mary and the Moslem World**, is not currently a leading issue in the literary market. Nor does it stir a productive output similar, for instance, to that inspired by Priesthood.[1] A quick survey of the Marian bibliography in the last two decades however, shows that there is, among a discreet handful of experts in Islamic and Mariological theology, a resurgence of interest in that theme, worthy not to be overlooked. In their eagerness to find out what place does Mary occupy in Islam, these Scholars have taken the subject to heart; they have delved into it deeply, some more and others less diligently; they have exposed their findings on it, some more and others less extensively; and they have indicated the sources of it, some more and others less competently.[2]

---

1. According to *Bibliographie Internationale sur le Sacerdoce et le Ministère*, published in 1971 by the "Centro di Documentazioni e Ricerche di Montreal," nearly seven thousand books and articles on the theme came to light in 1969 alone.

2. We shall give at the end of this study an alphabetical list of the main authors we've consulted, with a conventional abbreviation for each name for easier reference.

Their efforts contributed, as one can see, either to the development of the general theme, Mary in Islam,[3] or to essays of more modest dimensions, such as the Meccan History of Mary and Jesus;[4] Islam and the Immaculate Conception;[5] Mary's Assumption in the Koran;[6] the Mariological Preparation for Christ in Islam;[7] the Koran and Islam regarding Mary's Life and the Marian Theology;[8] Mary in the Doctrine and Piety of Islam;[9] the Islamic Cult of Mary in Syria;[10] the Islamic Cult at Mary's Tomb;[11] Islamic Reactions to Recent Catholic Manifestations, Doctrinal and Cultic, toward Mary.[12]

It has long been my intent to investigate *Islam's genuine*

---

3. Cf. JAL. I, *op. cit.* — IDEM, *El Islam ante la Virgen María* in Arbor, (1951), p. 1-27. — IDEM, *Islam and the Virgin Mother*, in *The Marian Era*, 2 (1961), p. 75-88. — IDEM, *María in Islam*, in *Mariolog. Stud.*, 3 (1964), p. 215-225. — COURTOIS V., *Mary in Islam*, Calcutta, The Oriental Institute, 1954. — ZARA PHILIPPE, *Marie et l'Islam*, Centre Marial Canadien, "Les tracts Marials," 45 Nicolet, (1954). — HARRY M., *La Sainte Vierge et l'Islam*, in *Revue des deux mondes*, 16 (1954), p. 623-638. — HAYEK MICHEL, *Marie dans le Coran et la tradition musulmane*, in *Bulletin du Cercle de St. Jean Baptiste*, 5 (1957), p. 160-165. — MOREIRA PORFIRIO G., *Maria no Alcorão e no tradição musulmana*, in *Volumus* (Cucujaes), 1958, p. 67-92. — CHARLES-BARZEL R., *La Vierge et l'Emir Abdou*, Paris, La Colombe, 1963.

4. BELLI A., *Storia meccana di Maria e di Gesù* (Sura 19, 1-33), in *Aevum*, 24 (1959), p. 442-466.

5. ANW., p. 447-461.

6. HEN., p. 288-292.

7. PEIR., p. 43-50.

8. FAKH., p. 724-741.

9. TOD., p. 208-218.

10. HIND., p. 268-275.

11. ARCE AUGUSTIN, O.F.M., *Culte Islamique au Tombeau de la Vierge*, in "Atti del Congresso Assunzionistico Orientale, organizzato dalla Custodia di Terra Santa," Jerusalem, 1951, p. 177-193.

12. MUL., p. 268-275.

thought on Mary and bring to light its authentic and original expression. As I am at it today, I deliberately prefer to focus my attention upon the *one Koranic text,* above and beyond any other incongruent and exotic import. It is overly known, in fact, that the unbridled imagination of the *qussàs* (storytellers, or writers), the credulous simplicity of the commentators,[13] and the unabided-by literary critical sense in almost all the Moslem historians, have overwhelmingly contributed to swelling and contaminating the already overflowing river of Islamic tradition. And this contamination is not limited to the so-called "stories of the prophets" *[qìsas il àmbiya]* in general related by the Koran, but also goes down to details such as the events of Mary's life. Taken all alone and as they read in their Koranic narrative, these events are of a mild and praiseworthy sobriety; but still they have been desecrated with whimsical embroideries[14] which

---

13. Including also very famous exegetes like MUQATIL IBN SULAIMAN (+767), labelled by Fr. Nwyia as the "first great exegete" of the Koran (NWY., p. 25). — In his plain effort to clarify the terms by resorting to the context and opportune parallelisms and analogies, Muqatil also falls victim to the *qussàs'* lethal influence. And in his *Tafsìr* he gathers "an enormous quantity of imaginary details, some invented by himself and others borrowed from the popular conscience, but whose spokesmen were the *qussàs* themselves" (NWY., p. 63). What makes his commentary voluminous is the mass of "legends, frivolous tales, symbols and myths" he piles up (*ib.*, p. 66).

No different are other exegetes. Their tomes, to believe Zakarias, are "indigestes, amusants, dans lesquels la fantaisie, l'imagination, quand ce n'est pas la ruse, tiennent une place prépondérante." ZAK. II, p. 292. — With regard to the Koranic commentators and their prince also, At-Tabari (+922), writes Blachère: "On demeure frappé de la place qu'occupe le merveilleux dans l'exégèse telle que la conçoit At-Tabari [...]. Le texte coranique, généralement sobre de détails ou même très sommaire, constitue le point de départ d'amplifications incroyables. Au cours de la transmission, ces données, semble-t-il, se chargent de nouveaux éléments, se dédoublent ou donnent lieu à d'autres combinaisons." BL. I, p. 236-237. — Also Fr. Abd El Jalil, OFM., and an ex-Moslem, recognizes the flaws of the Moslem commentators: "information légendaire, anachronismes, confusion, etc." JAL. I, p. 5.

14. To help the reader form himself an idea, we shall give in notes, whenever the case calls for, some of these more relevant *embroideries*. All extra-Koranic, the popular fancy has weaved them around the Marian "facts"

have, to a great extent, dulled their original charm and simplicity.

Therefore, all through this investigation, I will stay away from the more or less dependable legends, the more or less arbitrary conjectures, the more or less brain-sick amplifications. I will limit myself to mentioning them, if ever, in the critical apparatus and data occasione. Meanwhile, the Scripture of which I'll make use and depend upon, shall be basically, not to say exclusively, the Koran. No norm can be more effective for a scientific research of this sort. It responds better to the world's modern needs and, more important, tunes itself in more perfectly with the present atmosphere of "aggiornamento" — an updating which in the definition of Vatican II stresses in whatever sector the "return to the sources." Furthermore, I sincerely believe that, by these preliminary precautions and the initial exposure of the problem, the scholar will be able to sift wheat from chaff and rid himself in his research of overstructures which can be so disforming and cumbersome. Only thus will he succeed in discovering, in its limpid mainstream and free of muddy leaks and deplorable contaminations, the original nucleus of the Koranic teaching on Mary.

On the other hand, it does not appear to me that an extensive study, thus conceived and thus outlined, has so far been accomplished. A task of such competence was expected of Fr. J. M. Abd el-Jalil, O.F.M. In his book *Marie et l'Islam*, labelled as "the best synthesis of Islamic Mariology"[15] and considered "the most complete work on Koranic Mariology to date,"[16] he gave it a good try, but fell short. Despite explicitly stating that he would not yield to the temptation in front of graceful tales and would avoid scholarly and enjoyable excursions through Islam's general

---

reported explicitly or insinuated by the Koran, e.g. Mary's parents, her presentation in the Temple, retreat in the *mihràb*, the annunciation, the childbirth, etc.

15. ANW., p. 448.

16. PEIR., p. 88.

literature,[17] he did not know how to disentangle himself from the dozens of Moslem exegetes or historians, nor avoid encumbering his exposition with a lot of heterogeneous material. The same remark is true of the Paulist, Fr. P. Fakhoury, in his article;[18] and of the specialist and great Islamologist, Fr. Yussuf Durra Haddad. In his study *Mary Mother of Christ in the Koran*,[19] Haddad also falls victim to this organic defect in outlining the question. Instead of investing his efforts in sounding the Koran's depths and displaying its text and context, he often ends up by relating one gloss after the other, gleaning them as he goes along from various Koranic exegetes.

The Koran shall consequently be the basis of my present dissertation. I will make use of the original text as it has been set, even for the numeration of verses,[20] in the ultimate edition

---

17. JAL. I, p. 5.

18. FAKH., p. 724-741.

19. HAD. I, p. 141-189. — With the intent of replacing everything where it belongs and emphasizing the imaginative nature of the Koranic production in general, here is the severe but objective opinion of an authentic Moslem, the Turkish writer Riza Tewfic, suggested to him "by a life of study and discussion": "[...] mais j'ai constaté que malheureusement la plupart des historiens en Orient sont dépourvus de sens critique, et l'histoire, — jusqu'au commencement du 19ème siècle, — a conservé chez nous son caractère primitif: celui d'être platement anécdotique. Quant aux commentateurs, ils ont accumulé, — au nom de traditions qu'ils considèrent comme des vérités évidentes par elle-mêmesl, — un tas de superstitions inventées par l'imagination populaire [...]. Ils en ont tant abusé, que les commentaires sont pleines de ces anécdotes stupides qui, loin d'éclairer la signification du texte, la ternissent plutôt; celà embarrasse l'intelligence des gens simples et ébranle leur foi." *Sur la génèse et l'origine de l'Islam*, in *Les Cahiers de l'Est* (Beyrouth), II ser., vol. 1 (1947), p. 68.

20. In Cairo's typical edition, the verses amount to 6236 according to the computation by the Kufis who reproduce the division made by Ali, ben Abi Taleb. — To other editions other figures. VINCENZO CALZA, *Il Corano* (Bastia, Fabiani, 1847), has 6242. — LAURA VECCIA VAGLIERI, *Il Corano*, (Napoli, Pironti, 1946), has (p. 47) 6206. — MASS. (I, p. 16), has 6226. Likewise HAY. (p. 29), who also reports between brackets other figures. — JAL. II (p. 73) says that the verses are in all 6211. — GAR. (p. 22) follows Massignon, 6226.

prepared and supervised by Azhar University Doctors, published in Cairo in 1913 under the auspices of King Fouad I.[21]

According to a steady tradition, the Koran "descended" on the Prophet, or was "recited" by the early epigones of the Prophet, in seven different "letters." Initially then it would have been susceptible to at least[22] seven different dictions, or "readings," all nonetheless concordant in meaning. The present version, the Koran used today, has survived a drastic and general extermination. It is known, in fact, that in the year 650 (i.e. twenty-eight years after the Hegira and eighteen after Mohammad's death) the Third Caliph, Othman ben Affan, had by means of iron (sword) and fire (burning) made all the current copies disappear from circulation. Into the same sword and fire also went the one compiled, in chronological order of the "descents" or revelations, by Ali, the Prophet's brother-in-law, and its destruction has been an irreparable loss for Islam and history. An outstanding mind of all times in Islam, Ali was the live depository of Mohammad's thinking, spirit and theology; the confidant and eye-witness of his revelations; the Founder's heir not only to the Caliphate but mainly to Islam's spiritual legacy. Had his authoritative version survived, it would have thrown so much light on our Koranic researches. But Othman's ambition to the Caliphate decided otherwise. With draconian decrees he im-

---

No wonder, consequently, if the quotation of verses is not always the same. There is in general a difference of two to three verses. A classical example on that is G. FLÜGEL, *Concordantiae Corani Arabicae* (Lypsiae, typ. Caroli Tauchnitii, 1842). He follows the division adopted in 1694 by Hinckelmann.

21. In the Koranic quotations, the first Arabic number will indicate the Sura; the second, the verse, separated by a comma; the passage, however, from one Sura to another will be indicated by a semicolon.

Because the subject is like a new world for many, we shall be rather generous with illustrative notes.

22. Cf. SAL., p. 170; GAND., p. 35-40; HAD. II, p. 207-216. — MUHAMMAD DRAZ reports the following *hadith* by the Prophet: "En vérité, le Koran est révélé en sept lectures, ou variantes; récitez-le suivant celle d'entre elles qui vous sera facile." DR., p. 27. Incidentally, the Arabic translation by Abdel

posed on all Islam as the one official text the version that is in our hands today. Helped by ad hoc committees, he pieced it together by himself; and he textured it in the "letter" or language of the Quraish tribe, the purest[23] and most elegant among the not less than fifty tongues (idioms or dialects) spoken throughout the Arabian Peninsula in Mohammad's time.

Needless to say, the Koran as we have it today has gone through hard and critical historic vicissitudes. The particular issues dealing with its original and fundamental wording, its final graphic setting, its integrity through successive transmissions, its compilation frequently manipulated or mutilated or increased, will always be the researcher's incurable headache and frustration; they will always torture him with saddening ques-

---

Adhim Ali [Kuwait, 1971], p. 42, does not contain the clause "ou variantes." However, Draz asks himself, and rightly indeed, if the word *seven* means exactly the number seven, or an undetermined multitude. His answer is: "La *question est controversée.*" DR., p. 27, in note.

23. In terms of linguistic perfection, it is known that the Koran — "*The best thing ever after Allah*" in the expression of TIRMIDHI (ap. HAY., p. 29) — is praised as the top and inimitable (17, 88) model of Arabic literature. "Il est une oeuvre que certes la piété interdit d'imiter, mais qui, malgré ses liens avec la tradition littéraire arabe, en renouvelle splendidement le fond et la forme, et inspire jusqu'à nos jours, dans cette forme comme dans ce fond, indissociables, la pensée et l'expression de pensée des peuples musulmans." GAUD., p. 76. — That is a known fact. What perhaps less known, is the fact that, according to the accurate analysis of Siyuti, there are 700 terms not used in their original meaning; several others, though Arabic, don't belong to the idiom of Hijaz; and nearly one hundred barbarisms, properly so called, of Persian provenance, Hebraic, Syriac, Coptic, Abyssinian, Greek, or Latin. Cf. respective lists in HAD. III, p. 143-137; 137-141; 141-145. — Blachère, to the contrary, thinks that the Koranic language is not rooted in the Meccan dialect, but in "l'idiome des poésies 'préislamiques.' Cet idiome est une *koiné* comprise sur une aire géographique très étendue." BL. VI, p. 79. — On the inimitability of the Koran, cf. bibliography *ibid.*, p. 236.

A. JEFFREY, *The foreign Vocabulary of the Qor'an* [Baroda, 1938], has studied the vocables alien to the Koran's idiom. R. BRUNSCHVIG instead examined in *Simples remarques négatives sur le vocabulaire du Coran*, and in *Studia Islamica*, V, 1956, the terms which were supposed to appear, but do not, in the Koran. Cf. SAUV., p. 123.

tions to which no plausible, adequate and convincing answer has so far been possible.[24]

But aside from these less than lucky events, we can still positively assert that the *Vulgate*, i.e. today's official Koranic version, is substantially authentic. Indeed all Moslems, Sunnites and Shiites, despite their conflicts and not always small differences, admit unanimously that the Koran expresses faithfully and indisputably the revelations sent by Allah to his Prophet. We therefore disagree with Zakarias in this regard;[25] we accept today's Koran with no serious reservations as to the substantial authenticity or integrity of its content, and will use it just as it is in universal use today.

The Koran, "a text often obscure and enigmatic, always hard to follow as it evolves,"[26] was across the centuries "read"[27]

---

24. Contrary to DRAZ' statement (p. 23-24), Othman's compilation did not go through smoothly and "with no contradiction." Apart from the storms it immediately raised within the Moslem community (cf. BL. I, p. 62-63), it leaves the reader dubious and tossed about by many a question mark (cf. *ib.*, p. 55-57; BL. VI, p. 204-205). Despite all the efforts that were invested, the history of the present Koranic "vulgate" remains "*confuse, mystérieuse, insaisissable sur des points essentiels.*" BL. I, p. 1-2. Behind the scene, it seems, a political movement played the culprit (cf. *ib.*, p. 57-60; BL. VI, p. 200-203, with bibliography).

25. Against the Ps.-Zakarias' opinion ["*Un Mahomet illettré ne peut être l'auteur du Coran*"], II, p. 12-13, the Koran's authenticity, as to the substance, is admitted by all scholars. As to the modality of this authorship, however, we abide by PAREJA's remark relative to the fundamental difference between Koranic studies conducted by Moslem authors and those by non-Moslem scholars: for the first, Mohammad is not at all the "author", but simply a "transmitter" of God's word, the Koran. Cf. PAR., p. 597.

26. "*Texte souvent obscur et énigmatique, toujours difficile à suivre dans son déroulement.*" BL. IV, p. 13.

27. Qur'an means properly a *reading*, but recited, declamatory and psalmodic. Its root is the Arabic verb Qara': to read aloud, recite, to psalm (73, 4, 20). GUIDI sees in the word a recall of the Aramaic *qeryana* "already in use at Judaic and Christian centers in Arabia, which, in liturgical language, means the solemn recital of the sacred texts." GUID., p. 348.

and meditated upon from three different viewpoints. And this triple psychological attitude has, in turn, originated three distinct hermeneutic methods, namely: the *tafsìr* — which clings tenaciously to the letter and explains it [sharaha] according to the obvious meaning of the words and phrases, helped usually by the philological, grammatical, historical, dogmatic and juridical expedients; the *taawìl* — which goes beyond the letter, considered as a simple shell, and points to the substance held within an interpretative sense we would call allegorical, or "sensus plenior" (fuller sense); the *istinbàt* — which, while resorting to methods not rarely arbitrary, toils to extract from the text a mystical, symbolic, sense very close to the "accommodative" one of the Bible. Though defended by Sufism, this latter was rejected by the official Islam: by the Sunnites, strenuously advocating the *tafsìr*; and by the Shiites, preferring the *taawìl*. Such an interpretation, in fact, would empty the text of its true and proper content, and fill it instead with allegorical senses based on intuitive and symbolic ways of thinking.

Every exegesis abstracting from the historic environment in which a particular Scripture came to light or evolved, runs the high risk of offering only a disfigured interpretation. That is the pit we are trying not to fall into. We are trying to avoid the danger of going into subjective, whimsical, not to say ridiculous, interpretations. We're conscious, in other words, that we should not be won over by a subconscious mania, the will of "soliciting" the text, of "looking in it deep down to the bottom" and finding in it at any cost the allusions or implications we've just forced out of it. No! Our hermeneutic criterion will be the one suggested by Blachère.[28] Scientifically, we believe, it is far more sound and more sure. Practically also, it matches the type of exegesis which blends better with Mohammad's historic back-

---

28. "Entre plusieurs interprétations, il paraît préférable de retenir celle qui, confinant au concret, représente le mieux celle qui s'était offerte à l'esprit de Mahomet et de ses contemporains mékkois, médinois ou bédouins, celle aussi qui a été retenue par la plus ancienne exégèse traditionnelle." BL. I, [IV. Ressources fournies à l'exégèse orientaliste par certaines "sciences coraniques"], p. 220.

ground; and while orchestrating more harmoniously with his positive and realistic spirit,[29] it reflects more probably the ideas that would have loomed in the minds of his first hearers, or the Koran's first readers. These were all people of humble social class, such as the slaves or the bedouins of the desert, although not totally alien to Hijaz' more advanced centers such as Mecca, Medina and Khaibar.

That will easily explain why our eventual recourse to one Moslem exegete or another, in order to clarify the ambiguity of a text and determine as probably as possible the genuine meaning of it, will go preferably for the *tafsir's* sponsors. Among these, for broad learning and sharp intuition, and by the unanimous testimony of the erudite, towers El Tabari (+922), who is rightly hailed as the father of all Koranic exegetes. His opus, a colossal commentary, gathers together all the hermeneutic data, whatever their nature, that up to his time were uttered concerning the Islamic revelation. It constitutes indeed "an inexhaustible mine of doctrinal and historic information," which Orientalists of both worlds have always worked over.[30]

With these cautions presented then as a necessary methodological preliminary, I shall divide my dissertation in two fundamental parts:

---

29. "Dans l'Islam, le haut idéalisme s'associe à un sens pratique essentiel. Mahomet a été *un homme pratique exalté.*" Ess., p. 80. — The mentality and the intellectual level of Mohammad's historic environment are thus described by Blachère: "On y découvrira non seulement *l'esprit réaliste* des marchands mekkois, mais ce sens du concret, cette capacité à s'évader du matériel et du sensible, qui caractérisent le bédouin et font sa force et parfois sa granduer. La pensée, dans le Coran, apparaît essentiellement concrète." BL. I, p. 219. Italics are ours.

30. Cf. JAL. II, p. 128; BL. III, p. 84-85. — "La méthode d'at-Tabari est à la fois accumulative et méthodique; il s'en dégage le sentiment que le *Coran* peut recevoir son explication, sans que ce soit faite référence à une discussion personnelle des problèmes." *Loc. cit.*, p. 85.

In the first, *analytical*, I shall expose in chronological order the Marian Facts, called "historic," emerging from the Koran.

In the second, *synthetical*, I shall attempt to bring together, within a global structure, the other Marian elements that are also found in the various Koranic Suras.

In the conclusion, I will first try to localize the historic and Scriptural sources of Mohammad's Marian teaching. Then I will close with two remarks: one theological and the other ecumenical, or pastoral, in nature.

Chapter One

ANALYSIS

Mohammad never dreamed of setting up "a religious and dogmatic organic system."[1] Neither was it his intention to consign in the Koran "a systematic exposition of Dogma, or a complete code of jurisprudence."[2] On the contrary, he only provided a casual recording for the received revelations; just as casual were his religious experiences, and as unforeseen were the practical occurrences which demanded then and there an appropriate solution.[3] Especially since the "descents," or revelations, would not have ended until the effective death of the Prophet. The

---

1. GUID., p. 348.

2. PAR., p. 599.

3. There is no evidence that Mohammad tried effectively to set up a corpus for the received revelations. The contrary is true, notes Blachère. Serious proofs

Koran in its present version is not of the Prophet's own direct making. The same is said of its division in *Suras* (chapters) and *ayàt* (verses), of the titles heading each Sura, of the *Bàsmala*, or the invocation at the beginning of Allah, the Compassionate and the Merciful. Therefore, the Koran is universally retained as a non-original arrangement, not binding, but conventional and optional. It is not ultimate, but susceptible to change. It is consequently *tawfiqi* (conventionally adjusted, accommodative), not *tawqìfi* (set, established, unchangeable).[4]

The transcription of the revelations started probably during the Medinian period.[5] Up to then, memory was the only trustworthy recipient. Initially, the sacred verses were recorded upon any available material, often quite rudimentary, such as white and smooth stone slabs, sheep or camel shoulder blades, animal skins, and hard-pressed palm leaf braids.[6]

The authors of the official compilation under Othman have unfortunately taken no account of the *chronological* succession; they neglected to mark down the time in which the individual communications either "descended" on the Prophet or were "recited" by the Prophet to his early followers. Nor were they aware of the necessity of adopting some *logical* criterion. From

---

are there to make him believe that "une telle entreprise n'a même pas été projetée par lui." BL. I, p. 21.

4. Cf. GAND., p. 48. — An indication of that is the fact that while the *Suras* are invariably 114, the *ayàt*, or verses, vary in number as we have seen earlier (note 20, *Foreword*).

5. Cf. BL. IV, p. 19. Blachère himself, however, has written in his *Introduction* that "dès qu'une révélation était transmise à Mahomet, des scribes, selon la Tradition, la notaient." BL. I, p. 13.

6. Cf. NOL. I, p. 14-18; BL. I, p. 13-14. At the Prophet's death, the Koran existed only in loose fragments in possession by different faithful. The first ones who were in charge to put it in writing, numbered twenty-six, according to some; others raise that number to forty-two. Cf. GAND., p. 41.

their hands, in other words, came out an authentic jumble: a fragmentary work randomly pieced together. And this very serious defect, which we may label as technical and literary, is our major headache today. Not only does it prevent us from seeing clearly the origin of Mohammad's prophetic call and following step by step its further development, but it keeps us in a nightmare of doubt and perplexity, unable by ourselves to pinpoint the epoch to which a verse or a complex of verses belong.[7] Hence the necessity and the urgency, felt at once by the Moslem Exegetes themselves, to set up a whole series of Koranic disciplines in order to ease the problem. One of them, "*asbàb un-nuzùl*" (the motives of revelation), aims particularly at determining the contingence of time, of place, and the motives which caused the individual "descents" or revelations.

The only norm adopted, but not always rigorously observed, was to begin the Koranic Body with a sort of general introduction: the *Fàtiha*, or Exordium. This is the *Bàsmala*, a kind of Islamic doxology which later became the Moslem's typical prayer, as "Our Father" is for the Christian. Then followed the Suras in decreasing order; i.e., the longest coming first after the *Fàtiha*, the next longest after that, and so forth to the end. Thus in the Vulgate, or the official text in use today, the shortest Suras are found relegated to the end of the book, although they are

---

7. J. LA BEAUME, adopting KASIMIRSKI's version (1840), has published the Koran *per materia* and distributed its verses under generic titles. His opus was also published in Arabic. Of *Mary* he treats in paragraph III (p. 203-206) of section VI, where, among others, he gathers the Koranic data concerning Jesus (p. 206-214) and the Trinity (p. 214-215).

Others, to the contrary, have worked hard to reconstruct the Koran according to the closest chronological order possible. Thus in England, ROD-WELL A., *The Koran. Translation with the Suras arranged in chronological order* (London, 1861); in France, RÉGIS BLACHÈRE, *Le Coran. Traduction nouvelle*; in Germany, TH. NÖLDEKE, *Geschichte des Qorans*. After patient and accurate research, he gives a chronological list which was revised by F. SCHWALLY, and, later, by BERGSTRÄSSER and PRETZEL. Though not definitive, such list is certainly a valid help for orientation; and is "generalmente accettata dagli orientalisti europei, almeno come ipotesi di lavoro." BAUS., p. 46. Cf. such list in BAUS., p. 46; and in PAR., p. 600-601.

chronologically of earlier date; while those textually more extensive come at the beginning, despite the fact that they go back to the Medinian period and are therefore, chronologically, of later time.

In the absence of a logical and chronological plan, it is no wonder that reading the Koran becomes so dull and tedious, especially in its translations, however most accurate. In this respect Guidi rightly says: "Such variety of arguments, the lack of an orderly nexus, the sudden switch from one theme to another, disorient and often wear down whosoever with no adequate preparation reads the Koran."[8]

And that concludes our preliminary remarks.

Coming now to the core of the subject, we say that there are thirteen Koranic chapters, i.e. Suras, in which Mary is explicitly mentioned: *four* belong to the Meccan period, and *nine* to the Medinian period.[9]

The four Meccan Suras are: Sura 19, *Maryam*; Sura 21, *The Prophets*; Sura 23, *The Believers*; Sura 43, *The Ornaments of Gold*.

---

8. GUID., p. 349. — "C'est ce qui donne une désagréable impression de désordre, et c'est ce qui rend la tâche des historiens fort difficile." JAL. II, p. 73.
Blachère has beautifully described the reader's discomfort at his first contact with the Koran, in these terms: "... dès les premières pages la déception commence. D'abord, il s'étonne de rencontrer cette prose sèche et sans éclat où il retrouve les rythmes habituels du français des sociétés savantes. Bientôt il est dérouté par l'allure chaotique d'une révélation où se mêlent les exhortations morales, les dispositions juridiques, les récits édifiants, où la pensée s'efforce de retrouver un lien qui n'existe point. Enfin, s'il poursuit sa lecture, il se lasse de ces récits bibliques ou légendaires constamment repris et que le Pentateuque ou les Évangiles lui donnent sous des aspects d'ailleurs assez différent. Finalement, il cède au découragement; il jette le livre après en avoir parcouru d'un oeil distrait les derniers chapitres qui lui semblent une apocalypse sans originalité et sans grandeur." BL. I, p. 273.

9. The only chronological indication given by the Koran's publishers is the distinction between Meccan Suras and Medinian Suras.

The nine Medinian Suras are: Sura 2, *The Cow;*
Sura 3, *The Imrans;* Sura 4, *The Women;* Sura 5, *The
Table;* Sura 9, *The Repentance;* Sura 33, *The Confederate
Tribes;* Sura 57, *The Iron;* Sura 61, *The Battle Array;*
and Sura 66, *The Prohibition.*

To define the epoch[10] in which these thirteen Suras have
been revealed is what we are about to do timidly, in so far as
their Marian role is concerned.

The two major Suras, the 19th (Maryam) and the 3rd
(Imrans), will be taken into consideration later, separately. It is
enough for now to note that they date respectively back to the
beginning and the end of Mohammad's career: around 615 for
the 19th, and around 631 for the 3rd. A quick confrontation of
them both brings us at once to this important truth: that not
only does the mention of Mary's name occur time and again with

---

The division into two periods, *Meccan* and *Medinian,* separated by Hegira
(622), is of utmost importance. It helps to give a clearer insight into Mohammad's prophetic activity, to follow the Koranic revelations in their ascensional
curve and determine exactly their meaning.

In the *Meccan* period (c. 612-622), Mohammad abides by a program
markedly religious. He's the warner (*mùndhir*) for the Last Day, and the proclaimer (*mubàsshir*) of the faith in Allah. His opponents: the Quraishi Oligar-
chy of Mecca, and the *mushrikùn* (the Associators).

In the *Medinian* period (622-632), he declares himself a prophet
(*nabì*) and a messenger (*rasùl*) sent by Allah to the Arabs. He displays his
political and military genius in favor of the new, "middlemost" (2, 143) and
theocratic Community. His enemies: besides the *mushrikùn,* are the *munafiqùn*
(the hypocrites); then, the Jews; and around the end, the Christians, or Judeo-
Christians (*nasàra*).

10. The three *epochs* of the *Meccan* period are thus earmarked: in the
first (612?-615), under the Christian influence [the "nasàra"], eschatological
preaching; in the *second* (615-618), under the vetro-testamentary influence
["stories of the prophets"], persistent call to monotheism; in the *third* (618-622),
beginning of the emancipation from the "People of the Book," and institution of
the new and "middlemost" Community. Cf. HAD. II, p. 373-438; 439-576;
577-645.

no break as to continuity,[11] but that the Prophet's teaching regarding Mary and his attitude toward Mary have also persisted fundamentally as identical, unaltered, and with no relevant variations — a thought of high regard and esteem; an attitude of warm sympathy.

The Marian content of these two basic Suras and of the other Suras hitherto mentioned as well would, in Fr. Haddad's opinion, have been "interpolated."[12] And Othman is the culprit. While patching together the official version, he had intentionally excised the sections relative to Mary from their original context and inserted them elsewhere. What were the reasons behind that? Merely polemical! He intended to use them as a tool to stir anger and aversion against the Christians.

In the attempt to determine at least approximately the dating of the other Suras, we will, as a rule of thumb, abide by Fr. Haddad's conclusions; between the traditional positions of the Moslem exegetes and the scholarly researches of the two eminent orientalists, Nöldeke and Blachère, he knew how to keep a sound balance.

The 43rd Sura (Ornaments of Gold) is unanimously remanded to the second epoch of the Meccan period. The two other Meccan Suras, the 21st (Prophets) and the 23rd (Believers), Haddad assigns to the third epoch of the Meccan period, while Nöldeke wants them in the second.

For Nöldeke there are no epochs in the Medinian period: the decennial going from 622 (Hegira) to 632 (Mohammad's death) constitutes one solid and indivisible period. Haddad, on the con-

---

11. "Le nom de Maryam se trouve dans le Kur'an depuis les plus anciennes parties jusqu'aux dernières surates médinoises." WENS., p. 358. — Cf. S. 19, *Maryam*; and S. 5, *The Table*, which mark respectively the beginning and the end of the Prophet's mission.

12. Cf. HAD. II, p. 299-305. — It is rather Fr. Haddad's thesis that whatever is closely related to the *nasàra*, or to that form of Christianity known to Mohammad at the time, was arbitrarily misplaced in the Koran for mere polemic reasons. Cf. HAD. V, p. 19-55.

trary, distinguishes in it two epochs;[13] to the first (622-628) would belong all the Medinian Suras mentioned above except the 5th (Table) and the 9th (Repentance), which fit better in the second epoch (628-632).

Scholars are of dissenting opinions as to what place each individual Sura occupies in the global series established according to the chronological order of the revelations.[14]

Finally, the *ayàt* (verses) dealing directly or indirectly with Mary form a complex of approximately seventy.

The passages more relevant as to length and importance are: 15 verses of Sura Three, *The Imrans* (v. 33-37, 42-51); 17 verses of Sura Five, *The Table* (v. 17, 46, 72-78, 110-117); and 20 verses of Sura Nineteen, *Maryam* (v. 16-36).

In the remaining Suras we find another partition based on one single verse in seven Suras;[15] two verses in two Suras;[16] and three verses in only one Sura.[17]

To judge from the quantity, it will be a rather forced choice to admit that the material gleaned is very scanty. I would almost say "discouraging," mainly if compared with the 114 Suras and

---

13. The *first* Medinian epoch is characterized by intense political and military activity to establish, defend and consolidate the newly born "middlemost" Community. The *second* is characterized by the expansion and assertion of the Islamic era on the heels of the violent liquidation of its adversaries (Jews and Associators); by the recapture of Mecca and with it the Ka'ba; and by the delegations to Mohammad, now the only umpire of the situation in the whole of Arabia. Cf. HAD. II, p. 723-908; 909-1015.

14. Cf. HAD. II, p. 299-305. — For the Medinian Suras, cf. NOL. I, p. 133; 213-215.

15. The Suras with only one Marian verse: 9, 31; 21, 91; 23, 50; 33, 7; 44, 57; 57, 27; 66, 12.

16. Cf. 2, 87, 253; 61, 6, 14.

17. Cf. 4, 156, 157, 171.

6,236 verses composing the Koran's bulk; and also with the 36 Suras and their respective 502 verses speaking of Moses; and again with the 25 Suras and their respective 245 verses related to Abraham. It must be added, though, that this small harvest is sufficiently rewarded by the quality of the material. Far from being worthless or negligible, the Marian material in the Koran is rather conspicuous, relevant and not void of charm, as will later be seen at the end of this dissertation.

In the further process of our analysis we will first make an appropriate presentation of the major *sources* for the Marian teaching, as a premise; and then set to investigate and display the *content* of the Marian material that has been found.

And I explicitly repeat: *Marian material*, not *Mariological*. The *technicality* in the expression justifies the rigor of the term.

I believe in fact that it is historically false and technically improper to speak of *Islamic Mariology* or of *Koranic Marian Theology*.[18] For one reason: "Mariology," or "Marian Theology," is a "sacred science" with a specific task to examine, down to the grass-roots and under the light of the divine revelation, the mystery of Mary. In terms of how to conceive this revelation, Islam and Christianity are as far apart as are the Gospel and the Koran. For another, Mary's Divine Maternity is the basis upon which rises the whole structure of the Marian science — and Mary's Divine Maternity is unquestionably excluded from the Koran, definitely rejected by Islam.

––––––––––––––

18. "Il y a donc une *esquisse de Mariologie en Islam*; on en trouvera ici un bref exposé, destiné à en souligner les principaux aspects." JAL. I, p. 55 (Problèmes de Mariologie). — "The best synthesis of *Islamic Mariology* is the precious book of Father J. Abd El Jalil." ANW., p. 448. — "Sulla *Mariologia del Corano* si legga il recente ed equilibrato opuscolo." BAUS., p. 590. — "Giungiamo alla prima fase importante della *Mariologia Coranica*." PEIR., p. 46. "*La teologia mariana coranica*." TOD., p. 209. — Italics are ours.

I. THE SOURCES

The sources are predominately those Suras speaking mostly of Mary: those in the Vulgate bearing respectively the distinctive numbers **Three** and **Nineteen**.

Sura 19 is chronologically prior to Sura 3. From the historico-doctrinal viewpoint, however, both claim prime importance in the Marian sector. Thanks to these two Suras, today we are able to gauge how deep was the influence Christianity exercised on Mohammad's mind with regard to Mary on one hand (S. 19), and on the other, to follow throughout the Koran the Marian trajectory and trace it back to its source. The event that triggered that trajectory was the Christological controversy that Mohammad sustained in 631 with the members of Nejran's Christian delegation (S. 3). The compromising attitude adopted by both sides on the heels of that dialogue delineated it as it is in the Koran forever. Such controversy, it is known, broke off with each of the opposed parties rigid in its doctrinal position; it ended up with the prospective of a *mubàhala*, or ordeal,[19] removed thereafter with a *musàlaha*, agreement or compromise.[20]

---

19. "La *mubâhala* consiste primitivement en une triple mimique: un prélude, *juthuwu*, l'action de s'accroupir, les mains sur les genous, prêt à se mettre debout pour contredire; un invitatoire, *tashbîk*, où les deux adversaires entrelacent leur deux mains droites; une élévation, *raf'*, des deux mains vers le ciel, en écartant les doigts, et en prononçant la formule." MASS., (*La Mubâhala de Médine et l'hyperdulie de Fatima*, 1943-55. Étude sur la proposition d'ordalie faite · par le Prophète Muhammad aux chrétiens Balharîth du Nejrân en l'an 10/631 à Médine), I, p. 551. — In a separate brochure (Paris, Libr. Orientale et Américaine, 1955). — Cf. BOUB. I, p. 107, 124-125.

20. According to GARDET, the Christians of Nejran could have been considered as a small republic of *Nestorian faith* (GAR., p. 31, 58). But that is an oversight. To the contrary, they were of *Jacobite faith*: Monophysites consequently, not Nestorians; they were also in connection with

1. Sura 19, Maryam

A) *Time:*

The Sura is certainly *Meccan*. The unanimous testimony of the Islamic tradition in that regard is endorsed by a solid confirmation from the *internal critique*; and specifically from the concurrence of several criteria[21] diligently formulated after an accurate analysis of the text. Commonly accepted, these criteria are the norm in current use by Orientals and Orientalists as well, to decide whether a particular passage (Sura, àyat) is respectively Meccan or Medinian. In fact:

a. — In Sura 19 we do not yet find the Koran as a "Book" distinguished from the other sacred books of the previous revelation, Jewish or Christian (Torah, Gospel), as will later be the case in the Medinian period.[22]

b. — The Sura contains an explicit recall of the day of judgment with the expectation of the inexorable and final sanction: a scourge (v. 75) or a reward (v. 76, 96). And this recall of the last judgment is known as an oratorical explo-

---

the Christians of Abyssinia, likewise Monophysites. Cf. HAD. V, p. 125-147. Rather, according to HADDAD, the only Christians with whom Mohammad had contacts were all Jacobites, Nejran's delegates included. *Loc. cit.*, p. 15-18.

By virtue of the compromise between Mohammad and Nejran's delegates — a compromise that should have served as a model for all subsequent arrangements between a Moslem State and Christian minorities — Allah's benediction and the protection of the Prophet would have covered "all the goods of the Christians, their persons, the exercise of their cult, their present and absent ones, their families, their churches, and all that whichever way belongs to them, whether small or large." As a sign of political subjection, however, the Christians should have paid an annual tribute to the Prophet. Cf. GAR., p. 32.

21. A list of the main criteria used generally to determine the Meccan or Medinian nature of the Koranic Suras is found in SAL., p. 181-184; HAD. II, 290-298; GAND., 34-35; BL. I, p. 240-263.

22. Cf. S. 19, 12, 16, 30, 41, 51, 54, 56.

sion of "eschatological piety". And as such, it is a distinctive mark of the Meccan period, mainly in its early beginning, characterized by fiery invitations calling man to consider his last things,[23] rather than by the religious, political, or military activity so distinctive of the Medinian period.

c. — In Sura 19 Mohammad does not proclaim himself yet a prophet (nabì) and a messenger (rasùl) as he will do in the Medinian period, but merely a "proclaimer of good tidings" and a "warning giver" — " li-tubàsshira wa tùndhira" (v. 97) — on behalf of ar-Rahmàn (v. 96), the Merciful.[24]

d. — Contrary to what we know of the Medinian period, the incriminations read in the second half of the Sura are not directed against the "People of the Book" — *Ahl al-Kitàb* — a denomination that would be looked for in vain in all of Sura 19; but against the *kafirùn* (unbelievers, infidel), branded as wrong-doers (v. 72), erratic (v. 75), polytheists (v. 81), unbelievers (v. 83), sinful (v. 86), associators (v. 88) — all denominations so typical of Mohammad's enemies in the Meccan period.[25]

e. — The polemic, which looms up in the second part of Sura 19, makes no mention of the *munafiqùn* (the shaky, skeptical, hypocrites), nor does it assail them for that matter, as will later happen in the Medinian period.[26]

---

23. In the third part of his book *Les origines de l'Islam et le Christianisme* (trad. de l'allemand par J. Roche, Paris, Librairie d'Amérique et d'Orient, 1955), TOR ANDRAE speaks at length of Mohammad's "eschatological piety," p. 67-199.

24. "The Suras and the ayàt in which Mohammad is proclaimed a "bearer of good news" [bashìr] and a "warner" [nadhìr] are Meccan; those others in which he declares himself a "prophet" [nabì] and a "messenger" [rasùl], are Medinian instead." HAD. II, p. 298.

25. "Every Sura in which an attack occurs against the Associators [mushrikìn] is Meccan; every other in which there is an attack against the 'People of the Book' [ahl al-kitàb], is Medinian instead." HAD. II, p. 291.

26. "Every Sura, or ayàt, mentioning the hypocrites [munafiqìn] is Medinian." HAD. II, 292-293.

Fr. Haddad would refer Sura 19 to the first *Meccan* epoch;[27] or, more exactly, to a phase of transition that would have closed the first epoch and marked the passage to the second.[28] And he establishes a tight relationship between its revelation and the first Hegira, the transmigration to Abyssinia of the Prophet's very first followers. Reportedly, these refugees would have shown Sura 19 to the Negus, and they would have it recited to him by Jaafar ben Abi Taleb, Mohammad's cousin (who headed those emigrants), as a symbol of faith in Christ and Mary identical to the creed formula professed by the Abyssinians.[29] That Sura consequently would have marked the highest apex of Christian influence on the Prophet and the Koran.[30] And therefore, chronologically, Sura 19 would have existed, at least in its primitive Christo-Marian part (v. 16-33), even before 615, the date of that little Hegira to Abyssinia.

However, all pros and cons impartially weighed, I strongly doubt that such seniority could be attributed to Sura 19, even reduced to its primitive nucleus. I'm rather inclined to assign it to the *second* epoch of the Meccan period.

In fact, it reflects an historical environment, which is more evolved, certainly after the first Meccan epoch: an environment

---

27. HAD. II, p. 301, 310, 315.

28. *Loc. cit.*, p. 395.

29. It probably happened in 615. A scared group of Mohammad's followers, to escape the constantly increasing harassments and the harsh language by the Quraishis, decided to take refuge in Abyssinia, with the Negus, encouraged in that by the Prophet himself. We don't know if the Negus knew the Arabic, or the Koranic Arabic, to understand Sura 19's lecture by Jaafar, as tradition has it. For the emigration to Abyssinia and the motives that led to it, cf. WAT. I, p. 190-192.

According to GAUD., p. 90-91, there were three successive emigrations. There is doubt whether the understanding between the emigrants and the people of the Negus was complete. "The Judeo-Christianity, which inspired certain verses of the Koran, was of Nestorian origin. Abyssinians were, by contrast, Monophysites." GAUD., p. 90.

30. Cf. HAD. II, p. 460.

in which the *narratives* [qìsas], biblical and extra-biblical, already appear.

Now, by Fr. Haddad's own confession,[31] the Suras which include narratives [qìsas] belong to the *second* Meccan epoch, while those without them belong to the first. And so — because Sura 19 is (in its "historic" portion at least) a full sequence of narratives and biblical allusions, e.g. Yahia's (John's) birth (v. 1-15), Issa's (Jesus') birth (v. 16-33), the remembrance of Abraham (v. 41-50), of Moses and Aaron (v. 51-53), of Ismael (v. 54-55), of Idris (Enoch) (v. 56-57), of Noah and other prophets (v. 58) — it is right and logical to attribute it to the *second*, not the first, Meccan epoch.

Another criterion, equally valid for Fr. Haddad, leads us to the same conclusion, and that is the appellation of the divine Majesty — ar-Rahmàn.[32]

If we examine diligently the whole of Sura 19 in both its original and accessorial portions, and if we can stay away from an almost sure interpolation (v. 35-40) and (according to Fr. Haddad) from three appendices (v. 59-74) which he thinks were inserted at a later date,[33] we will realize that Sura 19 is structured fundamentally on the majestic name ar-Rahmàn rather than on the supreme name of Allah.

Elsewhere, in fact, the name ar-Rahmàn is never used

---

31. "The Suras where the 'narratives' are missing belong to the *first* Meccan epoch; those with the 'narratives', on the contrary, belong to the *second*." HAD. II, p. 292.

32. The criterion appears in the eleventh place in HADDAD's list, and reads: "The Suras and the verses containing ar-Rahmàn must be reported to the Meccan period; more exact, they belong to the *second* epoch of the Meccan period." *Loc. cit.*, p. 293. — Likewise Bausani: "Rahmàn, come nome divino, compare di preferenza nelle sure del *secondo* periodo meccano; è anzi dagli orientalisti considerato un segno probante dell'appartenenza a quel periodo." BAUS., p. 585. Italics are ours.

33. Cf. HAD. II, p. 467.

with such frequency or insistence. Never. Not even in the Sura bearing for its own and proper title ar-Rahmàn, in which this divine epithet occurs no more than once, at the beginning (55, 1). Throughout the rest of the Koran, we find ar-Rahmàn used in the proportion of only once in nine Suras, twice in two Suras, four times in four Suras, five times in five Suras, and seven times at most in only one Sura.[34]

In Sura 19 instead, ar-Rahmàn surfaces sixteen times, i.e. twice as many as Allah's name, which appears eight times only.[35]

All that brings us to necessarily conclude that Sura 19 is un-questionably Meccan, and belongs not to the first but to the *second* epoch of the Meccan period. It consequently came down on the Prophet after the return from Abyssinia of the first emigrants: therefore after 615. Not without motive, Bausani notes: "According to most authoritative exegetes, the Sura chronologically belongs to the *second* Meccan period, even though it includes some occasional Medinian additives and re-manipulation. It is therefore old; or more accurately, it is the first Koranic treatise of John's, Jesus' and Mary's histories.[36]

---

34. The nine Suras mentioning ar-Rahmàn once each are: 2, 163; 13, 30; 17, 110; 26, 5; 27, 30; 41, 2; 50, 33; 55, 1; 59, 22. — The four Suras mentioning it four times each are: 20: 5, 90, 108, 109; 21: 26, 36, 42, 112; 36: 11, 15, 23, 52; 67: 3, 19, 20, 29. — The Sura where the epithet recurs seven times is 43: 17, 19, 20, 33, 36, 45, 81.

HADDAD states that God's title ar-Rahmàn comes originally from Abyssinia; it was introduced in the Hijaz by the immigrants while returning from their "little Hegira". Cf. HAD. II, p. 379, 442. The divine name more in vogue, at the time in the Hijaz, was that of Allah; in the South of Arabia, that of ar-Rahmàn; in the North, instead, ar-Rahìm. Cf. Loc. cit., p. 293; NOL. I, p. 112-113; JEF., p. 140-141.

35. The 16 verses of Sura 19, where ar-Rahmàn recurs explicitly and in relation to God, are: 18, 26, 44, 45, 58, 61, 69, 75, 78, 85, 87, 88, 91, 92, 93, 96.

Allah's name is read in the following eight verses of Sura 19: 30, 35, 36, 48, 49, 58, 67, 81. In the Medinian Suras, to the contrary, it is read at every step. In Sura 2, *The Cow*, Allah's name is read 216 times; in Sura 3, *The Imrans*, it is read no less than 209 times.

36. BAUS., p. 590. Italics are ours. Likewise NOL. I, p. 130.

B) Structure:

The Sura bears "Maryam" for its own title, taken from the 16th and the following verses. It is probably *tawqîfi* if one takes into account a *hadith* (oral tradition) reported by Tabarani.[37] It dates back to Mohammad himself. And based upon the same *hadith*, the Sura was revealed during the night rather than in daytime.

Its title, however, only expresses the Sura's material inadequately.[38] So do all other Koranic titles. Most often inappropriate to the content of their own chapters, they're picked up from a verse, a word, or even from a simple alphabetic letter.

In Cairo's typical edition, Sura 19 consists of 98 ayàt; while in other editions, or redactions, it carries 99 verses: a slight difference that makes no dent in the substance, resulting as it does from the different criteria used in dividing and numbering the ayàt.

The Sura's verses are rhymed prose: a peculiar note, this one, of the very early days of Mohammad's career. Then fresh in

---

37. A certain individual, called Ghassani Abu Maryam, was introduced to the Prophet and said: "O Messenger of Allah, last night a baby girl was born to me." The Prophet answered him: "*And last night came down onto me the Sura, Maryam.* **To the newborn baby girl you shall give the name of Mary.**" Cf. SAL., p. 171.

How much we can trust this episode, is hard to tell. What is absolutely sure is the fact that Mohammad could not yet speak of a "Sura," **Maryam**, as of an all too fresh revelation downed right that night. There was no Koran compiled in Suras at the time, not even in its graphic transcription.

38. Concerning the *titles* of the Koranic Suras, Marracci writes caustically: "Hae vero tam ridiculae epigraphae vix umquam Suris suis in argumento conveniunt: non secus ac si quis cerdo, vel barbitonsor apponeret tabernae suae cauponis, vel myropolae: vel si quis Ethnicus subscripsisset Jovi simulacro: **Mercurio Sacrum.**"* MAR. I. [De Alcorano], p. [47].

(*). "These *titles* are so ridiculous in that they never agree with what their Chapters (Suras) speak about; any more than if a craftsman, or a barber, had identified his shop with a sign, reading: 'a tavern', or 'perfumery'; or as if a non-Roman looking at Jupiter's statue said: 'It's Mercury's'." (Fares)

his call, he used to find himself caught up in the fervent whirl of his religious visions, all calling men to the frightening awareness of the account that each and all should give before Allah, the ultimate Judge beyond whom there is no appeal.

According to Blachère the Sura is composed of three parts. According to Haddad, on the contrary, it is the sum of two Suras joined together by juxtaposition; the *original* part (1, 33) includes the "histories" of Yahia's birth (v. 1-15) and Issa's birth (v. 16-33); the *accessorial* part instead (v. 75-98) reports strong volleys of invectives against the Associators *[mushrikùn]*, those mainly who feel no shame to ascribe a son to the Merciful. The rest would all be interpolated.[39]

Having taken into account both the diversity of the content and the variety of the final assonances, Haddad should be credited with being on the right side.

After some mature reflection, however, it seems to me that Sura 19, *Maryam*, shows a unitarian character hardly traceable in other Suras — except for the 12th, which deals with Joseph's "story." This unitarian character nonetheless does not necessarily indicate that the Sura's components have to be assigned to the same epoch, or period.

I have reservations particularly for a passage of seven *ayàt* (v. 34-40). There is no doubt in my mind that they are an *interpolation*. Either in content or form, the section gives the impression of an erratic bloc, out of place, forcibly wedged there in the context for polemic intent, and pointing toward the end of the controversy with Nejran's delegates.[40]

---

39. Cf. HAD. II, p. 460-468. — And, as for Blachère, the three mentioned groups would be these: v. 1-63; 64-74; 75, 98. Cf. BL. III, p. 329.

40. Of the same opinion are HAD. II, p. 465; and BLACHÈRE: "Ce vt. et les suivants sont sans doute une addition introduite plus tard au moment où Mahomet a engagé la lutte contre la doctrine chrétienne de Jésus fils de Dieu." BL. III, p. 332, in note; NOL. I, p. 130, in note.

As a matter of fact, the *content* of the passage clashes harshly with the calm, idyllic intonation of the preceding recount. Like a whip, it poignantly lashes those who dare confess that Jesus is God and do not shy from attributing children to the Divine Majesty (v. 35). And this is all the more emphasized when one considers that Mohammad never had any problem with the "nasàra" (Christians) during all the Medinian period, i.e. up to 631, the year of the delegation, and much less during the Meccan period.

And as to the form or style, the redactional anomaly pops out at once to whosoever reads the Koran in the original script. From verse 35 on, the reader notices a blunt, unexpected change in the final rhythm of the verses: after the unique and unaltered assonance in -*iyan*, characteristic of all prior narrations, a shocking variety follows — five different assonants for only seven verses (v. 34-40).

All in all, therefore, and after discarding the passage just mentioned, Sura 19 may well be divided logically into two parts.

The first part includes the first 58 verses. In it there is fundamentally the question of the *dhìkr*, remembrance, of five divine interventions in the history of salvation. Each of these is easily identified by the introductory phrase, *"Remember in the Book!,"* repeated after Zachariah (v. 2), with regard to Mary (v. 16), to Abraham (v. 41), to Moses (v. 51), and to Idris (v. 56).

The second part is no longer historical but parenthetic and comminatory. In it God's final verdict is put in perspective: a reassuring verdict with the reward the Merciful (v. 61) has in store for His adorers (v. 85), for the believers and the just (v. 96); and a desolating one with the scourge the same Merciful has prepared for those who rebelled against Him, ar-Rahmàn (v. 69); or who obstinately wished to ascribe to Him, ar-Rahmàn (v. 91), a son (v. 92).

It is a Christian story on one side, and a battle against the *mushrikùn* (the associators) with the Merciful [*ar-Rahmàn*] on the other. The typical elements are those of the Meccan period. Accordingly, they seem to favor Sura 19's Meccan origin.

2. Sura 3, The Imrans

A) Time:

The Sura is certainly *Medinian*. It therefore takes us to the period begun in 622 with the *Hegira*, the migration to Yathrib, called later Medina, the City (of the Prophet). While historically a quite modest event per se,[41] the Hegira had decisive consequences for the fate of Islam,[42] and uncounted repercussions on mankind's very history.[43]

In Medina Mohammad is another person. In control now of his own destiny on the wake of so many tragic and often successful vicissitudes, the great Arabian marked the second half of his career with a predominantly political, social and military ac-

---

41. Anything but "spectacular," as some put it, this flight was as modest as ever. In a hurry, and stealthily, Mohammad sent away his family first in July of 622; later, the following September, he rejoined them at Yathrib. And his entry into Medina was anything but triumphal, as Ess., p. 137, figures it.

42. Without the Hegira, "Islam probably would not have been other than a religion, or rather a mere Arabic religion, doomed not to cross the borders of the Arabian Peninsula which gave it birth." NAL. II, p. 194-195.

43. It is known that the Hegira was, seventeen years later, taken as the beginning of the Moslem era; and this reckoning is still in use in Islam today. Had the Hegira not been the memorable event it was, "several centuries of the European Medieval history would have taken a quite different turn. One can say the same of the many European issues regarding Oriental or colonial policies; [...] these would either have never existed, or, if they did, they would have taken another form." NAL. II, p. 195. Cf. WAT. I, p. 190-192.

tivity. His faithful, constantly increasing in number and influence, needed the juridical and theocratic structure[44] he intended to give.

A change of attitude is immediately noticed in him. His opposition to the Associators [*mushrikùn*] tapers off; instead his struggle becomes greater against the Hypocrites [*munafiqùn*], and likewise the Jews, who refused to acknowledge in Islam a teaching in accord with the primitive revelations.[45]

The Koranic Vulgate, the Moslem exegetes, and Specialists, all retain the Sura as Medinian.[46] They also recognize the endorsement by the *internal critique*. More than one "criterion," in fact, favors their opinion. We quote some:

a. — *Relation with the "People of the Book."* — In Sura 3 the sacred Books are no longer pointed to generically, but designated by their proper names — Torah and Gospel (v. 3, 48, 65). The polemic with "*Ahl il-Kitàb*," mainly Jews, is mentioned more frequently and is bitterly engaged[47]

---

44. "Such are the bounds set by Allah [*hudud Allah*]. And he that transgresses Allah's bounds [*hudud Allah*] wrongs his own soul" (65, 1). Cf. 2, 229-230. *The expression [hudud Allah]*, so typical of the Medinian period, is here to signify God's absolute sovereignty and unalienable rights as Lord (*rabb*) of the new, "middlemost" and basically "theocratic" Community.

KELLERHALS describes thus the *theocratic* nature of Islam: "In Medina wurde er zum politisch-militärischen Herrscher der sichtbaren Teocratie, zum irdischen Stellvertreter Gottes, zum Gründer und Führer des neuen Gottesvolkes, der allein wahren, Gott wohlgefälligen, zur Weltherrschaft bestimmten Gemeinde Allahs." KEL., p. 72. — Cf. also Ess., p. 244-249; WAT. II, p. 267-316.

45. With the three Jewish clans at Medina, furious and irreconcilable enemies, Mohammad used extreme violence. Cf. DIN., p. 185-6 (against the Qainuqa); p. 187 (against the Banu Nadir); p. 187-88 (against the Quraiza); p. 188-193 (against the Jews of Khaibar). Cf. also WAT. II, p. 252-254 (Qainuqa); p. 254-57 (Banu Nadir); p. 257-58 (Quraiza). — Whenever he used kindness and clemency, "that was only for economical reasons." GOT., p. 10.

46. Cf. HAD. II, p. 304, 312.

47. For attacks against the "*People of the Book*," cf. 3, 64, 65, 69, 70, 71,

— which is evidence of harsh feelings so typical of the Medinian period. The exclamation in addressing the crowds is the same one proper of the Medinian period: no longer the generic *"O Men,"* or *"Sons of Adam"* as in the Meccan period; but *"O You, who have believed."* And Mohammad keeps on using it exclusively.[48] An instance of that is Sura 5, *The Table,* one hundred per cent Medinian and, to believe some authorized sources, the last one in the series of the descents, or revelations. The exclamation in this 5th Sura, *"You, who have believed,"* reoccurs sixteen times.[49]

b. — *New style.* — The style is calm, reasoned, objective: more serene, more positive, as becomes a farsighted legislator. It is no longer imaginative as was before, or provocative and reactionary, or strewn with oaths which the enthusiasm, triggered by prophetic inspiration, has caused.

The material length itself, 200 verses, is also an index of the Medinian climate. We know also that the Meccan Suras could have been composed of only three verses, and the verse, or àyat, of only two words.[50]

c. — *Historic references.* — If the Koran's allusions to historic events are generally sibyllic and subject to diverging

72, 75, 98, 99, 110. — "Scripturales: hoc nomine intelliguntur semper Judaei et Christiani, vel simul, vel disiunctim." MAR. II, p. 122. — "Dignum peculiari nota est quod Mahumetus distinguat Scripturales, nempe Judeos et Christianos ab Associatoribus, nempe idololatris, seu plurium deorum cultoribus." Ib., p. 140.

48. For the exclamation form: "You, who have believed," cf. 3, 100, 102, 118, 130, 149, 156, 200.

49. For the exclamation in Sura 5, cf. vv. 1, 2, 6, 8, 11, 51, 54, 57, 87, 90, 94, 95, 101, 105, 106.

50. For the composition of the Suras, cf. 108, Al-Kàwthar (The Abundance) (3 vv.); 110, An-Nàsr (The Triumph) (3 vv.). — For the ayàt, cf. 107, Al-Ma'ùn, (The Alms), 7 (two words); 112, Al-Ikhlàs (The Unity), 2 (two words); 114, An-Nàs (Men), 2 (two words), 3 (two words).

interpretations,[51] here, in Sura 3, the hints appear clear and with no doubts involved; and they also refer to facts that certainly took place after the Hegira — therefore in the Medinian period.

Examples of that are: the allusion to the victory over Quraish in 624 at Badr (v. 13, 123); to the defeat suffered the following year at Uhud (v. 121-171); the *mubàhala* proposed in 631 to Nejran's delegates (v. 64). Thereupon it is concluded that the Sura could not, in its main portions at least, be earlier than the above-mentioned events.

In that light Blachère was able to assert that Sura 3 was born[52] of elements that took place in the years 624 and 625. Not so, believes Montet. Arguing from the constant recall of Uhud's defeat, which then must have been still recent, and of the confidence in Allah's protection, he proposes as a date the Hegira's sixth or seventh year, i.e. "the period from May 23rd, 627 to May 1st, 629." He adds at once, however, that it is quite difficult to fix "even approximately" the exact date of this Sura, formed undoubtedly of "Medinian fragments."[53]

B) *Structure:*

The title is taken from verse 33. In number of ayàt and in length, this Sura takes fourth place following, as it immediately

---

51. "Le Coran fournit uniquement des indications fragmentaires, souvent sybillines, presque toujours sujettes à des interprétations divergentes." BL. IV, p. 17.

52. "Elle est constituée en fait d'éléments, dont la venue se situe au cours de l'année 624 et 625." BL. III, p. 75.

53. "Les allusions positives à la Bataille de Badr (624) et à celle d'Ohod (625), et surtout l'insistance avec laquelle le Prophète revient sur la défaite d'Ohod, montrent que ces événements importants ne sont pas encore bien éloignés dans le temps. On pourrait donc proposer comme date de cette sourate l'an 6 ou l'an 7 de l'Hégire, c'est à dire la periode qui s'étend du 23 mai 627 au 1er mai 629." MONT. I, p. 83.

does, Sura 2, *The Cow* (286 vv.), Sura 26, *The Poets* (227 vv.), and Sura 7, *The Heights* (206 vv.). For amplitude and extension, however, it takes second place. That is why in Othman's compilation it was placed immediately after *The Cow's* Sura.

Its title, *The Imrans*, or The Imran Family, does not correspond to the content except by one-eighth of a fraction, i.e. 26 verses (v. 33-59) out of a total of 200.

An extremely complicated Sura like this one cannot possibly be reduced to a unity. Blachère[54] discovers in it five blocs of different revelations: 1-32; 33-63; 64-115; 116-180; 181-200. Of a contrary opinion is Haddad. He first lays aside the two sections considered interpolated and which concern the Banu Qainuqa Jewish tribe of Medina (v. 10-17) and the birth of Mary and Jesus (v. 35-64) respectively. Then he distinguishes the following: a sequence of controversies with the Jews (v. 7-97); a trace of sermons addressed to the Jews and to the faithful Moslems (v. 98-120); details relating to the defeat at Uhud (v. 121-122, 144-155); hints of the second incursion at Badr during the spring of 626 (v. 176-179); a debate with the Jews (v. 180-188); an exhortation on the value of suffering and witnessing with bloodshed (v. 189-195); and finally a Medinian account written during the Hegira's fourth year (v. 196-200).

As one can see, the Jews occupy a preponderant portion in this Sura — a fact which once more corroborates the argument for its Medinian nature.[55]

---

54. "Ces éléments sont groupés autour de *diverses idées centrales*, en sorte qu'il est impossible de distinguer entre plusieurs séries." BL. III, p. 75. — Italics are ours.

55. After quoting ZAM. and BAYD., Marracci thus describes him who reads Sura 3: "Qui legerit Suram in qua commemoratur Familia Amran, die Veneris: Deus et Angeli orabunt super eum donec Sol occubuerit [...]. Pro unoquoque versiculo illius dabitur ei immunitas a carcere gehennae." MAR. II, p. 106. — A similar reward is promised those who recite Sura 18, *Al-Kahf* (The Cave), which is, in Massignon's opinion, a permanent spiritual call by Elias (Hebrew saint) and the Seven Dormant (Christian Martyrs). Cf. MASS. (*Elie et son rôle trans-historique, Khadiriya, en Islam*, 1950), I, p. 154.

In terms of our theme, Sura 3, when compared with the
19th, proves itself to be far richer with Christological details
about the person and mission of Jesus placed at the core of the
controversy with the Nejran's delegates. In it Jesus is a messenger
to the children of Israel, largely provided with charismatic
powers (3, 49), and has come expressly to confirm and enforce
the Torah revealed by Allah to the first Fathers (3, 50).

To integrate the Marian material of Sura 3, I believe it is
not untimely to mention here a section of Sura 4, *The Women*,
so close to the subject we're dealing with. It relates Mohammad's
charges against the Jews (v. 155-161): They have violated the
Covenant, negated the signs of God, practiced usury while they
were forbidden it, and cheated others of their property. But
these were not all their major sins. The bitter bile of the Prophet's indignation pours mercilessly on them for two other crimes:
they have killed Christ, whom in reality they did not kill, and
they have dared to tarnish the stainless image of Mary by attack-
ing her with a "monstrous falsehood" (4, 156).

It is the famous calumny of πόρνεια (fornication), talmudic
in origin, that the Prophet took to heart to refute in Sura 19, using the mouth of the child Jesus vicariously (19, 27-32).

II. THE CONTENT

Sura 19 deals with four events in its Marian section
(v. 16-33): the separation of the child Mary from her own family, the annunciation, the childbirth, and the defense against an
outrageous calumny. Sura 3, however, besides relating the an-

nunciation episode, mentions Mary's nativity and adds further accounts about her secluded life in the Temple.

Putting the content of the two Suras together, we come out, in chronological order, with five events of Mary's life here on earth. They are:

1. *The Nativity* (3, 33-37);
2. *The Retreat into the Temple* (19, 16-17; 3, 37b, 42-44);
3. *The Annunciation* (19, 17b-21; 3, 45-51);
4. *The Childbirth* (19, 23-26);
5. *The Defense against an Outrageous Calumny* (19, 27-33).

We shall first speak of each separately and according to the Koran, and then we shall deal with:

6. Mary's *Eschatological Events*.

1. Mary's Nativity

THE TEXT:

"Truly Allah exalted Adam and Noah, Abraham's descendants and the descendants of *Imran* above all his creatures. They were the offspring of one another. Allah hears and knows all.

"Remember the words of Imran's wife: 'Lord,' she said, 'I dedicate to you that which is in my womb — as totally free of the world and vowed up to you. Accept this gift of mine, since you're the One who hears and knows all.'

"And when she was delivered of the child, she said: 'Lord, I have given birth to a daughter.' —

Allah well knew in advance of what she was delivered. — 'The male is not like the female; but I have called her Mary, and placed her and her descendant under your protection from Satan, the Accursed One.'

"Her Lord graciously accepted her. He made her grow a goodly child and entrusted her to the care of Zacharias." (3, 33- 37a)

In contrast with the degree of priority and importance that the Sura's title would have one assume in the weaving of the narrative, the protagonist here is not Imran, the main stem of the family, but his wife. This latter substitutes for her husband and performs as a principal actor, although she is not called by her proper name.[56] Of Imran the text makes no other mention but the name.

And his name — inserted in the list of Allah's chosen ones beside Adam, Noah and Abraham (v. 33) — might easily support an identification with the biblical Amran, Moses and Aaron's father;[57] and, thereby, a confusion between Maryam, the mother of Jesus, and Myriam, Amran's daughter and the sister of

---

56. This silence is a proof and a confirmation of the willful purpose not to mention, in the Koran, any woman by her own name except Mary, the mother of Jesus.

57. With regard to Mary's parentage, here are some "embroideries" by Moslem authors. Her father, Imran, was of a noble and regal ancestry; he descended from David through Solomon; and was of Mathan's tribe, who presided over the leaders and doctors of Israel. IBN ATHIR, THA'LABI, KISA'I (ap. HAY., p. 67). Her mother, Anna, was advanced in years, and sterile up to then (cf. note 67, p. 65). Imran would have died before Anna would have given her birth. IBN ATHIR, THA'LABI (loc. cit., p. 68). Cf. AMEL., p. 469.

Mary was related to Elizabeth, Zachariah's wife and mother of Yahia (cf. note 129, p. 90), and some state that she was a descendant of Aaron, forefather of the class of the Levites [ahbàr]. TABARI, IBN ATHIR, THA'LABI (ap. HAY., p. 83). But she was no "sister" of his, in strict terms (cf. note 59, p. 62).

Aaron.[58] Although explicitly admitted by several authors, mainly Westerners,[59] the implication was decidedly rejected by Moslem

---

How close Mary and Elizabeth were, cannot be determined from the Koran. Together with Zachariah, Yahia and Issa, both were part of *"Imran's Family."* Some, exegetes or historians, think Elizabeth to be Mary's *sister.* Cf. IBN ATHIR (ap. HAY., p. 67); SAB., p. 100, 203; AMEL., p. 461; and WENS., p. 359, who, while not agreeing with this opinion, quotes in his favor TAB. and MAS'UDI. — Others pretend Elizabeth is Mary's *maternal aunt*, and consequently sister to Imran's wife [Anna]; in other words, Imran and Zachariah may have married respectively two sisters. Cf. TAB. VI, n. 6914 (p. 352), n. 6915 (p. 353); IBN ATHIR (ap. HAY., p. 51); ZAM. I, 357; BAYD. I, 136; GEL., p. 73. BOUB. (I, p. 614), instead, believes Elizabeth to be "Mary's older cousin."

58. "Sumpsit ergo Maria prophetissa, *soror Aaron*, tympanum in manu sua." (*Ex.*, 15, 20).

59. Marracci had already expressed his ruthlessness and retained this confusion as *"crassissimus Mahumeti error"* and added textually: *"Distorqueant quantum volunt Mahumetani expositores verba Alcorani: numquam Prophetam suum ab hoc errore potuerunt vindicare."* MAR. II, p. 107. Cf. *ibid.*, p. 453. — Ullman sees here an *"anachronismus."* Ull., p. 246. — "Aaron's sister and daughter of Imran (*confusion*, therefore, between Mary, mother of Jesus and Mary, Moses' sister)." NAL. I, p. 608. — "Mary, sister of Moses, and at the same time mother of Jesus. Several such mistakes must have been already in circulation and accepted in the Prophet's days." BON., p. 11. — *"Confondant la Vierge avec Miriam, soeur de Moïse et d'Aaron, Mahomet donne à son père le nom d'Imran."* SID., p. 141. — "De là la *confusion* commise par Mahomet entre Miriam, soeur de Moïse et d'Aaron, et Miriam, mère de Jésus." MONT., p. 88. — *"L'identification* de la Vierge Marie et de la soeur d'Aaron n'est donc pas un fait isolé dans la sourate 19. Elle fait partie d'un système généalogique délibérément inventé par le rabbin. Et cette *identification* constitue un acte d'impudence notoire. Elle entre dans le plan général de la judaisation des données évengéliques que nous trouvons dans le Psuedo-Coran." ZAK., p. 295. — We ought to note here that Zakarias does not hesitate to label the Koranic "confusion" as a *"fraudulent trick"* genially conceived by the famous Rabbi (Zk., p. 162). This latter, to make fun of the Arabs (p. 161) — people ignorant (p. 212) and stupid (p. 200) — would have jumbled the chronological data just to empty his documents of any Christian content (p. 153). But we're allowed to ask Zakarias if the "trick" could have passed smoothly and unobserved by the Arabs — brainless people, who would have easily "swallowed" this and other "balivernes" (nonsense) of the sort (p. 162). — The "gross genealogic trick" (p. 212), *confusing* two persons separated in time by 1800 years, could not have passed unnoticed by the reported opponent of the

exegetes,[60] and prudently discarded by others.[61]

The Koranic expressions, as they clearly read in the text, show at once the confusion. Analyzed, however, in the light of their context, they make one feel that they probably hide, in between their lines, some kind of *spiritual* kinship rather than a

---

Rabbi, the Pastor and Bishop of the Christians of Mecca — could it? Bishop Waraka, history knows, was a figure of high standing, and erudite (p. 145). — Italics are ours. — Cf. JEF., p. 217, 262; GAUD., p. 384.

60. Blachère thinks that the polemic around the confusion of the two Marys would have been stirred by Nejran's delegation. And the Islamic exegesis, sensitive to the attack, might have suggested seeing here in Aaron a personage other than the brother of Moses, or given to the term *sister* the meaning of Aaron's *descendant*. BL. III, p. 331. — BOUB. [I, p. 612]; "il s'agit en l'occurrence, non d'un lien direct de parenté, mais d'une lignée généalogique et d'une communauté de pensée religieuse." Therefore, "nulle part dans le texte sacré et dans ses commentaires, on ne trouve trace de cette prétendue confusion" (BOUB. I, p. 117).

For the reportedly existing distinction between two Imrans, and, consequently, two Aarons, and two Marys, all apart from each other by a lapse of time of no less than 1800 years, cf. TAB. VI, n. 6855 (p. 328), n. 6895 (p. 332); ZAM, I, p. 335; BAYD. I, p. 136.

61. "The problem of Aaron's sister could be resolved on the lines of that of Christ's brothers." ANW., p. 458. — "On a supposé ... le fait que Maryam est donnée comme soeur de Harun (surate 19, 29) est dû à une confusion entre les deux Myriam de la Bible. Sale, Gerock et d'autres pensent qu'une telle confusion est improbable." WENS., p. 359. — "Quoiqu'il puisse être du Coran, il faut s'abstenir d'accuser l'islam de faire une telle confusion." JAL. I, p. 13. — "Respingiamo l'interpretazione corrente di questo vocativo come un anacronismo dovuto ad una visione storica sfasata in Maometto, per cui la Maria di Mosè sarebbe stata confusa con Maria Madre di Cristo. Dolendoci di trovare tra i sostenitori di tale teoria persino l'informatissimo Ahrens (*Christliches im Qoran*, ZDMG. N.F., 9 [1930], p. 167), sottoscriviamo piuttosto su questo punto la tesi del Torrey [*The Jewish Foundation of Islam*. New York, 1933, p. 120]. BEL.,p. 460. — "Sembra difficile che *Muhammad*, che, senza essere uno storico, conosceva certo la enorme distanza di tempo che separa Gesù da Mosè come risulta da tutto il Corano, abbia potuto fare una simile confusione." BAUS., p. 519.

true and proper consanguinity.[62] Born of the similarity in the way people lived and thought, this kinship was nurtured and sustained by their faith in the one and true God and the fidelity to the common covenant with God. In virtue of this covenant, and that faith, the successive generations *[dhurriyàt]*, from Adam, to Noah, to Abraham, to each member of Imran's family, may have mutually seemed to each other so connected, almost blended, that they were able to call each other "brothers" and "sisters"; they thus constitute all together only one descendant whether Imran be retained as *carnal* father of Moses, Aaron and Myriam, or whether he be considered the spiritual primogenitor of Zachariah, Yahia, and Mary, Issa's mother. Especially if one keeps in mind that the terms of relationship do not always bear the same identical meaning in both the Semitic and Indo-European languages — as notes Boubakeur. "In Arabic, in Hebrew, in Aramaic, etc. words like *abb* (father), *umm* (mother), *ukht* (sister) *bint* (daughter), *amm* (paternal uncle), carry a significance which is not strictly limited to ties of carnal kinship."[63]

In Mary's case here, direct mention is made of Aaron rather than of Moses, maybe because of a biblical reminiscence: "*Maria, prophetissa, soror Aaron*" (*Ex.*, 15-20) — "Mary, the prophetess, the sister of Aaron"; or because of an intended allusion to the priestly race of which Aaron was the head, and to which Mary, the mother of Jesus, was supposed to have had at least some spiritual link.[64]

---

62. Unlike others, TABARI puts in emphasis the factors of religious and moral unity, which bind together the generations favored by Allah in the persons of their respective foreparents, Adam, Abraham and Imran. Cf. TAB. VI, n. 6850 (p. 326), n. 6854 (p. 327-28).

63. BOUB. I, p. 612.

64. Reacting to a comment by WHERRY *["Because she was of Levitical race"]*, Belli states that the reason why Aaron is mentioned here, and not Moses, is because he is the "forefather" of the Priestly Cast; and Priesthood appears as a prerogative for his descendants only. And adds, besides, that the term "sister", *[ukht]* is understood "in a large sense of parent, descendant, like all the parenthood words in the Orient." BEL., p. 460.

After unquestionably using Christian sources, Moslem authors call Mary's parents *Joachim* and *Anna*.[65] On these two names, however, the Koran is entirely silent. Likewise, it does not remember the particulars of Anna's sterility and old age,[66] which particulars, the sterility at least,[67] we find recorded by the exegetes subsequently to James' *Proto- evangelium*.[68]

While pregnant, and with high hopes that she will give birth to a baby creature of male sex, the future mother thinks at once of consecrating to God the fruit of her womb, thus expressing herself: *"Lord, I dedicate to your service that which is in my womb: a gift totally free (muhàrrar) from the world and solely vowed to you. Accept it from me, you who hears and knows all."* (3, 35)

The term *muhàrrar*, in its actual passive participial form at least, is a rarity. Nowhere else in the whole Koran is it found in this grammatical construction. To explain it, the hermeneutics have tried to give various interpretations which, despite some small nuances,[69] all fundamentally agree.[70] What we are concerned about so far, is our preference for the explanation pro-

---

65. Cf. TAB. VI, no. 6855 (p. 328), n. 6875 (p. 332); ZAM. I, 355; BAYD. I, 136. — Cf. STR., p. 68, 70, 82, 96.

66. The Koran describes Abraham's wife as old (11, 72) and sterile (51, 29); and Zachariah's wife as sterile (19, 5, 8). But it is silent with regard to Imran's wife.

67. Cf. TAB. VI, n. 6785 (p. 332); ZAM. I, 355; BAYD. I, 136. — "Anne était vieille et stérile." IBN ATHIR (ap. HAY., p. 67-68).
Moslem exegetes (cf. TAB. VI, n. 6860-6869 [p. 331-32] [p. 330]; IBN ATHIR [ap. HAY., p. 68]; ZAM. I, 355; BAYD. I, 136) depend on the Apocrypha for the detail which stirred in Anna's heart the desire for a son, despite her known sterility. Cf. *Proto-ev. of James*, III, 2: "She saw in the laurel tree a nest of sparrows, and at once she made a moan." STR., p. 74.

68. Cf. *Proto-ev.*, II, 1; IV, 4. — Cf. STR., p. 68, 82.

69. For such nuances cf. TAB. VI, n. 6860-6869 (p. 331-32).

70. Cf. in NWY., p. 50, the explanations given by Ga'far Sadiq, Termidhi Hakim, Sahl Tustari, Nuri and Abu-Uthman.

posed by Muqatil (767). According to him, *muhàrrar* indicates the type of person who is free from the worries of the world, not tied by engrossing temporary commitments, and engaged in the service of the Temple for the glory of the Lord.[71]

By using this accurate term right from the very start of Mary's earthly existence, the Koran intends to present the Child to us in the light of God, as someone totally dedicated to Him and exclusively intended to give Him honor and glory with all her powers. The pious mother's most ardent wish was consequently this: to offer her offspring to serve the Lord in the Temple.[72]

Moments after childbirth, the mother does not hide her surprise and frustration, and appears to be crushed by sorrow.[73] She had brought forth into the world a baby girl, knowing well in advance that the baby, if female, will not be welcome to serve in the Temple. And without hesitation she expresses her disillusion and grief, pouring out her heart before the Lord in these words: *"Lord, I have given birth to a daughter."* (Allah well knew of what she was delivered.) *"The female is not as fit as the*

---

71. "Le *muharrar* est celui qui ne travaille pour ce monde, qui ne se marie pas, et qui se consacre aux oeuvres de l'Au-delà, en s'attachant au Sanctuaire pour y adorer Dieu" (ap. NWY., p. 50).

72. According to Moslem authors, the *presentation in the Temple* would have been accomplished by the pious mother immediately after the birth of the daughter (cf. ZAM. I, 357; BAYD. I, 135; SAB., p. 199). According to others, instead, when Mary was an adolescent and bereaved of her father (SHAR., p. 172); or, even, of her mother (SAB., p. 199). At the beginning she would have been entrusted to Zachariah, with no dissent by, or contention with, the Levites; and in Zachariah's home, near Elizabeth, she would have spent her tender years (*ibid.*). Only later, she was offered for the service of the Temple, to fulfill the vow of the religious mother. Cf. TAB. VI, n. 6914-6915 (p. 352-353).

73. Koranic exegetes have all noticed in the pious mother this sense of surprise and bitterness when, instead of a baby boy, she brought forth a baby girl. Cf. TAB. VI, n. 6876 (p. 334), n. 6878-6979 (p. 335), n. 6881 (p. 335); ZAM. I, 356; BAYD. I, 136; SHAR., p. 172; SAB., 198; AMEL., p. 470.

male! I have called her Mary, and placed her and her descendant [dhurrìyat] under your protection from Satan, the Accursed One!" (3, 36)

The text gives no explanation for the name Maryam. [74]

It limits itself to making understood, implicitly, that Allah has largely responded to the pious mother's plea while explicitly emphasizing that the vow she expressed to him was graciously accepted (3, 37a): Mary, although a female, was received into the divine service. [75] And the sovereign complacency was quite obvious by the singular watch over the person and vicissitudes of the newborn Baby, to the extent that Allah deigned to make her grow (3, 37a) as a goodly child, [76] with common satisfaction in conformity to the vow [77] of the religious and pious mother.

---

74. Exegetes give the name "Mary" the meaning of "devout." Cf. ZAM. I, 356; IBN ATHIR (ap. HAY., 68); AMEL., p. 470. This denomination, they think, was preferred to all other proper names because it expressed the full accord between the name imposed and the exemplary life of the favored Child. Cf. BAYD. I, p. 136. — BOUBAKEUR notes that the meaning of "devout", "pious" ['abidat], "s'inspire moins de la stricte étymologie que de la vénération que le monde musulman porte à la Vierge." BOUB. I, p. 611.

75. Only males were recipients of such promises. "Les filles, elles ne pouvaient pas l'être à cause du régime des impuretés physiques auxquelles elles sont soumises." IBN ATHIR (ap. HAY., p. 68). The service in the Temple expected by the vow extended itself until adult age. "C'est alors seulement qu'on lui laissait le choix soit de continuer à vivre dans le Temple, soit de le quitter pour vivre où il voudrait." *Ibid.* Cf. AMEL., p. 470.
The exegetes note that Mary's admission to the service in the Temple, although she is a female, constitutes an exception all in favor of her goodness. Cf. TAB. VI, n. 6876 (p. 334), n. 6878-6979 (p. 335), n. 6881 (p. 335); GEL., p. 72; HAD. I, 157; SHAR., p. 172.

76. The bloom in the growth of Baby Mary is, by authors, understood in two ways: physically and morally.
For GEL. (p. 73), her bodily growth in one day only equalled that of a whole year. — TAB. (VI, n. 6900; [p. 344]): Allah made her grow wonderfully, in the sense that He provided her with all the necessaries to become an adult, mature woman. — For ZAM. (I, 358) and BAYD. (I, 136), the growth was luxuriant, in the sense that Mary's education was excellent and it had an indelibly beneficial impact on her whole existence. Others prefer to insist on the

2. Retreat into the Temple

THE TEXT:

1. "And you shall remember in the Book the story of Mary: how she left her own people and betook herself to a solitary place to the east, and in their presence she took herself a veil." (19, 16-17).

2. "And Zachariah took her into his care. Whenever he visited her in the *mihràb* (Shrine) he found she had food with her. 'Mary,' he said, 'where is this food from?'

" 'It is from Allah,' she answered. 'Allah gives without stint to whom He will'. " (3, 37b)

Living beyond the *borderline* of the Byzantine Empire, in the far Hijaz, and deprived of accurate topographic notions about Jerusalem and her monuments, Mohammad could not have expressed himself here in more than a generic and laconic

---

moral aspect of this growth. For them, Mary grew constantly in goodness, chastity, obedience, loyalty and was wonderfully dedicated to all exercises of piety. Cf. SAB., p. 199; HAD. I, p. 157.

77. The Koran makes no mention of the Angel's apparition, reported by Proto-evangelium (IV, 1), subsequent to which Imran's wife had formulated her consecratory vow. Such apparition is recorded instead by the Ps.-Matthew along with the wish of the pious mother; and in that, it agrees with the Koran (3, 35). It words it differently however. First, it makes the mother express her wish, or vow, right from the beginning of her marriage; then, it explicitly states the mother's decision, whether the newborn be a male or a female: "You know, O Lord, that the very day I was married (ab initio conjugii mei) I made a vow that if ever I am granted a son or a daughter (filium aut filiam), either of them I would have offered to You in your holy Temple" (Ps.-Mt. II, 2. AM., p. 286). And this difference calls, in my opinion, for an oral dependence, not textual.

manner. The Koranic indication makànan sharqìyan (a place to the east) is thus vague and undetermined. In trying to localize it commentators have gone groping along, some locating it to the east of the paternal home, and others in the annex of the Temple, on the eastern side.[78]

This latter interpretation seems preferable, because it is more cohesive with the text and context.

Profiting, in fact, by the Koranic analogy, we should say that the "place to the east" of which Sura 19 speaks, ought not to be distinguished from the mihràb[79] mentioned by Sura 3. And this sort of mihràb must have been a building annexed to the Temple, on its eastern side, and destined to be lived in.[80]

---

78. Thus GEL., p. 404. — Cf. Also HAD. I, p. 144; ZAM. III, 9; BAYD. II, 24. — "A l'orient. A l'est de la sinagogue? Dans un lieu situé du côté de la maison de Zacharie? En un oratoire privé construit par Zacharie et attenant à sa demeure du côté est. Ce sont les questions que les commentateurs se posent en se demandant si ce n'est pas là la raison profonde qui explique l'orientation traditionnelle des églises chrétiennes vers le levant." BOUB., p. 619.
Besides the paternal home, ZAM. and BAYD., loc. cit., mention also the oriental part of the Temple. BAYD. adds further (ibid.) that the Christians had, for this reason indeed, fixed their own Kìbla toward the Orient. — SAB. (p. 200): in the "annex" of the Holy House, the Temple. — ZAK. II, p. 29: "Du côté de l'Orient, c'est à dire dans le sanctuaire du Temple orienté vers l'est."

79. In today's Mosques, the mihràb indicates the direction of the Ka'ba toward which the Leader [Imàm] and the faithful turn during public worship [salàt]. In the text, and more specifically in Zachariah's case (19, 11), mihràb means the Sancta Sanctorum of the Temple of Jerusalem as in Lk. 1, 9, 21. But in Mary's case (3, 37) it must mean quite another site. "Mohammad had no accurate notion of the Temple's locality, and therefore, he has confused it with some other suggested by some Apocryphum." BAUS., p. 445.

80. "L'enfant grandit dans une chambre du temple." WENS., p. 339. — The Proto-evangelium speaks of a sojourn in the very Temple of the Lord: ἐν ναῷ Κυρίου (8, 1 — STR., p. 100; cf. 9, 3 (p. 108); 15, 1 (p. 132); 16, 1 (p. 138); rather right in the very Sancta Sanctorum of the Temple: εἰς τὰ ἄγια τῶν ἀγίων (13, 2; 15, 3 — STR., p. 124, 134). And the Priests advised each other so that, coming to the age of puberty (12 years), Mary would not profane by her menstruation the Temple of the Lord: μήπως μιάνῃ τὸ ἀγίασμα Κυρίου (8, 2 — STR., p. 102).

If this interpretation is accepted, we will have in the Koran not one but two allusions to Mary's solitude: one is her presentation in the Temple,[81] already recorded in the Proto-evangelium of James,[82] and the other is her prolonged lodging near the Temple.[83]

It is worth mentioning here that the plasticity of movements is, by the Koran, attributed directly to Mary, not to her mother: The mother formulates the vow, and the daughter, Mary, fulfills it.

Mary abandoned her parental home and went to take another abode near the house of the Lord. There, for several years, she lived in solitude, protected by a *hijàb* — *curtain*-

---

The Koran's translators use different versions for the term *mihràb: santuario* (BAUS., p. 39), *sanctuaire* (BL. IV, p. 180), *Temple* (MAS., p. 65), *Kammer* (Ull., p. 56), *Zelle* (HEN., p. 69); Boub.: "nous traduisons, faute de terme plus approprié, par *sanctuaire.*" (I, p. 118). — More accurately MARRACCI: "morabatur in *Adyto Templi.*" MAR. II, p. 434.

81. Here are some "embroideries" regarding Mary's life in the Temple; or, better, in the *mihràb*. Some describe it as the most noble and respected site (TAB. VI, n. 6936 [p. 357]; ZAM. I, 358; SAB., p. 199); thus called, because *mihràb* is a "battlefield", from *[hàraba]*, to wage war against the devil (BAYD. I, 137).
Mary spent her years there under the rigorous and jealous tutorship of Zachariah. This, in the beginning, had provided her with a nurse. IBN ATHIR, THA'LABI, KISA'I (ap. HAY., p. 69). Only later he built her a separate room provided with a secret stairway to go in and out (ZAM. I, 358; BAYD. I, 137), reserved uniquely for him and her (GEL., p. 73). Each time Zachariah came to check on her, the trusted custodian made certain to lock hermetically as many as seven doors behind him. Cf. TAB. VI, n. 6930 (p. 355); n. 6936 (p. 358); ZAM. I, 358; BAYD. I, 137. From this usual abode — in the Temple, or near the Temple — Mary hardly went away for a notable time except during her periods; then, to avoid the profanation of the Temple, she would leave her retreat and spend a few days at her cousin's, Elizabeth; soon after her cycle, she would come back to her *mihràb* (ZAM. I, 9).

82. The Proto-evangelium delights in describing with pomp and majesty the presentation of Baby Mary in the Temple. Cf. 7, 1-3. — STR., p. 96-100.

83. Cf. 3, 37; 19, 16.

veil, or *mantle-veil*[84] — to favor her self-restraint and modesty and keep her away from any indiscreet eye: *"And in their presence she took herself a veil"* (19, 17a).

During her retreat, Mary spent her years tutored, protected and provided for by Zachariah (3, 37b). To him fell this honorific and dutiful charge in the wake of a challenge he won through an unusual miracle.[85]

Properly speaking, this miracle and that challenge[86] belong to the domain of the *ghàyb*, the world of arcane realities

---

84. Cf. for the word *hijàb*, 7, 46; 33, 53; 38, 32; 41, 5; 42, 51. — Translators and exegetes understand it differently. BAYD. II, p. 24; and GEL., p. 404, take it for a *curtain*. For others it is a *veil* with which Mary used to cover herself. Thus KASIMIRSKI (*loc. cit.*, p. 238): "Elle *se couvrit* d'un *voile* qui la déroba à leur regards." MONT. (I., p. 394): "Elle se *couvrit* d'un *voile* pour se cacher aux yeux de ses parents." — ULL. (p. 246): "und *sich* verschleierte." WAHL, by ULL. (*loc. cit.*) quoted in note, instead of using *Vorhang* (curtain), translates: "und den *Schleier* abgelegt." — HEN. (p. 287): "Und *sich* vor ihnen verschleierte." — And, long before, MARRACCI: "Et accepit clam ipsis *velum*, quo *se tegeret.*" MAR. II, p. 431. Italics are ours. — More than explicit is SAVARY: "Elle prit en secret un *voile* pour *se couvrir.*" And adds in the note: "Dès la plus haute antiquité, les femmes des contrées orientales ont été dans l'usage de *se couvrir* le visage." SAV., 325. — To the contrary BOUB. (I, p. 619): "Elle mit un *rideau* entre eux et elle." As to the meaning and use of the *Hijàb*, cf. CHELHOD J., in the new edition of EI [Leyde-Paris, Brill-Maisonneuve et Larose, 1971], III, p. 370-372.

85. The episode of the reeds, drawn for lots, is not mentioned by any Apocrypha; and much less in the Canonical Gospels.

86. Here are again some "embroideries" invented by Moslem authors around the debate, or challenge, which took place among the Levites of the Temple. The problem was, in the opinion of some Doctors, to find a substitute for Zachariah, now old and himself in need of others' help and assistance. Cf. TAB. VI, n. 6915 (p. 353). For others the question was who would initially assume Mary's tutorship, considered an honorific job; Zachariah would have availed himself of the title of his close parentage. IBN ATHIR, THA'LABI (ap. HAY., p. 68). Twenty-seven pretendants took part in the debate (ZAM. I, 357; BAYD, I, 136); the argument was hot, since it was around the daughter of Imran, a Leader and a Pontif. IBN ATHIR, THA'LABI, KISA'I (ap. HAY., p. 68). Upon reaching the river bank, probably the Jordan — KISA'I speaks of a fountain, "the fountain of Selwan" (ap. HAY., p. 69, note) — in the water

known to God alone.[87] Only through a special revelation did they come down to Mohammad (3, 44a). Soberly, and almost by short cut, both are insinuated by the Koran in these words: *"You were not present when they cast lots to see which of them should have charge of Mary; nor were you present when they argued about her"* (3, 44b).

If the miraculous intervention in casting the lots was a preferential sign for Zachariah against his competitors, the result, in ultimate analysis, was meant to be in Mary's favor: to guarantee her a trustworthy and visible custodianship. Which is, for us, another confirmation of that climate of delicate attention with which Mohammad wanted the person of Mary, the mother of Jesus, surrounded and almost enveloped from the very first moment of her mortal existence.

All the while Mary lived in the *mihràb*, Allah took care of her bodily needs providing for her abundantly; and the angels, His messengers,[88] were in charge of those of the spirit, delighting her with visions and revelations.

---

they threw their pen feathers, those which they had used to transcribe the Torah (TAB. VI, n. 6909 [p. 351]); and the only pen that remained afloat was that of Zachariah, which decided his selection for the job of tutoring Mary. Cf. Roschini G., *Dizionario di Mariologia* (Roma, Studium, 1961), p. 242; ZAM. I, 357; BAYD. I, 136; AMEL., p. 462.

We note incidentally that the controversy and the challenge were not among "the angels," as has been stated: G. Roschini, *Dizionario di Mariologia* (Roma, Studium, 1961), p. 242; but among the *Levites* of the Temple, one of whom was Zachariah. Likewise, the person to whom this news from the dominium of the *ghàyb* was communicated, was not Zachariah (*loc. cit.*, p. 241), but Mohammad himself.

87. "He knows the invisible [*al ghàyb*] and the visible" (59, 22). Cf. 62, 8; 64, 18; 72, 26.

88. Moslem authors have not failed, here also, to weave gracious "embroideries." To believe them, Mary, on a par with the baby Jesus, was favored with a premature speech; and, while a suckling, she could talk expeditiously. Cf. ZAM. I, 358; BAYD. I, 137. Furthermore, she never needed to be breast-fed (*loc. cit.*). Her food came to her from heaven [*jànnat*]. It was miraculously multiplied (cf. THA'LABI, ap. HAY. p. 70); or provided for in an exceptional

Upon visiting her, Zachariah found that she was plentifully provided with food supplied to her miraculously; and Mary admitted (3, 37b) to having received it from the hand of the Supreme Providence who imparts His gifts to whom He will, without favoritism or limit of any sort.[89]

Whether angels or angel — more exact according to the Koranic style of not infrequently using the collective for individuals — all loved to have a happy conversation with her. The angel, Gabriel,[90] for instance, was pleased to unveil to her, on behalf of God, her privileged situation in the design of salvation, her predestination, her sanctification and her glorification. He said to her: *"Mary, Allah has chosen you. He made you pure, and exalted you above all women"* (3, 42).

An exhibition so rich with divine complacence could not pass Mary by and leave her sensible soul totally indifferent; but should flood her with joy, fill her heart with love, and inspire her to fervor and activity. Mary understood that. And in the awareness that she had been elevated to such an honor, she

---

way: winter fruits during summer, or summer fruits during winter. TAB. VI, n. 6916-6936 (p. 353-358); ZAM. I, 358; BAYD. I, 137; GEL., p. 73; SAB., p. 199; IBN ATHIR (ap. HAY., p. 69. AMEL., p. 462).

89. To Allah, who lavishes His gifts without measure (2, 212), the Koran reserves the "most excellent names," e.g. *razzàk*, provider (51, 58); *wahhàb*, generous giver (38, 9); *khair ur-ràzikìn*, the best of providers (62, 11).

90. Many and varied are the tasks assigned to angel Gabriel by the exegetes. Among other absurd lucubrations, let what Muqatil allows himself to assert be an instance: in the Paradise runs the river of life. Every day, around tierce [nine a.m.], Gabriel [Gibril] takes a dip in it. He has two wings, which he displays in the water. And each wing bears seventy thousand feathers. As he comes out of the water after he's through bathing, a drop of water drips from each feather. Then Allah turns each drop into an angel who praises Him until the day of resurrection and judgment. Cf. NWY., p. 70. — Several honorific jobs were also assigned to Gabriel. One of them is particularly worth mentioning: to have cut the umbilical cord to the newborn and future Prophet, Mohammad, who came to light "net de toute souillure, circoncis naturellement" DIN., p. 17. Not to mention also the "wash of heart" to baby Mohammad. Cf. WAT. I, p. 61-62.

could not keep her soul from bursting into fiery songs of adoration and thanksgiving, thus putting into practice the angelic invitation: *"Mary, be obedient to your Lord; bow down and worship with the worshippers"* (3, 43).

3. The Annunciation

Unlike other Marian events, the annunciation is reported in
two Koranic Suras differing in time and content, Sura 19 and
Sura 3. Here is the text rendered, as usual, straight from its
Arabic source:

SURA 19:

"And We sent to her Our spirit in the semblance of a full-grown man. And when she saw
him, she said, 'I take refuge from you in the Merciful. If you fear the Lord, leave me and go
away.'

"He said, 'I am the messenger of your Lord,
and have come to give you an all-pure son.'

" 'How shall I bear a child,' she answered,
'when I am a virgin, no man has touched me
ever, and I am no prostitute?'

"He replied, 'So it shall be. For your Lord
had said, "That's an easy thing for Us. And We

will make of him a Sign to mankind, and a mercy
from Ourselves. That's Our established decree." ' "
(19, 17b-21)

SURA 3:

"The angels said to Mary: 'Allah bids you rejoice in a Word from Him. His name is the Messiah, Jesus the son of Mary, a noble in this world
and in the next, and one of the most favored by
Allah. He shall preach to men from his cradle and
in the prime of manhood, and shall be one among
the righteous.'

" 'Lord,' answered Mary, 'how shall I have a
child when no man has touched me?'

"The angel answered: 'Such is the will of
Allah. He creates what He will. When He decrees
a thing, He need only say, "Be," and it is. He will
instruct him in the Scriptures and in Wisdom, in
the Torah and in the Gospel, and send him forth
as an apostle to the Israelites. He will say to them:
"I bring you a Sign from your Lord. From clay I
will make for you the likeness of a bird. I shall
breathe into it, and, by Allah's leave, it shall
become a living bird. By Allah's leave I shall also
give sight to the blind man, heal the leper, and
raise the dead to life. I shall tell you what to eat
and what to store up in your houses. Surely that
will be a Sign for you, if you are true believers. I
come to confirm the Torah that has already been
revealed, and to make lawful to you some of the
things you are forbidden. I bring you a Sign from

your Lord: therefore fear Him and obey me. Allah
is my God and your God: therefore serve Him.
That is the straight path." ' "(3, 45-51)

The annunciation narrative in the two above-mentioned
Suras is based fundamentally on the announcement of Yahia's
(John's) birth brought to Zachariah. Though chronologically of
an earlier date, Yahia's news is also reported by our two present
Suras (3, 38-41; 19, 1-9). We limit our dissertation to these three
elemental points: the messenger, the message, and the
psychological reaction.

A) *The Messenger:*

In both events, the *angels* are the ones who bring the good
news respectively to Zachariah[91] and to Mary[92] as they had
brought it to Abraham for the birth of a son.[93]

The Koran more than seventy times makes mention of
angels; and always in the plural form (*al malà'ykat*), with one
exception only (17, 95). They are intelligent beings, capable of
entering into dialogue with God[94] and with men;[95] of rendering

---

91. "And as he stood praying in the Shrine *[mihràb]*, the *angels* called out
to him, saying: 'Allah bids you rejoice in the birth of Yahia (John)' " (3, 39).

92. "The *angels* said to Mary: 'Allah bids you rejoice in a Word from
Him' " (3, 45).

93. "Our messengers *[the angels]* came to Abraham with good news" (11,
39).

94. "When your Lord *said* to the angels: 'I am placing on the earth one
that shall rule as My deputy,' they *replied*: 'Will you put there one that will
do evil and shed blood?' " (2, 30). Cf. 8, 12; 15, 28; 34, 40; 37, 71.

95. "He (the angel) replied: 'Such is the will of Allah. He creates whom
He will' " (3, 47). Cf. 4, 97; 13, 24; 16, 32; 39, 73; 41, 1, 30-32.

witness,[96] of interceding and supplicating (42, 5), mostly in favor of Mohammad.[97] Gathered around the throne of Allah, their Lord, they adore Him (16, 49); they praise Him (13, 13); they execute His orders,[98] always faithful to His assignments (66, 6); always ready to go forth, as messengers,[99] to transmit to men His orders (16, 2, 33; 97, 4) and His threats (8, 50; 47, 27).

In Sura 19 Allah's envoy is called spirit, *rùh*, rather than angel: *"And We sent to her Our spirit [rùh-ana] in the semblance of a full-grown man"* (19, 17). And in the two parallel paragraphs elsewhere, alluding to the same fact, we find the same denomination: *"We breathed into her of Our spirit" [min rùhi-na]* (21, 91); and, *"Into whose womb We breathed of Our spirit" [min rùhi-na]* (66, 12).

To avoid equivocations, and despite the apparent identity in the denomination, the term *rùh* and the parenthetic *rùh-una* do in no way designate the Holy Spirit of the Christian doctrine.

As in other analogous terms — *rùh-ul'lah*, the

---

96. "Allah bears witness that there is no god but Him, and so do the angels and the sages" (3, 18). Cf. 4, 166; 37, 150.

97. "Indeed Allah and His angels pray upon the Prophet *[yusallùna ala nnabi]*. You that have believed, pray on him *[sallu alàihi]* and wish peace on him *[wa sàllimu]"* (33, 56). — "Prier et prière, dans la langue coranique, c'est invoquer la puissance suprême pour son propre bien ou pour celui d'autrui. Les commentaires sont donc à l'aise pour dire que prier est ici souhaiter et préparer le bonheur de quelqu'un. Mais ils se gardent de chercher devant qui Allah toupuissant et ses anges émettent ce voeu et en attendent la réalisation." GAUD., p. 215.

98. "And when We said to the angels: 'Prostrate yourselves before Adam,' they all prostrated themselves except Satan *[Iblìs]* who in his pride refused and became an unbeliever" (2, 34).

99. "He (God) chooses His messengers from the angels and from men" (22, 75).—"He makes angels and His messengers, with two, three or four pairs of wings" (35, 1). Cf. 6, 111; 8, 12; 15, 8; 16, 2; 17, 95; 25, 21. — Cf. MASSON (Les anges), I, p. 152-174.

spirit of Allah (12, 87);   *min rùhi-na*,   of Our spirit;[100]
bi rùhen minhu,   by a spirit (deriving) from him (58,
22);   *al rùh-ul kudus*,   the holy spirit;[101] * *bir-rùh-il
kudus*,   in the holy spirit;[102] *ar-rùh-ul amin*,   the faithful
spirit (26, 193) — the word *rùh*, spirit, in all of them
does not designate the Third Person of the Most Holy
Trinity. Mohammad never believed for one moment in
the Trinity. For that reason, we are not even allowed to
so much as think of the word's possible dependence on,
or conceptual affinity with, the Holy Spirit mentioned
in our canonical Books, the Gospels.[103]

The substantive *rùh*, spirit — not to be confused
with *rìh*, wind — recurs throughout the Koran exactly
24 times. It has a volatile meaning, with no definite

---

100. "Do not despair of Allah's spirit *[min rùh il'lah]* " (12, 87). — "We sent
Our spirit *[min rùhina]* " (19, 17). — "... of My spirit *[min rùhi]* " (15, 29; 38,
72). — "We breathed into her of Our Spirit *[min rùhina]* " (21, 91; 66, 12).

101. "Say, 'The Holy Spirit *[ar-rùh ul-qudus]* brought it down from your
Lord in truth to reassure the faithful" (16, 102). — The intermediary of the
revelation is Gabriel, called "holy spirit." Thus Muqatil also understands it (ap.
NWY., p. 57). "Quatre autres textes indiquent, du reste, clairement que *rùh* ne
peut désigner que Gabriel: ce sont ceux où l'esprit apparaît comme agent de la
révélation. On le nomme aussi *rùh al qudus* (16, 102; 19, 17; 21, 91; 26,
193)." NWY., p. 57.

(*). The expression "the Holy Spirit" is not, in my opinion, an accurate
translation of the Koranic *bi-rùh il-qudus* which means "with the spirit of the
Holy One". In this case, i.e. v. 2, 87; 2, 253; 16, 102; and 5, 110, the exact
Koranic version must read: "With, by, or through the spirit of the Holy One,"
i.e. God's. This spirit, as evidently appears from the literal text, is Gabriel.
Consequently, "With the spirit (sent) BY, or (coming) FROM the Holy One"
would be the real and exact sense of the Koranic expression. The version "Holy
Spirit," capitalized, is confusing; not only that, but then its original counterpart
should be *bi'r rùh il-qudus*, not *bi rùh il-qudus*. This last expression is the one
that Koran uses in the four instances quoted above. (Fares)

102. "We ... strengthened him with the Holy Spirit *[bi-rùh il-qudus]* " (2,
87). Cf. 2, 253; 5, 110. Muqatil says that this *rùh al-qudus*, i.e. Gabriel, was
sent to Jesus to confer on him the charisma of miracles. Cf. NWY., p. 75.

103. Cf. *Mt.* 1, 18, 20; *Lk.* 1, 35, 41, 66.

outline, and is hard to grasp.[104] In a situation like this, we conclude that it is far easier to guess what the term in the Koran may mean, rather than state what it really means.

From a diligent research that we conducted, the result we came up with shows that *rùh* is almost always,[105] and exclusively, used with reference to God. Without properly designating God in Himself, or a true and proper participation of His attributes, it indicates a reality strictly belonging to God[106] or emanating and coming from God.[107]

With respect to the angels, at least in four Koranic instances, *rùh* insinuates and presupposes a real distinction, if not truly an authentic opposition, between the two spirits i.e. the *Angels* and *God*.[108]

---

104. According to a tradition quoted by Maqatil, *rùh* would mean a "spirit," or an angel, with immense dimensions, inferior to none in size but to the *Throne*; his physiognomy is that of Adam's, though half fire, half snow. Cf. NWY., p. 57. — TIRMIDHI (+898), thinks that *rùh* constitutes the *first matter* out of which Allah had drawn all things into existence. Cf. NWY., p. 154.

We have to remark, however, that the term *rùh* — like *salàt, dhìkr, hùda, ràhmat,* etc. — includes according to the exegetes a plurality of meanings, v.g. command, revelation, angel, life, mercy, soul, Gabriel, etc.... Cf. HAD. III, p. 150. — The "Qommos" SERGIUS, in his booklet on the Trinity [Cairo, 1046], enumerates for *rùh* 19 different meanings (cf. 33-34). We are aware that the Koran itself (17, 85) avoids, and wants the faithful to expressly avoid any discussion on the nature of the "spirit" *[rùh].*

105. *Rùh* in the Koranic Text is used indiscriminately as a *subject*, cf. 16, 102; 29, 17; 26, 193; 70, 4, 38; 97, 4; as an *object*, cf. 15, 29; 32, 9; 38, 72 (for Adam); 21, 91; 66, 12 (for Mary); 40, 15; 42, 52; as a *Means*, cf. 2, 87, 253; 5, 110.

106. "When I have fashioned him and breathed of My *spirit* into him" (15, 29). Cf. 19, 17; 21, 91; 32, 9; 38, 72; 66, 12.

107. "Jesus the son of Mary, was no more than Allah's apostle and His Word which He cast to Mary, and a *spirit* from Him" (i.e. breathed by, or emanating from, Him) (4, 171). Cf. 16, 102; 58, 22.

108. For such opposition, cf. 16, 2; 70, 4; 78, 38; 97, 4.

In balance, we're able to establish the following conclusion: Despite the variety in the meanings and the elasticity in the use of the word, *rùh*, in the Koranic lexicon, implies a divine dynamism. It indicates in general a certain sort of emanation, of expansion, of efficiency of God: a breath of His, a blowing of His, an effluvium of His. A dynamism which, if not transforming man and causing him to be a sharer in the divine nature, still denotes Allah's special intervention in the events of man's life as a reflection of His might, His science[109] and His will ordaining the whole universe.[110]

To bring ourselves consequently to the parallel text of Sura 3 (3, 45), we may remember, with a solid foundation, that the parenthetic *rùh-una* (Our spirit) of Sura 19 signifies an emanation of God and His typical intervention, actuated in the history of salvation by means of an angelic spirit who appeared to Mary in the form of an accomplished man (19, 17).

And this angelic "spirit" was later identified by the exegetes in the person of Gabriel *[Gibril]*, three times mentioned explicitly by the Koran.[111]

B) *The Message:*

In both Suras, the angelic delegation carries the joyful news

---

109. Reflection of *might*, cf. 26, 193; 32, 9; 38, 72; 58, 22; 66, 12. — Reflection of *knowledge [wahi]*, cf. 21, 45; 42, 52; 53, 4; *['ilm]*, cf. 17, 85. In the early days of Islam *'ilm* meant the knowledge of the Koran and the Traditions, i.e. "knowledge *given* by revelation, or knowledge of truths revealed." BAUS., p. 579. — Only later it meant an acquired *knowledge.*

110. "By an order of His *[min àmrihi]* He makes the angels come down in the spirit on those of His servants whom He chooses" (16, 2). Cf. 17, 85; 40, 15; 42, 52. — On the rapport between *rùh* and *àmr* cf. the annotation by BAUS., p. 578.

111. "Allah is his protector, and Gabriel *[Gibril]*, and the righteous among the faithful" (66, 4). Cf. 2, 97, 98.

of, respectively, John's and Jesus' birth. The first is announced to Zachariah, and the second to Mary.

To Mary, the angels — or, as we have noted earlier, Gabriel, the most quoted among them — say: *"Mary, Allah bids you rejoice in a Word* [coming] *from Him. His name is the Messiah, Jesus the son of Mary, honorable in this world and in the next and one of the most favored by Him"* (3, 45).

Bids you rejoice in a Word: *kàlimat*. This substantive is attributed by the Koran to Christ in two facts of the same nature: first in the annunciation of the Baptist, recognized as the "confirmer" *[musaddeq]* of the Word deriving from God *[kàlimat min il-lah]* (3, 39), and then in that of the Messiah's, called expressly Word of Allah, *kàlimat min- hu* (3, 45).

In this latter instance — and heeding more the logical expression rather than the syntactic structure of it — we have to say that *kàlimat* performs in the phrase the role of complement of object for the verb *yu-basshìru-ki*, announces to you, or bids you rejoice; and that this complement is endowed with a proper name that is *his [ismu-hu]*, almost as a reminder that the *kàlimat* is not simply a dry utterance of the word — "flatus vocis" — but that it designates an individual subsisting, all distinct in himself, and is in turn entirely distinct from any other individual by his own proper and exclusive appellative: "Christ Jesus, the son of Mary" — *al Masìh, 'Issa b'nu Maryam* (3, 45).

What brings us to this conclusion is a passion-free and accurate reading of the Text. Therefore we reject, as non-objective and alien to the Text, the exegesis of Moslem commentators, already quoted at the time by Muqatil.[112] To the term *Kàlimat*,

---

112. "Par *kàlima* écrit Muqatil, Dieu signifie qu'il a dit à Jésus: soit! et il a été (kun, fa-kan), tout comme ce monde a été créé par un *fiat* divin." NWY., p. 57. — For an analogous sense go other exegetes, Cf. TAB. VI, n. 7060-7061 (p. 411); ZAM. I, 359; BAYD. I, 139; GEL., p. 76 — Disagrees BL. II, p. 81: *kàlima*: Verbe. — Le context permet de traduire ici par *Verbe*, sens que le mot

in this particular context, they assign no value beyond the mere divine command: a *fiat*, or a categorical imperative by which Allah brought into existence Jesus, the son of Mary. A divine order, passed under silence in John's case (3, 40), but explicitly emphasized in the case of Jesus for polemic reasons (3, 47).

If an hermeneutic of this kind were objective, if it indeed reflected the meaning intended by the Koran, how could it be explained that in the other seven instances where it is used,[113] the divine fiat means always and infallibly Allah's mere command, while here — and only here, in Issa's case — to the same *fiat* the Text assigns concrete features of a person existentially in act, quite discernible by a proper name and individual characteristics, i.e. **Jesus, the Messiah, the son of Mary?** And why are Allah's messengers never ever called *"Word"* of God, since, like Adam, they also were drawn from nothing by the same divine *fiat?*

Apart from polemic intentions permeating the Christological portion of Sura 3, I believe that the *kàlimat,* here, must be considered as a fair-and-square literal version of the New Testament's Λόγος. More than a bare command *[àmr]*, or a bare expression of the divine will manifested by the imperative *"fiat,"* it ought consequently to be intended as a *Word divine and subsisting;* a Hypostasis, a Person true and proper, endowed with a proper and personal name, exclusive to himself, not shared by others, and distinguishing himself from any other individual.

I feel another point should be clarified here. After examining the present Koranic Text and comparing it with the historic context of Islam, it can be easily realized that the *kàlimat,* attributed exclusively to Christ, is no more than a Christian reminiscence emptied of its original content and theological value. At most, it may be called a "resonance," merely verbal, of

---

n'a qu'exceptionnellement dans le Coran." BL. VI, p. 81, in note. — To the contrary BOUB. I, p. 125.

113. "He ordains life and death. If he decrees a thing, He need only say: 'Be', and *it is*" (40, 68). Cf. 3, 47, 59; 6, 73; 16, 40; 19, 35; 36, 82.

what the Orthodox Christian doctrine has always believed and maintained with regard to the person of Christ: Word [Λόγος, kàlimat] Incarnate.

What consolidates us in our present stand is the feeling of uncertainty and instability which assails the reader as he goes time and again through the Koranic verses relative to Christ's person. Gaudefroy-Demombynes put it in these words: "By reading over and over in the Koran the verses dealing with Jesus, one has the impression of being in a pendulum constantly oscillating between moments when Mohammad acknowledges to Jesus supra-human merits which make of him almost a divine hypostasis [...], and others when, sensing an impellent need, he could not help but remember his true human nature."[114]

C) *Psychological Reaction:*

The angel's apparition, with the unexpected message it brought, immediately provoked a visible reaction in the two events. It happened like a bolt from a blue sky. And more vivid and ostensible was its impact on Mary, a young virgin girl living almost isolated from any social gathering and in perfect solitude. To the contrary of what old Zachariah went through,[115] Mary was caught by a sudden blush of virginal modesty; and in her spontaneous concern to protect herself in face of the imminent

---

114. GAUD, p. 4 37.

115. Psychologically, Zachariah was in a waiting condition. He had addressed his petition to the Lord and was expecting an answer. *"He prayed to His Lord, saying: 'Lord, grant me from You an upright descendant' "* (3, 38). While caught by surprise, Mary makes use of a formula very frequent in Arabic: *"In God I take refuge from you [a 'ùzu bil 'lah]!"* Women use it most commonly whenever they unexpectedly face a dangerous situation. "La Vierge, loin d'être tentée par la beauté de l'ange sous sa forme humaine, use d'une formule propitiatoire par laquelle elle affirme sa chasteté et rappelle l'inconnu, dans la mesure où il craint Dieu, que celui-ci condamne tout ce qui est illicite *[haràm]*." BOUB., p. 619.

danger, she takes refuge in God, her only support, while at the same time she launches an appeal to the understanding of her visitor: *"I take refuge from you in the Merciful. If you fear God, leave me and go away"* (19, 18).

The Angel, Gabriel, is not worried about reassuring and encouraging her, as we read in St. Luke's relation;[116] but with an easy, speedy air that leaves no room for an answer, he declares he is the messenger of Allah, come with the purpose of giving her *[li 'àhaba la-ki]* a pure and innocent child (19, 19).

In both narratives, the psychological perturbation is outwardly obvious by the degree of anxiety in the identical interrogation. *"Lord, how shall I have a son?"* (3, 40) asks Zachariah. *"Lord, how shall I bear a child?"* (19, 20) demands Mary.

Identical is the interrogation, but different is the motive provoking it: old age, impotence, senility, in Zachariah;[117] virginity, freely chosen and jealously guarded, in Mary.[118] In fact, to the proposed maternity and to the invitation to solve its obligations, Mary at once opposes her condition of being a virgin; then by a sudden, almost instinctive, movement she answers back: *"How shall I have a child when no man has this far touched me ever, and I am no prostitute?"* (19, 20)

The objection raised by both, prompts, for both also, the ready and immediate solution: a peremptory solution from which one is not allowed to withdraw because it is endorsed by the om-

---

116. Cf. *Lk.* 1, 30-33. — Likewise the two Apocrypha which mention the annunciation: the *Proto-ev. of James*, 11, 3; and the *Gospel of the Nativity*, 9, 2.

117. "My bones are enfeebled, and my head glows silver with age" (19, 4). — "My wife is barren, and I am well advanced in years" (19, 8). — "I am now overtaken by old age, and my wife is barren" (3, 40). — "Il avait en effet quatre-vingt-douze ans." IBN ATHIR (ap. HAY., p. 54) . — "D'autres disent 99 ans. IBN ABBAS dit: il avait 120 ans, et sa femme en avait 98." THA'LABI (ap. HAY., p. 54).

118. "And of the woman who kept her chastity" (21, 91). Cf. 66, 12.

nipotence of Allah for whom the advanced age, the anatomical and physiological limitations pose no difficulty whatsoever: "*Such is the will of Allah,*" answers the angel to Zachariah. "*He does what He pleases*" (3, 40). And to Mary: "*Thus has the Lord decreed: 'For Me it is an easy thing to do'*" (19, 21). "*Allah creates what He will. When He decrees a thing, He need only say: 'Be', and it is*" (3, 47).

Absolutely true. In the Koranic mentality and understanding Allah is a reality tremendously alive and operative. He acts with an absolute and sovereign umpireship: He is *al-hàqq*,[119] the truth — and the truth in the fullest and unconditional sense of the term. Evident truth (24, 25), logical truth; but above all *ontological truth*. He is the One who, from the truth and in truth, has created the heavens and the earth.[120] Outside of Him, all is *bàtil*,[121] vain and inconsistent. Man himself, despite his spiritual assets — intelligence, will, freedom — is of no account in front of Him.

Thus, with this Koranic doctrine present in mind, it becomes clear why Mohammad allows Mary not even a minimal act of personal acquiescence to the irrevocable manifestation of God's will. And true enough, according to the same Koranic relation, Mary does not breathe or utter a single word — not even to profess herself as Allah's handmaid, ready to second His designs by a humble and unconditional surrender as becomes a good and brave Moslem woman "*ante litteram.*"

And the angel also, the messenger of Allah — in a typical

---

119. "Allah is the truth *[alhàqq]*, while that which they invoke besides Him is vanity" (31, 30). Cf. 41, 53.

120. "In truth *[bi-l-hàqq]* did God create the heavens and the earth" (29, 44). Cf. 30, 8; 39, 5; 45, 22; 46, 3.

121. "Such is Allah, your Lord, the True One *[al-hàqq]*. And what is outside the Truth but error *[dalàl]?*" (10, 32). — "Allah is the Truth *[al-hàqq]*; and vanity *[al-bàtil]* is all that is invoked besides Him" (22, 62). — "He will bring the vanity *[al-bàtil]* to nothing and vindicate the truth *[al-hàqq]* by His word" (42, 24).

Moslem tone and style — does not expect from Mary the slightest sign of consent. Above the activity of creatures, and beyond any man's free determination, exists Allah, the supreme, active and causative agent, who puts His plans in execution, with no obstacles or delay from the second cause: *"Thus has your Lord decreed: 'That is an easy thing for Me — so easy that I'll be able to make of him, from Our side, a sign and a mercy to mankind. And that's what will happen' "* (19, 21). Allah has thus decreed; no one could dare foil His design.

Mohammad himself is also said to be *ràhmah*, an exhibition of the divine mercy (21, 107). It does not result that he was sent or proposed as an *àyat*, a sign, at an equal level with Jesus and Mary, his mother (21, 91), as is mentioned here and as will later be seen at fuller length.

"It is a decreed thing" [*àmran maqdìyan*] (19, 21): a fact, in other words, to actuate which Allah had taken an irrevocable decision.[122] And Mary conceives (19, 22). "A pure soul — whom God has chosen to receive within her His Word, and whose womb He has purified to deposit in it His Spirit"[123] — already carries Jesus in the bosom: a sign of God's mercy, an act of His sovereign clemency to mankind.

And she has conceived him, following the breathing by the angel into her (21, 91; 66, 12): a gentle breath similar to that of Allah's (38, 72), from which Adam came into existence: a breath into the mud (54, 14), into the clay (38, 71), into the coarse clay (37, 11), to animate mankind's first parent (15, 29; 32, 9).

---

122. Tabari comments: "Et ce fut chose faite, c'est à dire qu'Allah en avait décidé la réalisation" (ap. HAY., p. 71). — And the translators agree on stating this sense of unrepealable decree. MASSON: "Le decret est irrévocable" (MAS., p. 373). — BLACHÈRE: "c'est affaire décrétée" (BL. VI, p. 331). — HENNING.: "Und es ist eine beschlossene Sache" (HEN., p. 288). — ULLMAN: "So ist die Sache fest beschlossen" (ULL., p. 246).

123. TABARI (ap. HAY., p. 77).

As we have already noted, the Koranic account is the most simple and sketchy ever. Complications and overstructures came later, born of the fancy of the *qussàs* (storytellers) and the mania of enriching the annunciation narrative with accessory details.

Be it enough for us to observe that the *place* of the angel's encounter with Mary, as reported by the Koran, must have been the *mihràb*, Mary's ordinary residence — as in the same *mihràb* the annunciation to Zachariah took place (3, 39).

A thoughtful reading of the Text does not seem to suggest a different place. The facts related are presented to us so continuously and meshed together that they exclude any contrary interpretation. Nor does the Text allow one to suppose, even as the faintest possibility, a location other than the *mihràb*.[124]

---

124. The fantasy of the *qussàs* and several other writers was very prolific in weaving "embroideries" around the event of the *annunciation*.

During the longest and warmest day of the year (IBN ATHIR, THA'LABI, TABARI, ap. HAY., p. 70), the angel, Gabriel, appeared to Mary while, out of her *mihràb*, she was strolling by the oriental side of the Temple to take some fresh air (SAB., p. 200). In another version, while she was taking a bath to purify herself of her period (cf. ZAM. III, 9). And in another, while, the jug in hand, she had gone out to haul some water at the fountain and was already in the cave. TABARI, IBN ATHIR, THA'LABI, KISA'I (ap. HAY., p. 70).

Gabriel appeared to her in the features of a young man. He was beautiful, stalwart, beardless, radiant, attractive, his hair black and curly, his aspect elegant and dignified, so that he could catch Mary's heart and have a decisive impact on her whole being. Cf. ZAM. III, 9; SAB., p. 200. Likewise was the description by Ps.-Matthew: "iuvenis, cuius pulchritudo non potuit enarrari" (19, 2; AM., p. 312). He first notified her of the reason why he was there. Then he blew his breath into the sleeve, or the cut, of her tunic that she had laid aside. When she took it on, the moisture of the angel's breath reached the womb, and it made it fertile. ZAM. III, 10; BAYD. II, 24; SAB., p. 202; AMEL., p. 474. — "*Marie revêtit sa tunique et conçut Jésus. Elle remplit ensuite sa jarre et revint au Temple.*" THA'LABI (ap. HAY., p. 73). — Others pretend, instead, that the angel's breath was blown into Mary's own mouth; from the mouth it ran down to her bosom, and fertilized it. Cf. SAB., p. 202.

We note here, however, that a tradition led by Muqatil offers a very grotesque explanation for Christ's virginal conception: The breath of the angel, Gabriel, would have been no less than "un germe séminal." Cf. NWY., p. 67.

The mention of the "fountain" is not of the Koran, but of the Christian Apocrypha: the *Proto-evangelium of James*,[125] and the *Gospel of the Nativity* of the Ps.-Matthew.[126]

Who was the first man to notice Mary's interesting situation? Her cousin (THA'LABI, ap. HAY., p. 69) and companion at work in the Temple (IBN ATHIR, THA'LABI, KISA'I, ap. HAY., 71), Joseph, the carpenter. He at once noticed her loss of weight, pallor and fatigue *(loc. cit.,* p. 72); he was shocked by it, although recognizing her virtue, and worked hard to protect her innocence *(Loc. cit.,* p. 71). He was tempted to get rid of her, and kill her. Gabriel intervened, ordered him: *"Hold up! Whom she is bearing in the womb is of the Spirit!"* (THA'LABI, ap. HAY. p. 80, in note). — Others try to console the poor Joseph. They make him hear from the mouth of the baby Jesus, the very day he was born, the following statement: *"Rejoice, O Joseph. Peace to your spirit. And be happy! My Lord has brought me out of the obscurity of the womb into the light of the world. I shall present myself to the children of Israel and invite them to the obedience of Allah!"* HALABI (ap. HAY., p. 84).

At the moment of the annunciation, Mary was seventeen years old according to MAS'UDI (ap. HAY., p. 66); thirteen, according to SABUNI (p. 200, 202); or only ten, according to others; and she had experienced two periods only (ZAM. III, 10; BAYD. II, 10).

While pregnant and alone, Mary had with Jesus, still in her womb, mutual and amorous dialogues. Whenever she was busy with some other people, Jesus inside her womb, and on his own, would sing hymns and lauds to God. ABU NU'AIM (ap. HAY., p. 73).

False is the annunciation narrative attributed to the Koran by some. "In Sura 3," they pretend, "the Book says that Mary was at the fountain getting water when the angels appeared to her and said: *'God has chosen you.'* " (ROSCH., p. 242). The Koran makes no mention of the fountain.

125. In the Proto-evangelium the annunciation is textured in two successive scenes: one *outside* the house, at the fountain where Mary had gone to draw water (11, 1 — STR., p. 112); and the other *inside* the house where, the jug laid down, Mary was sitting on her bench and spinning scarlet wool (11, 3 — STR., p. 116). The Koran is nowhere near.

126. The Ps.-Matthew mentions two distinct *"apparitions"*: one at the fountain, where Mary was filling her little jar (9, 1). The other *inside the house*, while she was busy working the scarlet (9, 2). And between either apparition there was a remarkable lapse of time: "in the third day" (9, 2).

Here is another disagreement between the Apocrypha: the Proto-evangelium makes no mention at the fountain of an "apparition", but of a "voice" only

4. The Childbirth

It is reported by Sura 19 in the following words:

"And when she felt the throes of childbirth she lay down by the trunk of a palm tree, crying: 'Oh, would that I had died and passed into oblivion!'

"But a voice from below cried out to her: 'Do not despair. Your Lord has provided a brook that runs at your feet, and if you shake the trunk of this palm tree, it will drop fresh ripe dates in your lap. Therefore rejoice. Eat and drink and be happy,* and should you meet any mortal say to him: "I have vowed a fast to the Merciful, and will not speak with any man today." ' " (19, 23-26).

With the Word of Allah in her bosom, Mary abandons her *mihràb* for good. It seems as though her prolonged retreat in the Temple was altogether, and exclusively, intended for Christ's conception. So she abandons the *mihràb* now and betakes herself to a faraway locality, *makàn-an qasì-yan* (19, 22), not well described.

The text, in fact, does not say what that locality was, nor where it could have been found. Nor from the commentators is one able to make out any sure and more concrete notion, since,

---

[φωνὴ-λέγουσα : 11, 1 — STR., p. 112]; the Ps.-Matthew, instead, speaks in both cases of an apparition: "The angel of the Lord appeared [apparuit] to her" (9, 1); "entered onto her [ingressus ad eam] a youth of an undescribable beauty" (9, 2. — AM., p. 312).

(*). Literally: "Wipe your eyes, keep cool and stop crying." (Fares)

in the matter, they all resort to the same obscure and enigmatic language.[127] I wonder whether this hasty[128] journey of Mary could be taken as a clue to her visit to Elizabeth, her aunt. Or whether it might mask some discreet allusion to the flight into Egypt, due to the known "distance" of that country.[129] Of these twin biblical episodes — the visit to Elizabeth and the flight into Egypt — the Koran makes no mention, at least in explicit terms, any more than it mentions the coming of the Magi, or the extermination of the Innocents.

What stands true and undeniable is that Jesus, in the Koranic description, did not come into this world born inside a manger, or in a grotto; but in the open,[130] by the trunk of a

---

127. Cf. GEL., p. 404: away from her own folks. — ZAM. III, 11: away from her parents, behind the mountain. — BAYD. II, 24: away from her parents, at the boundary of the paternal home. — ABU NU'AIM: "dans sa honte, elle s'enfuit du côté de l'orient, loin des siens" (ap. HAY., p. 79).

128. The hurry — "cum festinatione" (Lk. 1, 39) — can be concluded from the construction of the period: a pressing succession of two verbs that leaves no time for a pause: "She conceived him, and retired, to a far-off place" (19, 22).

129. Opinions are not unanimous around this trip. IBN ATHIR thinks it is a journey, a sort of a social visit to Elizabeth, whom he believes Mary's sister: "Elle s'est dirigée vers sa soeur qui était enceinte, car elle avait reçu l'annonce de Jean. Quand elles se rencontrèrent, la mère de Jean sentit que celui qui se trouvait en son sein se prosternait, confessant sa foi en Jésus" (ap. HAY., p. 79-80). — Belli, differently: "A noi sembra che il viaggio di questo v. 22 sia da intendere, con maggior probabilità di evidenza, come un viaggio-fuga (e non come viaggio-visitazione, o viaggio-prova), e da riferire alla fuga in Egitto." BEL., p. 452. Italics are ours.

130. Some "embroideries" the qussàs have weaved around Christ's birth. According to some, Jesus was unquestionably born in winter (ZAM. III, 10; BAYD. II, 24; SHAR., p. 174); and precisely on the twenty-fourth night of December, a Wednesday: MAS'UDI (ap. HAY., p. 66). His birth took place after a normal course of gestation, at the end of the ninth month (SAB., p. 202); or, as others prefer, at the end of the eighth, seventh, and even sixth month of pregnancy (ZAM. III, 10; BAYD. II, 24). A few think that the three operations through which the pregnancy with Jesus was achieved, i.e. the conception, the formation of the body, and the birth, took only three hours: one hour respectively for each function. Thus MUQATIL (ap. HAY., p. 78). One

palm tree.[131]

The imminent childbirth causes Mary to burst into a rather surprising, let alone disturbing, outpouring that reveals the depth of her pain and heartfelt sorrow: *"Oh, would that I had died! Would that I had fallen into total oblivion!"* (19, 23). Such out-

---

author reduces the time of gestation to one hour only: IBN ABBAS (ap. HAY., p. 78). So that Mary would have given birth to Jesus on the same day he was conceived; and precisely at sunset: MUQATIL (ap. HAY., p. 78); ZAM. III, 10; BAYD. II, 24. NAG., p. 378, and AMEL. 475 disagree, both retaining that Mary's pregnancy took its normal course and followed nature's laws.

The pains of childbirth first caught Mary while she was in "the House of the Prophecy." Overcome by a virginal shame, she ran away, confused, to a distant locality in the east. Against the trunk of a palm tree she leaned, and gave birth to her son, "cutting by her hands his umbilical cord." ABU NA'IM (ap. HAY., p. 79).

The *palm* near which the childbirth took place was, according to some, no more than an arid stump (GEL., p. 405); very dry, with no green foliage (BAYD. II, 24) or fruits (ZAM. III, 11; SAB., p. 205). It turned green and was loaded with dates by a miracle, to satisfy Mary's hunger and give her moral support. SHAR., p. 174. Cf. AMEL., p. 476.

As soon as Jesus was born, all *idols* were found thrown to the ground, all over; and all demons experienced a frightening panic, without knowing why. Satan, their head, wanted to find out. For three hours he went about searching, by land and by sea, from east and west. He wandered near the place where Jesus was born, but could not come close: the angels had built a tight ring around Mary to protect her newborn baby. By their shoulder tips they touched the limits of heaven; while planted in the ground their feet hit at the very bottoms of the earth. IBN ATHIR, THA'LABI, GHAZALI, ZABIDI, TABARI (ap. HAY., p. 82).

131. The description of the palm tree and the fountain (or brook) is not quite the same as in the Ps-MATTHEW, c. 20.

The differences the two reports carry, though marginal, are more relevant than the agreements.

The Apocryphum has Mary sheltered under the palm tree not fearing the imminent childbirth, as does the Koran (19, 23), but after the baby's birth which took place in a "grotto underground" [in speluncam subterraneam] (13, 2. — AM., p. 324); and precisely "on the third day" of her wandering through the desert, exhausted as she was by the parching sun (20, 1).

Furthermore, the palm tree under which she took rest, after Joseph had

pouring wells up from a pain hard to define, whether it is *physical* in nature — caused consequently by the torturing throes of childbirth common to women in general, or *moral* in nature — originating from a lucid prevision of her close, not to say immediate, parturition.

From somewhere around a mysterious voice[132] calls out to her unexpectedly. Several centuries earlier the same voice heard Hagar, the unfortunate mother, while she wandered throughout the desert with her son in her arms: Ismael, the proto-parent of all Arabs.[133] The voice comforts Mary. Then it invites her to feed

---

helped her dismount from the mare *(ibid.)*, was verdant, a bunch of fronds topping it, and "loaded with dates" *(ibid.)*. Not so explicit is the Koran.

The Koran reports Mary alone with the baby yet to be born; the Apocryphum, on the contrary, describes Joseph beside the baby, so worried about the shortage of water in the skins that he could not refresh the animals he had brought along *(ibid.)*.

Finally, the Koran — in a typically Islamic style which refers every event to God, the first cause in front of which every other causality vanishes — ascribes to Allah both the gushing of the brook and the bending of the palm tree, subsequent to the invitation by the mysterious voice (19, 24-25).

In the Ps.-MATTHEW, instead, the crystal clear and fresh water spurting and the bending of the palm down to the feet of Mary are attributed to the baby Jesus. Sitting in his mother's lap and smiling, he ordered: *"Bend down, O Tree, and with thine dates take away my mother's hunger [...]. Then let from thy roots gush that vein hidden under the ground, so the water may run to refresh and relieve us"* (20, 2).

132. The expression *min tàhtiha* (from below her) is an idiom foreign to the Quraishi language. It does not refer to the palm tree, feminine in its Arabic grammarial form, as would BELLI (p. 455); nor to "l'enfant qui était à ses pieds" (BL. III, p. 331); or "l'enfant qui se trouvait à ses pieds" (MARS., p. 373); but it means *"from her womb,"* i.e. Mary's. Cf. HAD. III, p. 142.

As to the source of the voice inviting, there is no agreement. It came from Gabriel: GEL., p. 405; ZAM. III, 12. — It came from Jesus, a baby still locked up in the mother's womb: BAYD. II, 25; HAD. II, p. 463; BL. II, p. 331; BEL., p. 455; MONT., p. 395. — In the Ps.-MATTHEW, it is Jesus who talks to the mother, but — mark it well — after he was born, not before: *"infantulus Jesus laeto vultu, in sinu matris suae residens, ait ad palmam"* (20, 2).

133. Mary's complaint and the providential answer find an echo in the "biblical episode of Hagar and Ismael, which Mohammad had certainly fused

herself with the delicious dates and quench her thirst at a fountain that Allah had bidden gush right at her feet: *"Shake the trunk of this palm tree, and it will drop fresh ripe dates in your lap. Therefore rejoice. Eat and drink and be happy..."* (19, 25- 26a).

The idyllic scene of Mary holding her infant in her arms under a lush green palm tree, seated at the bank of a fresh water stream made to flow especially for her, changes suddenly and takes on the tone of a violent contrast.[134]

The same voice presently tells the new mother to avoid meeting any other human,[135] excusing herself eventually in these words: *"I have vowed a fast to the Merciful, and will not speak to any man today"* (19, 26b).

Mary complies rigorously with the recommendation. She leaves to God alone the task of providing for her defense from malicious and unfair charges brought against her by her suspicious folks and tribesmen.

---

with the narrative of the Canonical Gospels and the Apocrypha to offer us an oriental setting for the birth of Jesus." PEIR., p. 52. — One should not, however, forget the difference already mentioned: i.e. Ismael was already born (cf. *Gen.* 21, 9-10); Jesus, on the contrary, was yet to be born.

134. PEIR., p. 52

135. Some authors believe that Mary's injunction to silence was meant to better emphasize God's intervention, through the baby Jesus, in defending his mother's innocence. Cf. ZAM. III, 14.

5. Defense against an Outrageous Calumny

SURA 19:

"Then, carrying the child in her arms, she went to her people, who said to her: 'Mary, this is indeed a strange thing! Sister of Aaron,* your father was never a whoremonger, nor was your mother a harlot.'

"She made a sign to them, pointing to the child. But they replied: 'How can we speak with a babe in the cradle?'

"Whereupon he spoke and said: 'Truly I am the servant of Allah. He has given me the Gospel and ordained me a Prophet. His blessing is upon me wherever I go, and He commanded me to be steadfast in prayer and alms as long as I shall live. He has exhorted me to honor my mother, and has purged me from vanity and wickedness. And peace was on me the day I was born, peace shall be on me the day I shall die, and peace shall be on me also the day I shall rise to life again' " (19, 27-33).

(*). Idiomatic expression for "saintly woman" in the image and example of Aaron, held by the Koran as a prophet and a saintly man. (Fares) — Cf. also notes 58, 59, and 61, above.

Back to her folks with the newborn in her arms, Mary heard herself at once addressed with sour terms of blame and condemnation, as though she had just been caught in a crude and flagrant crime. *"Mary,"* they barked at her, *"this is indeed a strange thing! O Sister of Aaron, your father was never a whoremonger, nor was your mother a harlot"* (19, 27-28).

The strange thing — àmran farì-yan: thing shameful, monstrous — with which Mary was rapped in the face, was really her maternity — an unexpected maternity, consequently illegitimate, and therefore disgraceful. A maternity all the more reproachable when one considers that Mary had always been considered an honest person, above any suspicion or blame in moral conduct; descending from a family — father, mother, brother[136] — well renowned for integrity of customs; living since her tenderest years under tight supervision, and never tied by a link to any legitimate marriage.

Despite her inner torture, the young mother shows she is calm, serene, and in her depths sure of her own innocence. She loses no composure, nor does she open her mouth. All she does is point to her Babe in a candid and pure gesture, almost saying: *"If you're seeking answers to the strange thing, he is the one to ask."*

---

136. As for Imran, so also for Harun (Aaron) the question was posed: who was he exactly?

Moslem commentators are inclined to make him contemporary with Mary, famous for his relatively honest or dishonest behavior. In that sense Mary also was compared to him: either in praise or in blame, depending on different opinions by authors. Cf. BAYD. II, 25.

ZAM. III, 14-15, is more favorable to an honest Aaron. At his funerary services, he says, more than 40,000 individuals took part, all bearing the same name. — In his commentary, p. 405, GEL. is decidedly for a virtuous Aaron, to whom Mary was believed similar long before her conception of Jesus. — BELLI rejects the identification of Aaron "with an unknown anonymous who was contemporary with the mother of Jesus, as some Arabic commentators pretend." BEL., p. 460.

And the Babe, still suckling,[137] takes the floor and begins to speak expeditiously, to the astonishment of his audience and the confusion of those who impudently dared to splatter with mud the reputation of his most pure mother.

An indirect refutation that was, but not less convincing. The sight of a suckling who begins to talk like an adult is no event of everyday life.[138] By his wonderful intervention, and by giving the lie to his mother's false accusers, Jesus wanted to do justice to her innocence. Allah Himself had done likewise before. By peculiar providence (19, 23-26), He proved her uprightness of character at the moment of the childbirth: "et il n'y a pas de plus véridique que ces deux témoins"[139] ("... and there is nothing more truthful than those two testimonies").

The prodigious child reveals himself, at the same time, as the servant (*'àbd*) and the messenger (*rasùl*) of Allah.

This assignment of his — servitude and mission — was activated by connatural solidarity with the condition of his mother. Seeing her the target of an infamous denigration, he hastens to make up for her hard feelings. He declares himself pious and obsequious, not certainly arrogant and insolent like those around who feel no shame in hurting and outraging their neighbor. He

---

137. The verb *kàna* (was), in the Koranic expression *man kàna f'il màhdi sabìyan* (who was in the cradle a child), has the value of a state of being, i.e. a circumstance abstracting from time; not the value of time already past, of an action already done in a remote or close lapse of time. Evidence of this is the context, so worded as to assert Mary's innocence by means of a miracle: the locution of a Baby still in swaddles and suckling. We disagree, therefore, with BELLI for whom "Jesus speaks not from the cradle, but as an adult mature enough to do it." BEL., p. 463.
The whole Islamic tradition maintains, besides, that the Baby Jesus talked right from the cradle: "Jésus ne parla plus par la suite avant l'age normal où tous les autres enfants parlent." IBN ATHIR (ap. HAY., p. 84).

138. According to IBN ATHIR (ap. HAY., 84), Jesus spoke three times from the cradle.

139. IBN ARABI (ap. HAY., p. 85).

finally closes his unexpected interference with the same formula he had already used before (19, 15) with regard to the Baptist: *"And peace was on me the day I was born, peace shall be on me the day I shall die, and peace shall be on me also the day I shall rise to life again"* (19, 33).

6. Eschatological Events

The Koran summarizes the life of Mary, the mother of Jesus, in the five episodes heretofore mentioned.

As to Mary's social events known to the New Testament — such as her attendance of the wedding at Cana, her occasional appearance during the public ministry of Jesus, her presence at the foot of the Cross, her relations with the newborn Church — the Koran does not make even the slightest allusion.

Likewise, it keeps a tight silence on the eschatological facts of the Virgin — death, assumption, glorification — notwithstanding the contrary opinion of a few authors who would like to see some indication of that in two verses: the 50th of Sura 23, *The Believers*, and the 17th of Sura 5, *The Table*.

My opinion is that such an indication or, rather, allusion, is void of a solid argument to prove it. It is more of a subjective inference than objective. Anyhow, it will not be a waste of time to consider for a little these Koranic verses.

A) SURA **23, 50:**

"And also We made the son of Mary and his
mother a sign to mankind, and gave them a
shelter on a peaceful hillside watered by a fresh
spring."

The Turkish writer Suad Yurdkoru[140] sees in the second
hemistich of the above verse an implication, not properly an explicit declaration, of Mary's last things, especially of her cor-
poreal assumption into heaven.

My impression, not to say conviction, is that the first
premise in Yurdkoru's argumentation is on the wrong track. He
reasons thus: "Donner abri à des êtres humains en un *lieu terrestre* (comme le supposent des commentateurs musulmans, qui
voient ici une allusion au refuge trouvé par Marie et Jésus en
Égypte) n'est pas un *signe* extraordinaire comme le serait leur
montée céleste."[141]*

---

140. In an unpublished statement sent to Msgr. MULLA on June 15, 1951,
and labelled as "très remarquable et objectivement fort vraisemblable." MUL.,
p. 276.
  Regarding Sura 23, 50, the same MULLA writes: "Seuls, à notre connaissance, quelques savants europeéns modernes, le P. Ludovico Marracci
[*Refutatio Alcorani*, in S. 23, nota ad v. 52], au XVIIe siècle, et, de no jours,
Ahrens [*Muhammad als Religionsstifter* (Leipsig 1935), 195] ont vu une allusion
au Paradis ou même une réplique confirmative à la croyance chrétienne à
l'Assomption de Marie en même temps qu'au dogme chrétien de l'Ascension de
Jésus." MUL., p. 275. — As for Marracci, he does not indeed speak of the
paradise "tout court," but of the *earthly* paradise. In fact, after quoting different opinions of authors (Jerusalem, Damascus, Palestine), he adds textually:
"Puto tamen Alcoranum loqui de *paradiso terrestri.*" MAR. II, p. 476 [not
376]. Italics are ours.

141. Cf. MUL., p. 276, in note. Italics are ours.

(*). "To give human beings refuge in a *terrestrial location* (as some Moslem
commentators suppose, who see here an allusion to the flight of Mary and Jesus
into Egypt), is not an extraordinary *sign* as is their *ascension into heaven.*"

The verse we're dealing with, and upon which Yurdkoru builds his argument, is composed of two hemistichs clearly discernible and opposed to each other by the two verbs in action: *We made* and *We gave*. The first verb concerns the sign *[àyat]*, and the other the refuge *[awaynà-huma]*.

One can clearly see from an impartial look at the text that the sign given — the extraordinary exhibition of Allah's power — is not in reference to the place of the shelter as Yurdkoru pretends, but properly and totally centers on the person of Jesus and Mary. *They are the sign.* It is both of them who, personally and by their exceptional gifts and prerogatives, manifest Allah's attributes of might and wisdom in an exceptional way. We have to conclude therefore that the referral to the second hemistich of what the text reserves exclusively to the first is in no way a justified hermeneutic, but simply an arbitrary illation.

Furthermore, the second part of Yurdkoru's argument does not seem to us very convincing either — which is thus expressed: "D'autre part, cette 'hauteur pourvue d'eau vive,' qui n'est pas de la terre et où Jésus et Marie sont ainsi receuillis, ne peut être que le *Paradis* que le Coran décrit habituellement comme un lieu élevé, sous les arbres duquel coulent des cours d'eau."[142]*

The argument, we ought to admit, does contain the outline of a truth. The aspects echoed and the elements advanced by the second hemistich are such that they might indeed be called typical of the *Islamic paradise*[143] conceived to satisfy basically the impellent environmental and personal needs of the Arabs, men "with the eyes scorched and the throat desiccated by the torrid

---

142. *Ibid.* — Italics are ours.

(*). "Besides, this 'elevated locality provided with fresh waters' — which is not on this earth and where Jesus and Mary are sheltered — cannot be other than the paradise that the Koran usually describes as a hillside, under the trees of which flow rivers of water."

143. Cf. MASSON *(Le paradis)*, I, p. 758-776.

whiffs of the desert."[144] Materialistic and voluptuous, as is well known, this paradise offers "all that the bedouin was deprived of in the desert — lush and umbrageous gardens, springs, company of beautiful women and untarnished virgins."[145]

The paradisiac components emerging from our verse would be the following: ràbwat, mound, hillside (idea of elevation); awaynà-huma: We gave them both a shelter — literally: We caused them both to have a shelter (idea of a safe refuge); qaràr, stability, peace-mindedness (idea of prosperity and stability in an abode); ma'ìn, fountain, spring (idea of freshness and irrigation).

Let us take a brief moment and define, according to the Koran, the exact meaning of those words, to see if they implicate or involve any allusion to the Virgin's last things.

The word ràbwat (mound, hillside) is read only twice in the Koran: once in the verse we're actually examining, and another time in another verse with reference to another garden also situated on a hillside (ràbwat) (2, 265). The context in this latter instance has nothing to do with paradise, the abode of the blessed. The term here is used as a comparison, or example, to illustrate another kind of hillside which is altogether different.[146]

---

144. GAB. I, (La legge e la fede dell'Islam), p. 36. — To the eternal verdict (joys of heaven and tortures of hell) SOUBHI EL-SALEH dedicates his book La vie future selon le Coran [Paris, Vrin, 1971], series Etudes Musulmanes, 13. After quoting the Koranic data (p. 13-22), he reports successively the traditional (p. 23-64), rationalistic (p. 65-87), mystical (p. 89-120) and modern (p. 121-136) exegeses.

145. LATOR ESTEBAN, Islam, in Enciclop. Filos. (Centro di studi filosofici Gallarate), ed. Sansoni, 1967, III, col, 1100.

146. "But those that give away their wealth from a desire to please Allah and to reassure their souls are like a garden on a hillside [rabwat]: if a shower falls in it, it yields up twice its normal crop; and if no rain falls upon it, it is watered by the dew" (2, 265). BAUSANI has in note: "Cf. nonetheless the wide differences, Matth. 13, 4 and foll. Then Mark, 4, 3 and foll. Also for 'rain', Matth. 7, 24 and foll." BAUS., p. 516.

The paradise, or the permanent home of the pious and Allah-fearing people,[147] is designated at times by words or by periphrases including the idea of *qaràr* (stability) and *mà'wa* (refuge). It is then expressly called: *dar-al qaràr* (40, 39), abode of permanence and stability; *jànnat al mà'wa* (53, 15), garden of refuge; or in the plural: *jannàt-il mà'wa* (32, 19), gardens of refuge; or simply *al mà'wa* (79, 41), the refuge par excellence. Only once, and tangentially, the concept of elevation occurs: *jànnat 'àliyat*,[148] garden high and elevated.

Habitually, however, the Koran uses other terminology to indicate the paradise: the proper and real paradise, I mean, the one that is the eternal (9, 22) delight[149] promised and prepared by Allah[150] as a reward and heritage[151] for those who believed

---

147. "As for those that fear Allah *[ittaqàu 'llah]*, theirs shall be gardens watered by running streams in which they shall abide forever" (3, 198). Cf. 13, 35; 15, 45; 25, 15; 50, 31; 68, 34.

148. "He shall live a blissful life in a lofty garden *[fi jànnaten àliat]*, with clusters of fruits within his reach. To your content eat and drink what you have already earned during the bygone days" (69, 21-24). — "On that day there shall be radiant faces, of men well-pleased with their labours, in a lofty garden *[jànnaten àliat]*, where no idle talk is spoken, where a fountain runs with fresh water; where beds to lounge are raised, and cups before them are set; and silk cushions in line, and carpets richly spread" (88, 8-16).

149. "The righteous shall surely dwell in bliss *[fi na'im]*. And the wicked shall burn in hellfire" (82, 13-14). Cf. 83, 22, 24; 52, 17.

150. "We have found that which our Lord has promised us *[wa 'adana* to be true. Did you, too, find that which your Lord has promised you *[wa 'adakom]* to be true?" (7, 44). Cf. 9, 72; 13, 35; 25, 15; 40, 8; 47, 15. — "Allah had prepared *[a'adda]* for them gardens watered by running waters" (9, 98). Cf. 9, 100.

151. "Such is the reward *[gazá]* of the good doers" (5, 85). Cf. 3, 195; 98 8. — "Such is the paradise We shall give in inheritance *[nurithu]* him who, among Our servants, was God-fearing" (19, 63). Cf. 43, 72.

and did good works,[152] whether men or women;[153] for those who
obey Allah and His Apostle (4, 13); for those who were steadfast
in prayer (70, 34); and those who sincerely humbled themselves
before Allah (11, 23).

To indicate this type of paradise the Koran almost always
resorts to two classic substantives: dàr (abode, stay, home) and
jànnat (garden, viridarium, green recreation park). It does
not ordinarily denote it with "ràbwat," hillside, nor with
"mà'wa," refuge.

In the text, in fact, we find that the paradise of the blessed
is signified respectively with dàr, or with jànnat. And the examples of that are not few.

The paradise is called simply dàr;[154] or dàr with
another specific predicative, e.g.: dàr al-'àkhirat (16, 30),
abode of the other life, the definitive abode; dàr al-
muqàmat,[155] abode of the perpetual stay; dàr as-salàm,[156]

---

152. "Those that have embraced the faith [àmanu] and done good [Amalus-
sàlihat], are the possessors of paradise, where they shall dwell forever
[khalidùn] " (2, 82). Cf. 4, 122; 11, 23; 14, 23; 18, 30-31.

153. "He has promised the men and women who believe [mu'minìna wa
mu'minatì] in Him gardens with streams running under the trees, in which they
shall abide forever" (9, 72). Cf. 40, 40; 48, 5. — BAUSANI notes: "The ignorance of this Koranic text has brought some Christian authors, even up to a
period relatively recent, to absurdly charge Mohammad of excluding women
from the paradise." BAUS., p. 524.

154. "Blessed is the final abode [ùqba d dàri] for a reward!" (13, 24). Cf.
38, 46. — Abode different from and opposed to the abode of fire reserved
to Allah's enemies, and called (once only) dar al-khulùd, abode of eternity
(41, 28).

155. "Through His grace He has admitted us to the eternal abode [dar
almuqàmat], where we shall know no toil, no weariness" (35, 35).

156. "The abode of peace [dar us salàm] with their Lord, shall be theirs"
(6, 127). Cf. 7, 46; 10, 25; 16, 31.

sojourn of peace; dàr al- muttaqìn (16, 30), abode of Allah-fearing people.

The paradise is also called jànnat, garden, in the singular; or jannàt, gardens, in the plural.[157] Garden, or gardens — they are so large, so spacious that they have a perimeter equal in dimensions to that of heaven and earth (3, 133; 57, 21). Gardens, viridaria, or recreational green parks — they are all refreshed by one (88, 12) or more water springs;[158] with a river (54, 45), or rather by more rivers[159] placidly running through.

Throughout the Koran we also find this paradise described with the following periphrases — all including the idea of garden, or viridarium (lush-green recreational park): jànnat na'ìm (56, 89; 79, 38), garden of pleasure; jànnat an-na'ìm (26, 85), the garden (singular) of the pleasure; jannàt an-na'ìm,[160] the gardens (plural) of the pleasure; jannàt wa na'ìm (52, 17), gardens and pleasure; jannàt 'àden,[161] gardens of Eden; jannàt el-firdàus,[162] gardens of the paradise.

---

157. "Enter the garden [jànnat]; no fear shall you find in it, nor regret" (7, 49). Cf. 2, 111; 3, 14; 4, 124; 46, 14; 76, 12. — "You, who believed, turn to Allah in true repentance, so He may forgive you your sins and admit you to gardens [jannàten] with streams running under the trees" (66, 8). Cf. 71, 12; 74, 40; 78, 16.

158. "But the God-fearing shall dwell amongst gardens [jannàten] and fountains [wa 'uyùn]: enter them in peace and secure" (15, 45). Cf. 44, 52; 51, 15.

159. "... gardens with rivers [anhàru] running under the trees, where they shall dwell forever"(3, 156). Cf. 2, 25; 4, 13; 5, 85; 10, 9; 16, 31.

160. "We will admit them to gardens of delight [jannàt in na'ìm]" (5, 65). Cf. 10, 9; 22, 56; 31, 8; 37, 43; 68, 34.

161. "The gardens of Eden [jannàtu Àdnen] they shall enter, where rivers run under the trees" (16, 31). Cf. 19, 61; 20, 76; 35, 33; 40, 8; 98, 8. — Cf. JEF., p. 217.

162. "Those that believe and do good works will possess the gardens of paradise [jannàt il firdàus]" (18, 107). — As mihràb is a barbarism of Ethio-

We consequently end up with these data in hand: to signify the paradise — or the abode of those who during their life have truly succeeded in obtaining the glorious (45, 30), magnificent (44, 57) and supreme triumph[163] — the Koran never makes use, never at all, of the substantive *ràbwat*.

On the other hand, the place of refuge given by Allah to Jesus and Mary according to the present Koranic verse, is never indicated by the classic terms, *dàr* and *jànnat*, usually used for the paradise.

Finally, neither does the verse call the place of refuge *qaràr*, abode stable and perpetual; but it qualifies it as *zàt qaràr*, pseudo-stable; in other words it is a locality which, beyond being watered by fresh waters, offers itself as suitable for a stable and tranquil abode, welcoming for a serene and pleasurable sojourn, fit for a safe, worry-free refuge.

In conclusion, we believe that the verse in question can ill afford to be stretched into sure and precise inferences because of the wording in it which is so vague and generic.

Its interpretation can vacillate in such opposite directions[164] that no positive and concrete conclusion can be drawn from it — an evidence and a confirmation of the verse's mercurial nature. The only note suggested almost unanimously by all exegetes is

---

pian origin (HAD. III, p. 461), so also is *Adn* (Eden) of Syriac origin, meaning "vineyard" (HAD. III, p. 142). Likewise *firdàus*, a barbarism of Greek origin (HAD. III, p. 142); or Iranian. — Cf. JEF., p. 224.

163. "Rejoice this day: Gardens shall be yours to dwell in forever, with rivers running under the trees. That is the supreme triumph *[al fauz ul 'adhìm]* " (57, 12). Cf. 9, 72; 48, 5; 64, 9; 85, 11.

164. The locality is not at all identified by Koranic exegetes. "Abdallah ibn Sallâm dit qu'il s'agit de Damas; et Abû Huraya parle de Ramla; Qatâda et Ka'b, de Jérusalem. Ka'b dit qu'il s'agit d'un endroit où la terre est plus proche du ciel. Abû Zeid mentionne l'Égypte; Dahhâk parle de l'oasis de Damas; et Abû al-'Aliya, de Jérusalem." THA'LABI, *Qisas*, 386 (ap. HAY., p. 80). — Cf. ZAM. III, 190.

this: The verse refers to the earthly life of Jesus and Mary, not to their last things, and less yet to their ultimate glorification.

With much probability therefore, if not indeed with an absolute certainty, we may say that this debated Koranic verse does not hit at Mary's eschatological "facts"; and neither does the text offer a solid foundation to adequately justify or sustain Yurdkoru's eschatological hypothesis.

It is not improbable that, in the verse, the Koran intends to emphasize Allah's providential concern by securing for Mary and her Child, astray since they abandoned the *mihràb*, a safe and pleasing refuge.[165]

What that refuge had been precisely, we have no way of defining.

I don't state categorically, but neither do I exclude, that that refuge might be identified with the same locality where Jesus was born. According to the Koran (19, 24), it ought not necessarily be called arid,[166] being near a spring which gushed out miraculously (19, 24) to make it a suitable and pleasing dwelling place.

The whereabouts of the "refuge," however, still remain obscure at this writing. With certitude it is known only to Allah,

---

165. SABUNI states with no reserve that right in that hillside, away from Jerusalem, Jesus had spent his early years, growing as he did under the tender care of his mother, Mary. Cf. SAB., p. 206. — THA'LABI places that elevated locality, or hillside, in Egypt. "Joseph conduisit Marie et son Fils sur le dos de son âne, jusqu'en Égypte. C'est là la Colline dont Allah a parlé: 'Et Nous leur avons donné refuge sur une colline de paix et d'eau rafraîchissante' " (ap. HAY., p. 80).

166. Moslem exegetes and historians are indeed the ones who, starving for the sensational, multiply the prodigious events around Jesus and his mother, reducing the palm tree to just a *dry* stump. The Koran says that Mary was told to shake the palm *trunk*, and that the tree should have dropped fresh ripe dates to her; no mention whatever in it of the winter season. — As noted before (n. 161), the Ps.-MATTHEW describes the palm tree as verdant and loaded with fruits.

whose knowledge nothing escapes, not even the arcane secrets of the realm of the ghàyb.[167]

B) SURA 5, 17:

"Who could prevent Allah from destroying the Messiah, the son of Mary, if He so wanted, together with his mother and all the peoples of the earth? His is the kingdom of the heavens and the earth and all that lies in between them."

Father Henninger,[168] subsequent to a review and a lecture given by Prof. Rudi Paret on April 25, 1953, revised his own position on Mary's assumption into heaven according to the Koran. Here in brief is his opinion:

a. He admits that there is in the Koran "ein interessantes (indirektes) Zeugnis" [169] to the Oriental Church's belief in Mary's assumption: a sign and a mark forerunning, at a century's distance, the homilies of John, the Damascene.

b. This sign, or indication, is not taken out from Sura 23, 50 [52] in which the very first thing one is aware of — "auf den ersten Blick" — is a great similari-

---

167. "He is Allah, beside whom there is no other god. He knows the invisible and the unseen [al ghàyb]. He is the Clement, the Merciful!" (59, 22.)

168. Cf. HENNINGER, JOSEPH, Mariä Himmelfahrt im Koran, in Neue Zeitschr. Miss., 10 (1945), p. 288-292. — My gratitude to Fr. Federico Ruiz, Director of Ephemerides Carmeliticae, who obtained for me a photocopy of this article. I had long and in vain searched for it elsewhere.

169. "Und doch haben wir hier ein interessantes (indirektes) Zeugnis für den Glauben der Ostkirche." (Loc. cit., p. 292.)

ty with the Koranic description of the paradise; but they are illusory similarities: *"diese Ähnlichkeiten sind trügerish."*[170]

c. That sign or indication is found, instead, in an interesting Koranic verse not sufficiently explored thus far or exploited — the 17th verse of Sura 5 quoted above. And based upon this verse, he thus reasons:

Allah, who had already wiped out whole cities with their people, might — according to the Koran — if He so wanted, do the same with Jesus and Mary: annihilate them completely because they are His creatures; mere creatures, not divinities.[171] Now, in order that this annihilation be real and effective, it should be supposed that Mohammad had considered Jesus and Mary as *actually existing:* that they were still in life and in a fully existential life, personal life, in body and soul.[172] Otherwise He could not in truth annihilate them.[173] This *"Fortleben von Jesus (und Maria),"* that is their survival, or perpetual vitality, must be supposed actual *in paradise.*

We know in fact that Jesus, according to the Koran, was not crucified, nor did he die of a natural death, but was raised alive into heaven. He will die, if ever, after the final resurrection. By mentioning Mary here at the side of Jesus, the thought that she went through the same fate as her son did, becomes urgent. On a par with him then she also enjoys a "reale Fortleben.[174] Thus, the more acceptable interpretation

---

170. *Loc. cit.,* p. 290.

171. *Loc. cit.,* p. 289.

172. *"Beachtenswert ist, dass die beiden dabei als wirklich exitierend gedacht sind."* *Loc. cit.,* p. 289.

173. *"(Sonst könnten sie ja nicht vernichtet werden)". Ibid.*

174. *Loc. cit.,* p. 291.

of the quoted verse 17 of Sura 5 must admit that, according to the Koran, both Jesus and Mary live together
in heaven near God in body and soul *("mit Leib und
Seele")*; and that they enjoy a real and physical existence identical to the real and physical existence of
those who were their contemporaries on earth.[175]

Now, to take the quoted verse as a basis and demand for
Jesus and Mary a "Fortleben," a personal and actual existence, so
that one might thence assert in truth that Allah might indeed annihilate them if He so wanted, seems to me an extorted and
totally gratuitous conclusion.

Upon mulling over the verse, as a matter of fact, one can
see that there is in it a *hypothetical* content formulated with connection to a condition. Well, in order that a condition result as
true or probable, it is not at all necessary that it be tied to a factor "actually" and *hic et nunc* present and living. So long as it is
a hypothesis, it requires nothing else beyond the absence of contradiction in its terms; and therefore, as a hypothesis, it prescinds
from categories limiting time and place. In other words, it
abstracts from the past, from the future, and even from the
present.

In the concrete cases of Jesus and Mary, consequently,
Mohammad might well indeed have forwarded his own
hypothesis, which would have certainly been logical and true,
saying that Almighty Allah could annihilate them both on a par

---

175. "*Die plausibelste Erklärung von Sure 5, 19 [17] scheint also die von
Paret gegebene zu sein*, d. h. nach der Überzeugung Mohammeds existieren
Jesus und Maria ebenso wirklich und leibhaftig, wie seine lebenden
Zeitgenossen auf der Erde. Weil aber Jesus nicht mehr auf der Erde lebt,
sondern lebendig zu Gott entrückt worden ist, muss dasselbe auch von Maria
angenommen werden; *mit anderen Worten*, Mohammed kannte und teilte die
Überzeugung seiner christlichen Gewährsmänner, dass Maria, ebenso wie Jesus,
mit Leib und seele bei Gott lebt." *Loc. cit.*, p. 292. — Italics are ours.

with the greatest prophets and messengers of the past, without having to necessarily suppose that both of them, and the biblical messengers as well, be yet retained in life, *actually* existing in body and soul.

And then, contrary to what Henninger adds, I do find it neither remarkable nor surprising [*Es ist auffällig*] that Mary's name appears here beside the name of Jesus.[176] I would rather say the opposite, induced to that by two motives suggested by both the remote and immediate contexts.

REMOTE CONTEXT: If Mohammad had here passed over in silence the name of Mary, that would have been really strange and extraordinary: a blow to his usual style. Because Mary and Jesus were in his mind tied indivisibly by one destiny, the Prophet had in fact taken the habit of always coupling their names and remembrance whenever they occurred. In the current verse, for instance, he places Mary beside Jesus in a way analogous to the coupling which follows in this same Sura, verse 75, where he states that Jesus, a messenger of Allah and yet a creature, did eat and drink. Instead of going far away in search of other individuals as terms of comparison, Mohammad settles for the one closest to Jesus, Mary, saying that, though mother of Christ — and yet a simple creature, she also, along with her son, did eat and drink and was subject to all the functions following the eating and drinking.

IMMEDIATE CONTEXT: It is precisely for the motive advocated by Henninger, a polemic one,[177] that Mohammad had to mention Mary explicitly in verse 17. Here, in fact, he wants to strike back at the Associators and all those who ascribe the divine nature to others besides the true and unique God. Nor should

---

176. "Es ist auffällig, dass in diesem Zuzammenhang Maria überhaupt erwähnt wird." *Loc. cit.*, p. 291.

177. "Für Mohammeds polemischen Zweck." *Ibid.*

one presently forget that Mary, together with Jesus, had been placed by some at the same level as Allah, thus coming up with the famous "triad" strongly reproved by this same Sura 5: "Impious are those that say, 'Allah is one of three.' There is no God other than Allah alone. And if they do not desist from so saying, a severe punishment will wait for those of them who thus blaspheme!" (5, 73). As insinuated by this same verse, this triad would consist of Allah, Jesus and Mary (5, 116). Consequently, in order to hit his adversaries with a complete and adequate demonstration, Mohammad had to make mention of Mary quite forcibly and exhibit her as a simple creature on a par with Christ, her son.

There is no question that the Koran professes immortality and knows man's survival in body and soul in the other world (21, 34). Nor is it excluded that the Book also grants this same survival to some individuals, such as Idris (19, 57) and Jesus (3, 55; 4, 157). But with regard to Mary's life in the world beyond, the Koran has not the faintest allusion.

The contrary is true. Pressured by the polemic debate raging mainly during the last years of his career, Mohammad had deliberately restricted the Koranic narratives concerning Mary to the episodes that are tightly connected with the person of Jesus, or uniquely related to the infancy of Jesus. From this abridgement, in fact, he could have thus drawn a valid argument favorable to the strictly human nature of Jesus, and without any pretense of a divine nature in Jesus.

Friend of Allah, and one of the most favored by Allah (1, 3, 45), Jesus, the son of Mary, "was but a messenger of Allah, like those who were sent before him" (5, 75). "Impious are those that say: 'The Messiah, the son of Mary, is Allah.' For the Messiah himself said: 'Children of Israel, serve Allah, my Lord and your Lord' " (5, 72).

As we will see later, such episodes of the infancy of Christ met a large response in the Christian literature of the early centuries especially in the Apocryphal Gospels. These were mainly conceived with a pre-set goal in mind: to make up for the reticences in the Canonical Gospels relative to Mary's birth and Jesus' infancy.

These episodes alone enjoyed Mohammad's favor and complacency. And them only he wanted to insert in his Koranic Message.[178]

Of the Marian events, including the eschatological ones, he does not say a word. He just did not want to speak.

In conclusion, as we've seen earlier, there is in the Koranic text and in the whole Islamic tradition as well no trace of Mary's death, of her assumption, and of her ultimate glorification.[179]

---

178. "Les histoires du **Transitus Mariae** n'ont pas trouvé place dans la tradition musulmane." WENS., p. 360.

179. The sheik MAHMUD SHALTUT, from Azhar, has made, among others, this declaration to the newspaper Al-Misri, on October 31st, 1950: "La croyance que Jésus-Christ est monté corps et âme au ciel était déjà très controversée [...]. Mais le Sacré Collège nous surprend aujourd'hui par une tradition dont il n'y a trace dans les Textes Sacrés ni dans la Tradition: Jésus ne serait pas, lui seul, monté au ciel corps et âme; sa mère le serait aussi." Ap. MUL., p. 272, in note. And BOUB. (p. 256): "Le dogme de l'Assomption instauré par le pape Pie XII (1946) [?], est en contradiction avec l'Islam."

Chapter Two

SYNTHESIS

Mohammad's attitude toward Mary was never irreverent or disrespectful. Never, ever! To the contrary, it was always saturated with esteem, admiration and veneration. Always steady, invariable and never betrayed to the end.

For Mary, the daughter of Imran and mother of Jesus, the Koran reserves a position of privilege — *singular and eminent* — shared by no other woman: not by the wives of the Prophet, nor even by his beloved daughter, Fatima. And it is this special position of honor that has motivated the scholars of all times, as it does nowadays, to bend reverently over the pages of the Koran and trace therein the most sweet and sympathetic image of Mary.[1]

---

1. "One of the aspects of Islam most likely to prove interesting in this

I. Singular Position

This singularity jumps out conspicuously from the exceptional way Mohammad treats Mary. He surrounds her with the highest regards of reverence and esteem despite his Semitic background which is not infrequently prejudiced against the fair sex. In the great Arabian, that is absolutely remarkable! Dealing with Mary, Mohammad ignores the code of values, proper of his time. He abides by another one. It is not the old Semitic mentality evaluating man by his sex, or, worse still, promoting the female's constitutional inferiority vis-à-vis the male.[2] In the old hierarchical scale of values, "men are slightly above women" (2, 228). To have mitigated this mentality to a great extent is one of the social reforms to be credited historically to the Koran.[3] But

---

Marian epoch is the place occupied by the Holy Virgin in Islamic doctrine." ANW., p. 447. — MARRACCI himself had already confessed that Moslem doctors "de Maria et Jesu honorificentissime loquuntur: et ea ipsa quae configunt, nihil indigni aut probrosi continere videntur." MAR. II, p.116. And Marracci is generally anything but tender with Mohammad. He calls him in fact, "non solum magnum peccatorem, sed idolorum quoque cultorem, saltem per plures annos" (MAR. I, [Mahumeti auctoris Alcorani vitae, rerumque gestarum Synopsis], p. 18); and elsewhere he calls him "women runner": "Mahumetus homo mulierosus" (MAR. II, p. 173). Italics are ours.

2. "A step higher!" (2, 228) because of their sex. "Bien que la mère soit cause de l'existence de son fils, son fils lui est quand même supérieur, à cause de la supériorité de son sexe masculin." IBN ARABI (ap. HAY., p. 76). This Koranic principle, at a practical level, provoked a real rupture between the two respective sectors, masculine and feminine. It subjected the females to a humiliating set of customs: cloister and veil; premature marriage at the whim of the father or tutor; right to divorce belonging to husband alone; and polygamy. Cf. GAR., p. 132.

3. Enough to mention, as an instance of this mitigation, is the reproval by the Koran of the barbarous custom in which the Arabs disposed of their own daughters, killing them or burying them alive soon as they were born. Cf. 6, 137, 140, 151; 16, 57; 17, 31; 81, 8-9. On the social condition of women before Islam, cf. DAR., p. 8-28; and after Islam, ib., p. 29-55. — Cf. also WAT. II, p. 330-345.

the mentality nonetheless still persists and surfaces into effect whenever there is in practice an attempt to delineate where man's and woman's duties and rights begin and end.

Mary is the only woman whom Mohammad remembers by her proper name. Of her alone, as of an individual, he discourses quite at length and with an out-spoken admiration. Witness to that is the actual Koranic script on which here we depend. Though the text contains perhaps some polemics and ill hides the Prophet's apologetic worries, it remains nonetheless an undeniable testimony of his high respect for the mother of Issa.

These polemic and apologetic flaws, if they exist at all, are not so relevant as to necessitate stripping Mary of her "Christian" faith and turning her exclusively into a "Jewess," or intentionally into an "anti-Christian" as would Zakarias — but with no foundation at all, as we will later prove at the proper time.

The Koran speaks profusely of women. "The Women" (Nisà) is the title of one of its longest Suras, the Fourth, which treats of the fair sex both in general and in particular.

In *general* it remembers the associating, or idolatrous, women (2, 221); the unclean women (24, 26); the believing women (24, 31); the honorable women (24, 23); the women praying, devout, sincere, etc. (33, 35); the women of the paradise (36, 56). In *particular* it mentions the Prophet's wives (33, 28, 35, 50; 66, 1) and his daughters (33, 59). *Individually,* Adam's wife (2, 35; 7, 19); Abraham's wife (51, 29); Lot's wife (11, 81); Faraoh's wife (28, 9); the Prince's wife (12, 30, 51); Imran's wife (3, 35); Zachariah's wife (19, 8); Abu Lahab's wife (111, 4); Lot's daughters (11, 78); the mother of Moses (28, 7); Moses' sister (28, 11); the Queen of Saba (27, 23).

But no woman other than Mary is mentioned by her proper name. No one absolutely.

Mary is the only feminine name that one reads explicitly in the whole Koran. It seems as though, in Mary's presence, all other women were something amorphous, evanescent, inconsistent; as though Mohammad wanted deliberately to cast on them all a shadow, and then place in the limelight the only woman truly worthy of this name — Mary.

Furthermore, from the beginning of his career, i.e. from the second epoch of the Meccan period, to be precise, Allah ordered Mohammad expressly to take care of Mary and make mention of her amongst His most favored friends.[4] *"Remember in the Book Mary,"* was enjoined to him a first time (19, 16); and then a second: *"Remember also the woman who kept her virginity and into whom We breathed of Our spirit"* (21, 91).

In the wake of this plan by Allah, it is no wonder that the remembrance of His chosen protégée recurs so frequently throughout the pages of the Book. Mary's name, in fact, appears explicitly in the Koran 34 times, a remarkable figure indeed, particularly when compared with the number of times in which the most prominent biblical personalities of either the Old or New Testament are mentioned.

Among the proper names therein quoted, the name of Mary, in fact, claims fourth place in terms of frequency of recurrence; it ranks immediately after that of Moses, of Abraham, and of Noah.[5] But it comes ahead of the name of Adam, of Lot, of Jacob, of Ismael, of Jonah, of Elias, of Zachariah, of Yahia, and of Jesus himself.[6]

---

4. Cf. 19, 41 (Abraham); 19, 51 (Moses); 19, 54 (Ismael); 19, 56 (Idris).

5. Moses' name recurs 169 times; Abraham's name, 69; Noah's name, 43. — Cf. BAQ., p. 680-82; 1-2; 722-23.

6. The name of Joseph and of Lot recurs 27 times in the Koran (cf. BAQ., p. 654, 733). — Twenty-five times the name of Adam (p. 24-25) and of Jesus (p. 494-495). — Sixteen times the name of Jacob (p. 733). — Twelve times the name of Ismael (p. 33-34). — Seven times the name of Zachariah (p. 331). — Five times the name of Yahia (p. 225). — Four times the name of Job (p. 108)

This practice by the Koran to address a woman exclusively by her own name, and to single her out from all other women, is quite unusual; it might induce someone to take it as a proof of Mohammad's open "devotion" to Mary. Her virginal, feminine figure had fascinated his heart in the same way God's memory had obsessed his whole being.[7] Allah's supreme name[8] in fact recurs on his lips throughout the Book no less than 2,697 times — and occasionally one, two, three, four, five and even six times in the same verse.[9]

---

and of Jonah (p. 775). — Two times the name of Elias (6, 85; 37, 123), and of Eliseus (6, 86; 38, 48).

7. "Il Corano fù il prodotto di una violenta azione monoteistica da parte del suo fondatore, certamente uno degli uomini che maggiormente nel corso della storia sia stato *ossessionato dal terrore dell'idololatria.*" QUADRI GOFFREDO, *Il pensiero arabo ed abraico del medioevo,* in "Grande Antologia Filosofica," diretta da A. PADOVANI, Milano, 1954, IV, p. 1048. Italics are ours.

8. *Allah* is not a name and a being invented by the Prophet of Mecca (cf. GAB. I, p.16). — Concerning the supremacy of this name above any other — particularly on *Hùwa* (p. 10-11), *al-Hày ul Qayùm* (p. 14-15), *Dhu'l Jalàl wa'l Ikràm* (p. 15) — cf. ANAWATI GEORGE C., *Le nom Suprême de Dieu (Ismu 'llah al A'zam),* in "Atti del Terzo Congresso di studi Arabici e Islamici," Ravello, 1-6 settembre 1966. (Napoli, Istituto Universitario Orientale, 1967, p. 216.) — Cf. GARDET L., *Allah,* in EI, t. 1 (nuova edizione), p. 418-429; JEF., p. 66-67.

The Arabic term *Allah* is a contraction of the article *al* and the word *Ilàh* (thus making: *Allah,* with the I dropped) which means "GOD." "Il est possible qu'antérieurement à l'époque de Mahomet les Méquois paiens aient usé de *Allah* pour désigner la principale divinité de la Kaaba." WAT. I, p. 51. Cf. "*Rabb al-Bait*" in the Koran (106, 3).

And for information on the cult rendered to Allah in the Hijaz before Mohammad, cf. HAD. II, p. 123-124. For HADDAD, the monotheism that already existed in Mecca before the Prophet — (who for his initial preaching had adopted an eschatological, not an anti-associationist, theme) — was a *monotheism* typically *biblical* coming from the "People of the Book" (cf. HAD. II, p. 26-39), especially from the Judeo-Christians, whose prominent Leader was Waraka Ben Nawfal. This latter was Khadija's uncle (others: cousin), and was committed to the translation in Arabic of the Holy Gospel. — Cf. HAD. VI, p. 292.

9. The *twin* recurrence of *Allah* in the same verse is quite common. An instance is Sura 2, *The Cow,* in the following vv.: 105, 174, 225, 268, 276. —

What undoubtedly betrays Mohammad's apologetic or polemic intent here is his insistence in the Book on speaking the name of Mary out loud. In 24 out of the 34 times where she is explicitly mentioned, her name for some reason never comes alone, but always associated with the name of Jesus.

In the Meccan period, which started and evolved under preponderant Christian or Judeo-Christian influence, Mohammad's plan was to steer away from Christ any concept of human paternity; by excluding from this latter any paternal reference, he wanted to stress more effectively Mary's virginity and Christ's virginal conception.

His attitude in the Medinian period was contrary altogether, emancipated as he was now from the "People of the Book," Christians and Jews. By enforcing the idea of a purely human origin to Christ, he intended to shut the door against any possibility of attributing to Mary's son a divine origin or affiliation.

The constant recourse by the Koran to Mary as "mother of Jesus" — and by correlative consequence, to Jesus as "son of Mary" — must be considered as a discreet but valid profession of monotheistic faith. It reflects Mohammad's tacit but impelling design to strike in a deadly way at any form of associationism (shirk) and to promote vigorously, though indirectly, the monotheistic dogma. Allah, One and alone, was the core of the Arabian's Koranic Message; the motive of his apostolate. To proclaim this creed the Prophet committed his life "with an ardor for both his time and society unsurpassed."[10] "Those who say, 'The Merciful has begotten a son,' preach a monstrous falsehood, at which the very heavens might crack, the earth break asunder,

---

For triple recurrence, also frequent, cf. 2, 140, 143, 213, 220, 228, 258, 259, 261, 284; 3, 31, 52, 78, 112, 159; 4, 139; 7, 158; 9, 37. — For quadruple recurrence, cf. 2, 187, 229, 247, 253; 3, 179; 6, 136; 29, 10. — For quintuple recurrence, cf. 2, 165; 9, 40. — For sextuple, cf. 2; 282. — Cf. BAQ., p. 40-75.

10. GAB. II [Il Profeta d'Arabia], p. 29.

and the mountains crumble to dust. That they should ascribe a son to the Merciful, when it does not become Him to beget one!" (19, 88-92).

"O 'kafirùn,' unbelievers, I do not serve what you worship, nor do you serve what I worship. I shall never serve what you worship, nor will you ever serve what I worship. You have your own religion and I have mine" (109, 1-6). "He is Allah: there is no god but Him. Praise is His in this world and in the next" (28, 70). "I am commanded to serve Allah and to associate none with Him. To Him I pray, and to Him I shall return" (13, 36). "As for myself, Allah is my Lord. I will associate none with Him" (18, 38).

II. Eminent Position

The great chosen ones of Allah had each a well-defined task to accomplish. In the final analysis, this task was reduced to bearing witness to the unity of God, creator of the seven heavens and of any other creature[11] on one hand, and on the other to call

---

11. Allah is creator *[fàtir]* of the heavens and the earth: cf. 13, 16; 35, 1; 39, 62; 40, 62. — Because He created *[khàlaqa]* every single thing (6, 101), Allah is the creator *[khàliq]* of everything (6, 102). — He is the maker *[bàdi']* of the heavens and the earth, for He creates and makes them all alone (6, 101). — "He has created seven heavens *[sab' samawàt]* " (65, 12). Cf. 2, 29; 23, 17, 86; 67, 3. — It is known that the division of the super-terrestrial world in "seven heavens" occurs all along in the Hebraic Apocrypha *[The Secrets of Henoch, The Testament of Levi]*; likewise in the *Ascension of Isaiah*, where the Jewish Prophet crosses seven heavens before reaching the Throne of the Most High. Same talk of the "Beloved," who went through seven heavens before coming

the errant to the "right path of Allah" (42, 53). It was then fundamentally a religious task, and ultimately a moral one.

Such was the task for Abraham (29, 16); for Moses (10, 84); for Jesus (3, 51). Such also for Mohammad himself, *"a witness and a bearer of good news and warnings"* (48, 8).

Likewise was it for Mary. Chosen and predisposed by God, she also had her own task to fulfill. Subsequent to her indivisible unity with Christ, her son, in mankind's religious history, Mary had to shine together with him as a prodigious sign *[àyat]* for the whole creation, and as a resplendent model *[màthal]* for all believers.

If these two terms àyat (sign) and màthal (model) were understood as intended, i.e. in their fullest sense and most fertile content, they would in my opinion offer the surest guideline for a synthetical and coordinated exposition of the Koran's teaching on Mary. Taken however as they read and sound, with no undue restrictions, they constitute the purest germ and the original and most authentic nucleus of Mohammad's Marian thought.

My purpose presently is to put together all the Marian elements, salient in the 13 Suras already mentioned, into a synthesis which is homogeneous and adherent to the text. With the comfortable feeling that I am not building on sand, I shall take as a solid and objective groundwork the two ideas of àyat and màthal. Generic indeed, but expressive ideas. And both of authentic Koranic coinage.

---

down to become flesh on earth. Cf. TISSERANT E., *L'Ascension d'Isaie*. Translation de la version éthiopienne, Paris, Letouzey, 1909. — Cf. MAS., p. 781.

According to Muqatil, the first heaven was created of a wave from the hollow sea. The second, of iron. The third, of silver. The fourth, of bronze. The fifth, of gold. The sixth, of red hyacinth *[yakùt]*. The seventh, of light. The thickness of each heaven, however, needs 500 years to be walked through; that is also the distance separating one heaven from the other. — Cf. NWY., p. 68-69.

1. Mary À y a t for the Universe

In two separate places the Koran applies to Mary the predicate à y a t. They are the two Suras belonging to the Meccan period: the 21st, *The Prophets*, and the 23rd, *The Believers*.

It ought to be noted here, however, that the predicate is of a particular significance, because it involves directly the person[12] of Mary and that of Christ, her son, as well. In fact, we do not find it thus stated of any other individual, not even of Mohammad himself.

In Sura 21, which Nöldeke ranks in place 16 among the Suras of the second Meccan epoch, the text reads: "Remember in the Book the Woman who kept her virginity, and in whom We breathed of Our spirit. We made her and her son a sign for the universe" (21, 91).

And in Sura 23, which according to Nöldeke ranks fifteen among the above-mentioned Suras, it is written (23, 50-51): "We gave Moses the Torah, so that his people might be rightly

---

12. The Ps.-Matthew offers us a clear insight of this *personal* glorification of Mary. To Joachim, found after he was lost, the angel bids: "Come down from the mountain and, secure and confident, return to Anna; the good deeds that you and she have done, are reported in the presence of the Most High; *et talem datum est vobis germen, quale numquam ab initio nec prophetae aut sancti habuerunt neque sunt habituri*" (III, 4. — AM., p. 292). In another apparition, the angel says also to Joachim, announcing to him the birth of the daughter: "This girl shall belong to the Temple of the Lord, and the Holy Spirit shall take abode in her. She will excel in bliss all women *[super omnes sanctas feminas]*, so that it never could be said that one has ever equaled her, or appeared to be like her in future time *"numquam erit ei similis ventura in hoc saeculo"* (III, 2. — AM., p. 288).

guided. Likewise, of the son of Mary and of his mother, We made a sign."[13]

À y a t, a sign; and a sign for the *u n i v e r s e*. That is Mary's first dimension as visualized by the Koran.

The term *à y a t*, so well in tune with the Islamic mentality,[14] is one of those common names most ordinarily recurring through the Koranic verses. It is found there no less than 360 times,[15] and it takes on the most varied attributions.

Qualified as a sign *[àyat]* is the creation of heaven and earth (2, 164). *Sign*, the creation of the first man from the dust (30, 20). *Sign*, the formation of the first woman, with the subsequent difference in sex and affections (30, 21). *Sign*, the diversity of men's tongues and colors (30, 22). *Sign*, the alternation of the day and the night (3, 190). *Sign*, sleep, restorer of human energies (30, 23). *Sign*, the winds raising the clouds (30, 46). *Sign*, the ships sailing the ocean with cargoes beneficial to man (2, 164). *Sign*, the lightning (30, 24). *Sign*, the water that Allah sends down from the

---

13. "àyat li'l alamìn" (21, 91). Fr. ANAWATI translates *alamìn* in its dual form *[alamàin]*, rather than *[alamìn]*: "as extraordinary signs (àyât) to the 'two worlds', i.e. *this and the next.*" ANA., p. 458. Italics are ours. — The Koranic text, is, on the contrary, universally read in the plural form *[alamìn]*; and has been understood for *the complex of the whole created world,* seen and unseen.

14. "Avec le Coran, le musulman ne dit pas, comme Bernanos avec l'Evangile, 'tout est grâce'; mais 'tout est signe de Dieu' (àyat min Allah), miracle." MASS. (*La "Poussée" de l'Islam,* 1959), I, 355. The *"all is grace"* is of Saint Thérèse, the Little Flower, (in *Novissima Verba*). — "Nella concezione mohammadica del costante, attivissimo intervento di Dio nelle cose umane, tutto è miracoloso e nulla lo è al contempo." BAUS., p. 523. — Cf. JEF., p. 72-73.

15. Cf. BAQ., p. 103-108.

sky (2, 164), which revives the dead earth (30, 24), turns it into a green vegetation (22, 63) and symbolizes man's final rebirth (22, 5-6) on the day of the resurrection of the dead (30, 50). *Sign*, the she-camel, drinking her share of water as men do (26, 155-158). Peculiar *Sign*, Allah's favor to protect His persecuted messengers (13, 38). *Signs of God*,[16] every paragraph, every verse *[àyat]* of the Koran, because the Koran is the proof (3, 50), or rather the supreme proof (28, 49), which confirms Mohammad's prophetic mission.

As one can see, the meanings that the word *àyat* carries along are not only numerous, but quite disparate. From a close and serene look, however, one can easily trace in them all a basic and minimal common denominator which helps reduce them into a *common sense*. Once found, this common denominator would bring to the fore *àyat's* radical concept: *a sign given by God to man so that he would recognize His intervention and the purpose of this intervention*. God's purpose is to coax man into the right faith in Him, to promote his spiritual and even temporal welfare, and establish peace and justice between him and his peers in a community. To make man well aware of all that, God resorts to different means of communication, or intervention. The one more immediate, more tangible, more convincing and in tune with man's nature, is the *sign*.

With regard to Jesus and Mary, it must be said that *àyat* represents an eloquent evidence of Allah's omnipotence.[17] It, in

---

16. "Such are the signs of God *[ayàt ul'lah]* that We recite on you in all truth" (3, 108). Cf. 4, 140; 6, 27; 7, 26; 8, 52; 16, 104. And elsewhere, *passim*.

17. ZAM. III, p. 10. — "Si noti che nell'assoluto teismo personalistico coranico non si fa alcuna differenza fra fenomeni che noi chiameremo naturali (l'alternarsi della notte e del giorno) e altri di ordine tecnico dell'uomo. Ogni *causa secunda* si affievolisce, tutta è diretta opera di Dio." BAUS., p. 510-511.

other words, denotes His singular intervention in their destinies. They then appear as a marvelous and splendid exhibition of the divine attributes.

That is true also of Mary. An *àyat* like her son, Jesus, she is in her own way another expression of Allah's wisdom and might.

In the actual plan of salvation, she also has her own mission, her own "task." For all men, whether believers or not, she is an outstanding expression of Allah's care for mankind. A portion of this divine care was made concrete in the plan of historic reality by the ineffable prerogatives that Allah was pleased to bestow on her. They may be reduced to the following ones:

A. *Her Predestination*

B. *Her Purification*

C. *Her Singular Maternity*

D. *Her Unity with Christ*

E. *Her Eminent Dignity*

Such five musical notes in a harmonious accord, these prerogatives orchestrate together into a soul-elevating symphony interpreting, in turn, the most stupefying complex of divine attributes called by the Arabs, *"God's Most Excellent Names."* [18] Of each prerogative we shall treat separately, and, exclusively according to the Koran.

---

18. "Allah has the *Most Excellent Names*" (7, 180). Cf. 17, 110; 20, 8; 59, 24.

A. Mary's Predestination

It is mentioned by Sura 3 when the angels, while entertaining a conversation with Mary during her retreat in the *mihràb*, said to her, "Mary, Allah has chosen you... [istàfa-ki]" (3, 42).

The verb *istàfa* — to choose, prefer, predestine — is classical in the Koran's terminology. Its use is infallibly called for whenever the Koran wants to emphasize Allah's preferential action toward an object (2, 132), a person, or category of persons.[19] Thus we find it used either with regard to angels chosen by God as His messengers (22, 75), or to men delegated by God for some particular mission to other fellow men. Such were Adam, Noah (3, 33), Abraham (2, 130), Moses (7, 144), and Saul (2, 247).

Now by the fact that Mohammad had selected the verb *istàfa* to establish Mary's destiny, we conclude with certainty that he intended to locate her, if not properly at the same level as that of the major prophets and apostles,[20] at least in the rank of Allah's most favorite. We further deduce from the same fact a transparently clear implication: that, in resemblance of the great divine messengers, Mary was the object of an absolutely special predilection, destined as she was to an exceptional mission — *to be the mother of Jesus*.

As an initial proof of this predilection, the Koran quotes Mary's lineage: a privileged race of Allah's dearest friends — Adam, Noah, Abraham, Imran. "Truly, Allah exalted Adam and Noah, Abraham's descendants and the descendants of Imran

---

19. For each person cf. 2, 247 (Saul); 3, 33 (Adam); 3, 33 (Noah); 3, 42 (Mary). For category of persons cf. 37, 153 (daughters instead of sons); 38, 47 (the good and the righteous).

20. IBN HAZM (ap. HAY., 77). He is, perhaps, the only Moslem author attributing to Mary a privilege "reserved to men alone," the prophecy.

above all His creatures. They were the off-spring of one another"
(3, 33-34). A carnal progeny. But above all a spiritual progeny,
because they were the descendants of a chosen squad of Moslems
"*ante litteram,*" i.e. adorers of the one, true God, "before Islam
existed."

Whoever thinks or assesses things from a Semitic point of
view cannot but ascribe an incalculable[21] value to this testimony
of preferential love for Mary.[22]

But Allah's complacency goes much further yet. To the
genealogy, even though spiritual, the Koran adds other testimonials of divine benevolence.

Prescinding for the time being from the concern for the intimate life of the Virgin,[23] we remember, along with the Koran,
that Allah had welcomed Mary into His service in the Temple
(3, 37a) despite the fact that she was a female;[24] had provided

---

21. Mohammad's followers had attached exceptional importance to his
descent from a noble lineage, or illustrious foreparents. To enhance his prophetic prestige, more than one Moslem author boasted of his descent from
Abraham: a carnal descent through Ismael, and a spiritual descent through the
same faith and religion. Cf. TAB. VI, n. 6853 (326-327); BAYD. I, 135.

22. "Le Coran reconnaît les privilèges accordés aux patriarches et à la tribu
à laquelle, selon lui, appartient Marie. Il fait précéder le texte relatif à sa
naissance par cette affirmation: 'En vérité, Allâh a choisi Adam, Noè, la famille
d'Abraham et la famille d'Imrân de préferénce aux mondes, descendant les uns
des autres.' " MASSON, p. 315.

23. Some commentators have tried to spotlight Mary's intimate life. TAB.
VI, n. 7025 (p. 393): He has chosen you and drawn you to His *obedience.* —
Ibid.: He has preferred you to all the women of the universe, because of your
obedience and submissiveness. — AR-RAZI (ap. HAD. I, p. 159): Allah has
made you ready for the exercise of *piety;* and enriched you, therefore, with
goodness and *rectitude.* — BAYD. I, 138: the first preference consists in His acceptance of her, though a woman, to His service, freeing her from any obstacle
and making her *worthy of offering God the divine worship.* — TIRMIDHI
(ap. HAY., p. 75): "Il fut exigé de Marie l'oraison intérieure, c'est à dire
qu'elle s'oriente de tout son coeur vers Allah, mettant son âme sous son ombre
divine."

24. Cf. ZAM. I, p. 362; BAYD. I, p. 470.

for her custody, assigning her to an honorable personage, Zachariah (3, 37b); had always catered miraculously for her with the needed food (3, 37c); had honored her with the company of angels (3, 42-43); had given her moral support and sustained her during childbirth (19, 23-26); had defended her innocence in the presence of her stone-faced false accusers (19, 27-33); and had finally offered her a spring-watered hillside to peacefully spend the rest of her days (23, 50).

B. *Mary's Purification*

It is mentioned in the second part of the angelic message just quoted: "Mary, Allah has chosen you, and made you pure... [tahhàra-ki]" (3, 42b).

The verb *tàhhara* — to purge, deterge, purify — is in the Koran and in common use as well[25] susceptible to various meanings depending on the variety or diversity of the stain from which one is purified. In concrete terms, in fact, this stain could mean a material filth, a physical defect, a social ill, or a moral shame: fault, crime, infamy, dishonor.[26]

---

25. According to lexicographers, the verb *tàhhara* means to clean, purify something from a *stain*. This could be *physical*, such as physiological defects and impurities; or *moral*, such as *sin*, or crimes. *Legal purity*, however, is the one declared by law, human or divine, or conventionally retained as such. Cf. GAND., p. 85.

26. Among the *legal*, or ritual, impurities in Islam are: bodily losses (urine, excrements, sperm, pus, flatulence, bloodshed, etc.); carrions (except those of

As defined by the Koran, the meaning of purification may stretch so as to include a blotch of mere *legal* order, and it is then cleansed by ritual ablution. Practically, it comes down to any dirt or pollution that has to be taken away from a garment (74, 4); or any unclean matter soiling one's face or hands that has to be eliminated with water — by ablution, or with fine sand — by rubbing oneself with it, before prayer.[27]

This stain may further be a *physiological* impurity coming, among other sources, from the regular menstruations of women (2, 222); from sexual relations, or even from the mere satisfaction of a natural need (5, 6).

It may also be of a *religious* nature. Stains, consequently impure, were the cultic and idolatrous practices (9, 28) that Abraham and Ismael had to wipe out (22, 26) by God's command, to make pure the *"Sacred House"* of the Ka'ba (5, 97); or the corrupt and corrupting association with the infidels and unbelievers, from which Christ was purified, i.e. freed and protected (3, 55).

The stain may finally be of a *moral* nature. It then means fundamentally an abominable thing — *rijs*.[28] It contaminates the individual whenever he sets his mind to intentionally (33, 5) commit proven sexual crimes[29] that Allah does not enjoin (7, 28)

---

fish and locusts); spoiled eggs; wine; pork; dogs. Cf. GAND., p. 94-104; TABB., p. 93-96.

Following the Koran and a steady tradition, "Moslem Jurists make it clear that the status of purity may be major *[janàbat]* or minor *[hàdath]*. BAUS., p. 528. The major impurity is taken away by a complete bath *[ghùsul]*; the minor by ablution *[wudù]*.

27. The purifactory action by either total bath or ablution is called tayàmmum. For its practice, cf. GAN., p. 124-128; TABB., p. 83-87.

28. "He will cast His abomination *[rijs]* upon the senseless" (10, 100). — Cf. 7, 71; 9, 125.

29. "Do not expel them from their homes, and let them not go unless they had committed a proven sexual crime *[fàhishat]* " (65, 1). Cf. 3, 135; 4, 15; 29, 28; 33, 30.

but rather prohibits and condemns (7, 33) because they're in-decent[30] and foul acts (7, 157).

These in practice are the evils,[31] the sins,[32] the in-iquities[33] of him who is an associator (4, 48); who is an unbeliever (6, 125); who is a hypocrite (5, 41); who practices superstition with divining arrows (5, 90); who communicates with the cowardly and the fallen-away from faith (9, 95); who falsely accuses the innocents (41, 112); who commits murder (17, 31) and fornication (17, 32); who drinks wine (5, 90), eats carrions, run-ning blood, and the flesh of swine (6, 145); and who practices the *màysir*[34] — or gambles.

---

30. "The believers, both men and women, do patronize one another. They enjoin what is right, and forbid what is wrong *[mùnkar]* " (9, 71). Cf. 3, 104; 5, 79; 9, 67; 16, 90; 24, 21; 39, 29.

31. "He that does evil *[saiy'àt]*, no reward shall evildoers *[sani'ù ssaiy'àti]* have but what they were perpetrating" (28, 84). Cf. 2, 81; 4, 18; 35, 10; 42, 25.

32. "Those that earn *[kàsaba]* evil and become engrossed in their sin *[khati'at]* are the heirs of hellfire" (2, 81). Cf. 4, 111; 6, 120; 10, 27; 5, 21; 111, 2. — "Those who invented that slander (Aisha's love affair with Safwan ben Moattel) were a number of your own people. Each one of them shall be punished according to what he had earned *[iktàsaba]* by his crime" (24, 11). — Cf. BAQ., p. 604-605.
Concerning the *earning* of sin *[khati'at]* and iniquity *[ìthm]*, BAUSANI notes that such a concept has been the starting point of a doctrine according to which man's actions are created, or produced, by God, but man acquires them by do-ing them freely. In any case, the word *earn* "which in the Koranic language means clearly 'to commit', allows a certain freedom to the human will." BAUS., p. 545.

33. "Do not support one another in committing sin *[ìthm]* or enmity" (5, 2). Cf. 2, 206; 4, 112; 7, 33; 42, 37; 53, 32.

34. The *màysir* (cf. 2, 219; 5, 90, 91) is a gambling game in common use by the Arabs of the *Jahilya*. Cf. in BAUS. (p. 513) its primitive form. MAR-RACCI notes in that regard: "Sed alii verius intelligunt latrunculorum ludum,

All these sinful practices, like a fatal disease, nestle in the heart (5, 41); the cleansing from which, or the remission of which, belongs to God; and cannot be granted by anyone else but by God (3, 135). He who lives unrepentant "will add abomination [rijs] above abomination (9, 125); disgrace in this world will be his reward (5, 41), and eternal fire in the other (2, 81)." Therefore the unbelievers,[35] the hypocrites,[36] the perverts,[37] the iniquitous,[38] the wrongdoers[39] — the sinners generally,[40] because they do Satan's deeds,[41] will draw upon themselves God's wrath and curse.[42] Allah, in fact, loves those that turn to Him in repentance (2, 222), those that are pure (9, 108), because He is the

---

quos vulgo *Scaccos appellamus*; et quo Arabes praecipue delectantur." MAR. II, p. 237.

35. "These are indeed the unbelievers [kafirùn], and for the unbelievers [kafirìn], We have prepared a shameful punishment" (4, 151). Cf. 4, 44; 42, 26; 61, 8; 64, 10; 67, 6.

36. "Be they men or women, the hypocrites [munafiqùn] are all alike. They enjoin what is evil, forbid what is just. ..." (9, 67). Cf. 8, 49; 33, 1; 57, 13; 63, 1, 7, 8.

37. "Those that hereafter rebel (to the Covenant) are impious [fasiqùn]" (3, 82). Cf. 5, 59; 24, 4; 46, 35; 59, 19; 63, 6.

38. "Those that do not judge according to Allah's revelations are the iniquitous [dhalimùn]" (4, 45). Cf. 2, 229; 6, 21; 14, 42; 29, 49; 49, 11.

39. "The wrongdoers [mujrimùn] shall not be questioned about their sin" (28, 78). Cf. 8, 8; 10, 50; 30, 55; 45, 31; 77, 46.

40. "Filth only shall be his food, the filth which sinners [khati'ùn] alone eat" (69, 37). Cf. 12, 29, 91, 97; 28, 8.

41. "Are abominations devised by Satan [min a'màl isshaytàn]. Avoid them" (5, 90). — Cf. 1 Joa., 3, 8; "ut dissolvat opera diaboli."

42. "Those that open their bosoms to unbelief, shall incur the wrath [ghàdab] of Allah" (16, 106). Cf. 4, 93; 7, 71; 16, 106; 42, 16; 58, 14. — "Those that will deny Me and die unbelievers, shall incur the curse [là'nat] of Allah, the angels and men together" (2, 161). Cf. 7, 44; 11, 18; 48, 6.

light most pure that excludes radically any shadow or stain.[43]

Having established this variety of accepted meanings, it should not seem strange that the attributes *tahùr* (pure) and *mutàhhar* (purified) should be applied by the Koran itself to persons and things indiscriminately, but obviously with a different meaning. Thus *pure* are the pages of the Book (80, 14; 98, 2); *pure*, the water raining down from heaven (25, 48); *pure*, the beverage Allah will give the believers in heaven (76, 21); *pure*, the daughters of Lot (11, 78); very *pure*, the wives of the Prophet (33, 33); *pure* and purified, the wives in paradise (2, 25; 3, 15; 4, 57); *pure* and purifying, the alms (9, 103).

There exists consequently, according to the Koran, a purifying dynamism determining two kinds of purity which are quite distinct: the external purity and the internal.

The *external* — legal purity — directly affects the body and man's social life more than it does the soul and the immediate relationship with God.[44] The *internal* — the purity of heart, the symbol of the affective sphere — directly affects man's rapport with God through faith, which eliminates incredulity; and through devotion, which eliminates vice and promotes virtue.

Speaking of Mary, the claim by some that the *purity* attributed to her by the present Koranic verse must be understood only and exclusively in a *legal, physical,* or *physiological,* sense[45] is a minimizing attempt nowhere near the point, and I do not

---

43. "Allah is the light *[nùr]* of heavens and earth" (24, 35).

44. For ritual purification by bath or ablution in preparation for prayer, cf. GAND., p. 105-124; TABB., p. 67-71 *(rules requested)*; p. 71-73 *(defects to avoid)*.

45. ZAM. I, 362: immunity of any shameful action and of the calumny by the Jews. — BAYD. I, 138: from the impurities peculiar to women. — GEL., p. 74: from any sexual relations.

hesitate one moment to denounce it as such. An interpretation of this sort does not, in my opinion, reach the bottom of the text and haul out all the richness and fertility it yields.

As ought to be granted, in fact, the peculiar benevolence of Allah toward Mary and the communicative dynamism so proper to love demand that the parenthetic *tahhàra-ki* be interpreted in the atmosphere of its immediate context, i.e. in the light of the preceding hemistich, *istafà-ki*. This latter verb in fact sets the dimensions of the term and energizes its content. Now, God's preventive love — and much more in our case, His preferential love — never halts itself idly at the surface of things. It goes beyond. It penetrates the substance of the being to its very depths, incising the spirit in its innermost recesses and permeating it with goodness: "*Creans et infundens bonitatem rebus*" (S. Th. I, 20, 2c).

The Koranic parenthesis *tahhàra-ki* must consequently be understood in the largest and fullest sense of the term: not only in a *physiological* sense — in the meaning that, by consigning Mary to the careful tutorship of Zachariah, God had preserved her immune from any carnal contact and solicited her to keep her virginity; but also, and above all, in a *religious* sense — in the meaning that God had flooded her soul with so much light that any stain of idolatry and any shadow of polytheist associationism[46] were wiped out; and in a *moral* sense — in the meaning that God had so rectified her will and other faculties against any perverted inclination that she came out as a model of honesty and rectitude: i.e. religiously "devout," and unconditionally surrendered to God (66, 12). And as notes ar-Razi (+1209): Allah "made her pure" from unbelief, from rebellion, from indecent acts, and from blameworthy habits.[47]

True. The Koran, we are well aware, does not apply to Mary those terms in use by the current Arabic lexicon to des-

---

46. TAB. VI, n. 7025 (p. 393): (He) purified your *faith* and your *religion* from doubt and from the stains that contaminate other religions.

47. Ap. HAD. I, 158-59.

ignate holiness, and which orbit around the verb qàddasa, to sanctify, to make holy.

Terms stemming from this root are found ten times in the text. Of them three[48] apply directly to Allah; four[49] refer to the word rùh,* otherwise understood; two[50] to Tuwà, the holy valley; and one[51] to the land promised by God to the Hebrews — the Holy Land.

To indicate Mary's purification, or better, her sanctity, the Koran uses the attribute siddìqat: "**The Messiah, the son of Mary, was no more than an apostle, like those who passed away before him. And his mother was a saintly woman [siddìqat]** " (5, 75).

The authentic siddìq is, at one time, a believer and a righteous, a faithful and a virtuous person: "**Those that believe in Allah and His apostle are the righteous men [siddiqùn] who shall testify in their Lord's presence. They shall have their guerdon and their light**" (57, 19). "**He that obeys Allah and the Apostle shall dwell with the prophets and saints [siddiqìn] the martyrs and saintly men [salihìn] on whom Allah bestowed his favors**" (4, 69).

---

48. "Will you put there one who will do evil and shed blood, where we are singing Your praises and extolling Your holiness [nuqàddisu làka]? " (2, 30). — "He is Allah, beside whom there is no other god. The King, the Holy [quddùs] " (59, 23). — Allah, "the King, the Holy [quddùs], the Mighty" (62, 1).

49. "We gave Jesus the son of Mary evident proofs and strengthened him with the Holy Spirit [bi rùh il-qùdus] " (2, 87). Cf. 2, 253; 5, 110; 16, 120.

(*). Cf. note 101, p. 78. (Fares)

50. "Take off your shoes; you are now in the sacred [muqàddas] valley, Tuwà" (20, 12). Cf. 79, 16.

51. "Enter, my people, the holy land [al àrda 'l muqàddasat] which Allah has assigned for you" (5, 21).

Righteous [siddìq] was Abraham (19, 41); righteous [siddìq], Idris (19, 56); righteous [siddìq], Joseph, Jacob's son (12, 46). On a par with these, even Mary is proclaimed righteous [siddìq-at]. Her righteousness was far from being hypocrisy, or some fallacious, virtuous showiness. Hers was an exercise of solid virtue. A righteousness which, while rising on one hand on a granite substratum of rectitude, involves on the other an outwardly and inwardly honest behavioral attitude. Thus, with the Koran itself witnessing, we're allowed to assert that Mary — on a par with Abraham — was "devout" and of pure faith; that Allah chose her and guided her in the right path. Therefore, she also is "among the righteous," min as-siddiq-ìn.

The holy, the good, the virtuous person is normally designated by the Koran with the adjective sàlih, a synonym of siddìq.

Abraham (21, 130; 16, 122), Lot (21, 75), Ismael (21, 86), Isaac (37, 112), Jacob (21, 72), Jonah (68, 50), Zachariah (6, 85), Yahia (3, 39), Issa (3, 46) and Elias (6, 85) all were of the number of the salihìn: the goodly, the saintly. By believing and doing good,[52] they had earned Allah's complacency with the remission of their faults.[53]

The same we may say of Mary, based on the Koran's quoted testimony: she was a siddìq-at, and a sàlih-at.

Indeed this righteousness was required by her consecration to God from her mother's womb (3, 35-37); it was demanded by her destination to the office of mother, certainly worthy, of one of the prophets most pure (19, 19), the closest to God (3, 45), the

---

52. "Who believe in Allah and the last Day; who enjoin justice and forbid evil and vie one another in good works. These are among the righteous [min as salihìn]" (3, 114). Cf. 27, 19; 28, 27; 37, 100; 68, 50.

53. "Those that accept faith and do good works shall be admitted among the righteous [salihìn]" (29, 9). — "Whoever believes in Allah and does good, Allah will forgive him his sins" (64, 9). Cf. 20, 82; 25, 70; 26, 227; 29, 7.

saintliest (3, 46). Of him it has been rightly affirmed, later, that Allah has made his body pure from any natural uncleanness; and He purified his soul by "preserving him from the effects of the natural elements and from the carnal desires, and by supporting him with the virtue of the Holy Spirit, whose image he was bearing."[54]

This supposition allows no doubt that Mary's purification took place in depth. God's benevolent and preferential love did not linger around at the outer part of her being. It landed at the core of it, touching down at the very roots. It freed her from all stains, moral mainly and religious; and it made her as pure as her ontological situation was receptive of, and as intensely as her psychological disposition was hungry for.

I would like to take another step further here. I want to explore the limits of goodness of Mary's moral character, and, if possible, measure the dimensions of her personal holiness. In other words, I would like to find out if the Koran — I repeat, if the Koran *per se* and without the *Hadith*[55] and subsequent com-

---

54. QASHANI (ap. HAY., p. 91).

55. It is read in the collections of MUSLIM, *Sahih*, II, 224; and BUKHARI, *Sahih*, III, and IBN HANBALI, *Musnad*, II, 233, 274, 288.

Based upon this *hadith* (tradition), exegetes — Moslem and others — state that Christ and his mother alone were protected from Satan's touch at the moment of their respective birth. Their statement calls to mind St. Ephrem's passage: "*Tu et mater tua soli estis qui omni ex parte omnino pulchri estis*" (*Enchir. Patris.*, 1959, n. 719).

Such *hadith* is reportd by all commentators quoted in this study, and by several others. For instance: THA'LABI, *Qisas*, 372 (ap. HAY., p. 78), obviously with some variants. Cf. TAB. VI, n. 7887-98; ZAM. I, 356: BAYD. I, 136; GEL., p. 73.

Here are the variants according to TABARI: every newborn — except Jesus and Mary — emits a scream (VI, n. 6898 [p. 343]) at the moment it comes out of the maternal womb, because Satan touches it with *his finger* (n. 6887 [p. 338]); *squeezes* it once or twice (n. 6892 [p. 339]); *grabs* it and *makes* it

mentaries — ascribes to Mary such a total and radical purity that it includes also her exemption from the stain of the original sin. I realize at once that I'm moving gingerly, like one struggling in the dark.

Some experts have touched[56] or extensively discussed[57] the problem of the Immaculate Conception in the Koran and in

---

his own (n. 6893 [p. 340]); he pricks it in the side (n. 6895 [p. 341]); he hits it with a dart (n. 6897 [p. 342]).

This satanic blow did not reach Jesus or Mary. Instead of striking their person directly, it hit the hijàb (veil) raised between Satan and them both (n. 6884 [p. 336]; n. 6885 [p. 337]; n. 6895 [p. 341]; n. 6898 [p. 343]).

One of the variants mentions sin. Mary and Jesus, it says, unlike Adam's sons, did not commit dhunub (sins) (n. 6895, [p. 341]). Of same opinion is THA'LABI: "On nous a rapporté qu'ils ne commettaient pas des péchés comme les autres hommes" (ap. HAY., 78).

In the present hadith — whose authenticity is brought into question by ZAMAKHSHARI (I, 357) — some authors either read Mary's exemption from the original sin (cf. HIND., p. 271); or notice "an 'allusion' to the peculiar privilege of immunity of any fault, including the original sin" (ROSCH., p. 241); or perceive an echo of the Christian dogma of Mary's Immaculate Conception (HAD. I, p. 173). In this regard MARRACCI had already noted: "Hinc opinantur aliqui innui immunitatem ab originali culpae Beatissimae Virginis, eiusque filii." MAR. II, p. 112.

Whatever the opinions, it is sure that the quoted hadith is not part of the Koran as has been erroneously stated (HIND., p. 270), and repeated (ROSCH., loc. cit.). Therefore it does not come within the scope of our investigation as we've conceived and outlined it from the beginning.

56. Cf. JAL. I, p. 17-20; FAKH., p. 726-27; HAD. I, 179, 187. — Cf. also ZAK. I, p. 239; "Comment ce pauvre homme de Mohammed aurait-il pu concevoir doctrine aussi subtile que la doctrine du péché originel?" GAR., p. 30: Islam "n'a pas le dogme du péché originel." — Massignon however does not hesitate to assert that Mohammad, disproving the blasphemies he heard in the Medinian environment, had maintained that Jesus and Mary, his mother, were not only pure, virgin and holy, but they have been the only human beings "dont la conception ait été immaculée, intouchée du Diable (Cor. 3, 31: prière de St. Anne". MASSIGNON, Signe Marial, in Rhythmes du Monde, 1948, III, p. 9.

57. ANW., p. 447-461.

Islam; the solutions they proposed are anything but unanimous and concordant.

To avoid repetitions, I shall limit myself to these few, but fundamental, points.

First of all, it is certain that the beginnings of Mary's earthly life were marked by tangible proofs of divine benevolence. As recorded by the Koran, these instances are: the consecratory vote of the pious mother; the offering to and acceptance of the divine service in the Temple; the answer to the plea for protection and defense from the snare of Satan (3, 36b), man's seducer (28, 15) and sworn enemy.[58]

One point here is worth making. The report, right at the moment of birth, of the simultaneous recurrence of Allah present, of Satan molesting, and of Mary as a person with a proper name, calls instinctively to mind an old Augustinian sentence; the three elements we notice in it are the same as those reported in the Koran, similarly tied with one another and in the very same instance: "Notwithstanding the obligation for Mary to contract the sin through her birth, she was not a slave to Satan, because the said obligation became inoperative by virtue of the grace of regeneration."[59]

However, we cannot forget that the Koran is the code of a religion which is flat and formalistic,[60] in which nothing tran-

---

58. "Satan is your enemy: therefore treat him as an enemy" (35, 6). Cf. 36, 60; 43, 62. — "Sworn enemy" (2, 168; 6, 142; 7, 22). — "Allah's enemy, and Gabriel's, and Michael's" (2, 98).

59. *"Non transcribimus diabolo Mariam conditione nascendi; sed ideo, quia ipsa conditio solvitur gratia renascendi."* AUGUSTINUS. *Op. Impf.,* IV, n. 122. — ML. 45, 1418.

60. Although religious formalism is not condemned by the Koran (2, 177; 107, 5-6), the cultic practices in Islam are "formalistic at a highest degree so that, at times, their spirit could be compared to the talmudic spirit. They are a body of a very meticulous and boring casuistry. Besides, the neglect of the rubric brings along the nullity of the whole action." NAL. II, p. 612.

scends the possibilities of nature and its requirements: in other words, it totally ignores the world of grace with all its supernatural wealth and wonders.[61] Islam is a religion that excludes categorically the entry into the mystery of God's intimate and trinitarian life (cf. 4, 171). Consequently, it forcefully ignores man's sublimation by means of a physical, and yet analogous, participation in the trinitarian life through the sanctifying grace. It does not know the soul's deific participation which will reach its full development in heaven, by the intuitive vision of God, One and Triune.

Furthermore, although the Koranic Message relates transiently the personal transgression of Adam and his wife, the protagonists of the first sorrowful event in the salvation's history (20, 119), it makes no mention at all of the transmission to Adam's descendants of an original sin [62] with all its deleterious consequences.

A religion of this kind has, therefore, no room for a dogma such as the Immaculate Conception of Mary. As long as Islam denies man's divinization by God's grace and his collective downfall through Adam's sin inherited by natural descent, there can be in it no statement, no allusion, no implication whatsoever of this Catholic Dogma.

---

61. St. THOMAS AQUINAS had already noted: "documenta etiam veritatis non attulit, nisi quae a quolibet mediocriter sapiente naturali ingenio cognosci possint." Summa c. Gentes, I, 6.

62. Fr. ANAWATI summarizes his investigation on Mary's immaculate conception in the Koran in the two following points: "1. Does the notion of original sin exist in Islam?" (p. 449-457). "2. Mary's conception and birth" (p. 457-60).
Regarding the first point he concludes: "But this fall had only personal consequences and they have moreover been forgiven. The notion of original sin transmitted by Adam to his posterity is absolutely opposed to the teaching of Islam" (p. 457). "Man has been created in order to be the vicar of God in the world. He is at the same time soul and body. From this duality results naturally a struggle between the two elements, but this is not the consequence of the original parental sin" (p. 457). Italics are ours.

The Immaculate Conception of Mary, one ought to remember, is a mystery implying in turn other mysteries, and has roots striking deep in a world essentially supernatural. It involves the original sin and the sanctifying grace as its two constitutive and indispensable components. That seems a paradox. But it is absolutely so! *S i n* and *G r a c e* are to the dogma its two opposite poles, the negative pole, and the positive pole. Each is with the other. And none is to be without the other. For the mystery both are unsuppressable, non-derogatory, irreplaceable. With either missing, the Immaculate Conception's dogma simply desists to be.

As one can see, we're here dealing with elemental principles from which none is allowed to depart. But truly it is the forgetfulness of the simple and elementary basics which often causes the leak and loss of human energies.

In his razor-sharp style, Zakarias writes: "L'immaculée Conception n'a absolument rien à faire avec cette déclaration du rabbin. Ceux qui affirment le contraire écrivent des romans du plus mauvais goût, fussent-ils d'éminents professeurs" (Zk. p. 228).

C. Mary's Singular Maternity

It is stated with such certainty as to exclude even the shadow of doubt. From the second Meccan epoch — with Sura 19, to the closing of the prophetic career — with Sura 5, the reference to Mary, *mother* of Jesus, and to Jesus, *son* of Mary, occurs continuously throughout the Koranic pages. Behind this steady continuity lurks a deliberate polemic plan: *to safeguard God's unity against any form of idolatrous associationism, and to defend Mary's virginal motherhood against the Jews who dared tarnish her candor by a slanderous lie.*

a. — The Virgin's motherhood in the Koran is unequivocally affirmed in two ways: *directly*, when Mary is explicitly called twice *wàlid-at* (5, 110; 19, 23), parent of Jesus; and four times *ùmm*,[63] mother of Jesus. *Indirectly*, but nonetheless with a convincing demonstration, when for 23 times the name of Jesus is infallibly followed by the apposition *ibn Maryam*, son of Mary, as we will later explain.

Such motherhood has been *physical*, truly and properly. It was not nominal, not metaphorical, not merely adoptive. The irrefutable proof of it is the annunciation event with its immediate impact on the person of Mary: she physically conceived Jesus in her womb (19, 22); really gave him birth (19, 23); and tenderly mothered him (19, 27).

b. — True maternity. But at the same time a *virginal* maternity.

Nowhere does the Koran call Mary "The Virgin," the Virgin par excellence, or "The Pure."[64] Neither does it seem to know the three classical aspects of Mary's integral virginity long established by theologians according to a triple

---

63. Cf. 5, 17, 75, 116; 23, 50.

64. "Le Coran dans ses versets 21-91 appelle Marie 'Celle qui garda sa verginite.' Il l'appelle 'vierge' par excellence, la 'pure'. " (HIND., p. 271). Thus it was written; and thus it was also repeated (ROSCH., p. 242).

The first part of the statement only is quoted by the famous v. 91 of Sura 21. The second is not quoted by the Koran, but in a letter (apocryphal) that Mohammad had reportedly sent to the Negus of Abyssinia. In it, the Prophet, among other things, says: "Je confesse que Jésus, fils de Marie, est l'Esprit d'Allàh et son Verbe, qu'il jeta sur Marie, *la Vierge, la Sainte, la Pure*" (ap. HAY., p. 86). Italics are ours.

chronological moment, e.g. the virginity *before* childbirth, *during* childbirth, and *after* childbirth.[65]

According to the spirit of the Koranic Message, however, not to say in adherence to the very textual letter of it, we may assert that the virginity of Mary *ante partum* is a positive datum, clear and irrefutable. It stands no shadow of doubt.

Already eloquent by itself is Christ's surname: *Son of Mary, "ibn Maryam."* Ignoring entirely the oriental practice, the Koran uses it continuously to identify Jesus with no reference to a "father."[66] The surname offers two unmistakable proofs: that Mary's virginity was blessed with a fruit, Jesus, born of her exclusively as a son; and that Jesus belongs to her alone as the only fruit of her womb and beyond any male involvement (3, 41; 19, 20).

We are moreover brought to the same conclusion by the Koranic insistence on Mary's seclusion from her tenderest

---

65. In the Ps.-Matthew the midwife, shocked with surprise, says: "No trace of impure blood came along with the newborn; no pain appeared either in the mother during childbirth. *Virgo concepit, virgo peperit, virgo permansit"* (13, 3. — AM., p. 326).

66. With regard to Joseph, or any other "father" to Jesus, we ought to grant that in the Koran "jamais le père n'est mentionné." WENS., p. 358. In Islam, Christ "reste comme un éternel orphelin, sans père connu ici-bas, et là-haut." HAY., p. 65.
We can't explain, therefore, what had prompted GARDET to write: "Un fonds de récits évoque maints Évangiles apocryphes: l'histoire de Marie au Temple, *son mariage avec Joseph* (période médinoise); la naissance de Jésus au désert sous un palmier." GAR., p. 29. The italic is ours.
During the annunciation, although Gabriel addresses Mary personally to deliver to her the message, he tells her nonetheless that Jesus, the Christ, shall be *ibn Maryam*, "the son of Mary" (3, 45). As it reads in the context, the clause is indeed strange, out of context. It justifies my belief in an interpolation inserted there during the Othmanian compilation for polemic reasons. Not all Moslem exegetes are of the same opinion. The clause is there, they conjecture, to emphasize the virginal conception by virtue of which Jesus did not have a "father," but only a "mother." He is exclusively "son of Mary." Cf. ZAM. I, 363; BAYD. I, 139; GEL., p. 74.

years, which can be verified also by the Apocrypha, mainly the *Proto-evangelium of James*. That seclusion was so strict that it cut Mary off completely from any social contact that may have blurred her virginal candor, or exposed to danger of violation her precious integrity.

Finally, at the moment of the annunciation, and while receiving the angelic message, Mary was still a virgin physically. Up to that time she had kept intact her virginal cloister.[67] And when she conceived her son in her womb, her happy event was not caused by a physical union with a man but by the sole virtue of Almighty Allah (3, 47), transmitted through a "breath" of His spirit (21, 91). In fact in reporting the first moments of the human existence of Jesus, the Koran follows the same guideline it once did for the first man, Adam. The proto-parent was drawn out of the mud with no physiological help by others to father him (3, 59). Christ came out the same way. He was molded, or better as the text puts it literally, *"created" [khàlaqa]*, without the interference of a third agent in a parental function. Whether

---

67. The Koran uses a term of a physiological, even anatomical, overtone: *Farg* (21, 91; 66, 12). All lexicographers whom I consulted stress the organic meaning of the word. Some examples: FREYTAG G.W., *Lexicon Arabico-Latinum*, t. III (Halis Saxonum, 1835). p. 327: "*Farg*: Pudenda. *Kam. Dj.* (tum maris tum feminae, antica *et* postica)". — KASIMIRSKI A. DE BILBERSTEIN, *Dictionnaire Arabe Français* (Paris, Maisonneuve, 1860), t. II, p. 562: "*Farg*. Fente, fissure, crevasse [...] Parties honteuses (tant de l'homme que de la femme, tant de devant que de derrière)". — WEHR HANS, *A Dictionary of Modern Written Arabic*. Edited by J. Milton Cowan (Wiesbaden, 1961), p. 702: "*Farg*. Opening, aperture, gap, breach; pudendum of the female, vulva."—HAVA J. G., *Al-Farid*. Arabic-English Dictionary (Beirut, Catholic Press, 1964), p. 522: "*Farg*. Gap, interstice. Space between the legs. Pudenda. Womb. Open place." — BELOT J. B., *Vocabulaire Arabe-Français*, Beyrouth, 1929), p. 578: "*Farg*. Fente, fissure, crevasse. Partie du corps que pudeur cache." — MAROUN C., *Vocabolario arabo-italiano* (Gerusalemme, 1933). p. 467: "*Farg*. Fessura, spaccatura, pudenda."

MARRACCI also had caught the right sense of it: "munitam servavit vulvam suam (id est fuit virgo intacta)". MAR. II, p. 455. And in a note on Sura 66, 12: "Vox arabica al-farg proprie significat cunnum muliebrem; hoc tamen loco honestius virginitatem seu verenda vertas." MAR. II, p. 735.

Adam or Christ, both came into existence through a divine "fiat."[68] Consequently, speaking of Jesus, with no prejudice of sorts to Mary's virginity.

The virginity of Mary *during childbirth* is not clearly stated in the Koran. But we find a clue to it in the fact that the Koran, unlike the Apocryphal Gospels,[69] gives no indication of the presence of a midwife on one hand, and on the other shows Mary in full possession of her physical vigor while being delivered; all alone she was able to "shake" (19, 25) the palm tree trunk at the foot of which she was bringing Jesus to light.[70]

A noteworthy indication, however, seems to stand against this theory, and it is the crucial pain the Koran describes Mary going through at the moment of delivery. Should this pain be proved to be only physical, then a serious difficulty would arise against the virginity *in partu*.

But one ought to keep in mind that the term *mikhàd*, throes, used by the Koran does not demand necessarily to be translated as *pains of labor*. Linguistically it may also mean the ordinary contraction of the fetus while forcing its way

---

68. "When He decrees a thing, He need only say: 'Be,' and it is" (3, 47). — "Jesus is like Adam in the sight of Allah. Allah created him of dust and said to him: 'be,' and he was" (3, 59). — Some exegetes think that, by His imperative "*kùn*", Allah wanted to show the infinite extent of His creative action which brought forth Adam without father or mother, Eve without a mother, and Christ without a father; all the rest came forth from a father and a mother. Cf. IBN ARABI (ap. HAY., p. 90).

69. Cf. *Proto-ev. of James*, 19-20 (AM., p. 250-256); *The Gospel of the Nativity*, 13, 3-5. — AM., p. 325-328; *The Arabic Gospel of Infancy*, 2-3.

70. Fr. ANAWATI also seems to subscribe to the opinion that Christ's birth, as well as his conception, had, according to the Koran, been *virginal*. He writes in fact: "The Koran indeed speaks of her in extremely laudatory terms, recounting some of the circumstances of her birth, and citing the special protection given her against Satan, the miraculous nurture sent to her, *the virginal birth of her son Jesus* and specifying the first rank she holds among all women both in this world and in the next." ANW., p. 447. Italics are ours.

out of the maternal uterus. Per se, that contraction does not connote suffering — and much less a crucial one, by the mother.

With the exception of some exegetes,[71] other commentators, even Moslem,[72] do not hesitate to understand Mary's pain in a spiritual way — in the sense, that is, of an agony assailing her from the clear and sharp foresight of her imminent dishonor. Her new condition as a "mother" was by no means easy to hide. And the news of it was going to spread around rapidly, passing from mouth to ear with no legal precedent to counterweigh or justify it — such as a previous marriage, or even an apparent wedding.

The virginity *post partum* may quickly be deduced from the concurrence of several elements duly put together and evaluated.

On one hand we have the Koran's tight silence over a spouse, or a legitimate husband, with whom Mary may have had conjugal relations; on the other, we have the choice moral qualities and psychological attitudes that the same Koran signals, or at least insinuates, in her at the time of the annunciation. We have, moreover, two incidents which clue to Mary's determination to stay virgin: one is her answer to

---

71. GEL., (p. 404) who takes *mikhàd* for throes, or physical pains of childbirth.

72. ZAMAKHSHARI is explicit in understanding *mikhàd* in a moral sense only, i.e. in an interior pain that Mary suffered from hearing the denigratory charges against her character. Her bitter complaint, however, did not mean rebellion against Allah's designs. ZAM. III, 12. Cf. BAYD. II, 24; HAD. I, 148. — SABUNI sees here two kinds of pain: one physical, which was so sharp that Mary had to grip onto the palm tree trunk in order to bear with it; and the other moral, or her immediate exposure to dishonor. SAB., p. 204. — Others, to the contrary, refer her moral anxiety to the sin that her folks would have committed by calumniating her; or to the sin, known by revelation, that the Christians would have committed by making her and her son as other divinities: "For such shame she would have wished herself death." Cf. FAL. I, p. 39, in note.

the angel, *"How shall I bear a child, when I am a virgin, no man touched me ever, and I am no prostitute?"* (19, 19). And the other, *"Lord, how shall I have a child when no man has touched me ever?"* (3, 46). These data allow no one to imagine that Mary had later behaved contrary to her habitual modesty and reservedness; they strongly suggest that she persisted to the end in the jealous custody of her precious treasure, her virginity.

According to the Koran, then, we have to say that Mary's motherhood was unquestionably a *true* motherhood; but at the same time a *virginal* motherhood.

c. — In no way *divine* motherhood.

The Koranic Message denies to Allah in the most categorical terms any *familial* relations, meaning fatherhood, motherhood and filiation.

To God belong the names, or attributes, most excellent.[73] But decidedly He is not a *father*. He has no *children*. Absolutely none. He is alone. Unique. Too glorious to need a *son*. He owns all that is both in the heavens and on the earth (4, 171); and Christ, included, is no son to Him, but a mere servant: *'abd* (4, 172).

In dealing with men, Allah is undoubtedly merciful,[74] clement,[75] benign,[76] compassionate,[77] forgiving.[78] But instead

---

73. Cf. MASSON *(Les attributs de Dieu)*, I, p. 15-83.

74. Cf. note 34, p. 50. — The two epithets rahmàn and rahìm appear often joined together: cf. BAQ., p. 307-309.

75. "He (Allah) is compassionate and merciful *[rahìm]* to men" (2, 143). Cf. 2, 182, 199, 218, 226; 3, 31, 89, 129; 59, 22.

76. "Allah is forgiving and lenient *[halìm]* " (2, 225). Cf. 22, 59; 35, 41.

77. "Allah is compassionate *[ra'ùf]* to His servants" (2, 207). Cf. 57, 9; 59, 10. The two predicates ra'ùf (compassionate) and rahìm (merciful) are by the Koran reserved to Allah. One exception only is Sura 9, which applies them to Mohammad.

78. "Allah will love you and forgive you your sins. Allah is forgiving *[gafùr]*

of emphasizing God's goodness and mercy, the Koran loves to stress the numinous idea of God — sublime, majestic, oppressing — to more easily imprint in the Moslem's mind the sense of Allah's greatness, sovereignty and transcendence.[79]

Allah is great.[80] Magnificent.[81] Sovereign.[82] Most High.[83] Strong.[84] Potent.[85] Almighty.[86] Ruler.[87] Conqueror.[88] First and Last One (57, 3). Transcendent and

---

and merciful" (3, 31). Cf. 4, 106; 34, 2; 35, 30; 49, 14. — Gaffàr (very forgiving): 38, 66; 71, 10. — Tawwàb (very indulgent): 2, 37, 54, 128, 160; 49, 12. Cf. JEF., p. 95.

79. "But the face of the Lord will abide forever, in all its majesty and glory [dhu'l jalàl wa'l ikràm] " (55, 27). Cf. 55, 78. — "To Him be majesty [kibriya'] in heaven and on earth" (45, 37).

80. "He is the High, the Great One [al-kabìr] " (34, 23). Cf. 4, 34; 13, 9; 40, 12; 22, 62.

81. "He is the Faithful, the Guardian, the Magnificent [al mutakàbbir] " (59, 23).

82. "He is the Exalted, the Immense One [al-Alìu l'Adhìm]" (2, 255). Cf. 69, 33.

83. "He is the Most High [ali] " (22, 62). — Alì-kabìr: 4, 34; 31, 30; 34, 23. — Alì- adhìm: 42, 4. — Alì-hakìm: 42, 51; 43, 4.

84. "Allah is strong [qawì] and hard when punishing" (8, 52). Cf. 40, 22; 57, 25; 58, 21. — Qawì-azìz: 11, 66; 22, 40; 33, 25; 42, 19; 57, 25. — Qawì-amìn: 27, 39; 28, 26.

85. "Allah is mighty [azìz] and capable of revenge" (5, 95). Cf. 5, 118; 14, 47. — Azìz-hakìm: 2, 129, 209, 220. — Azìz-halìm: 27, 78; 36, 38; 43, 9. — Azìz-rahìm: 26, 9; 30, 5. — Azìz-hamìd: 14, 1; 34, 6; 85, 8. — Azìz-gaffàr: 38, 66; 39, 5; 40, 42. — Azìz-gafùr: 35, 28; 67, 2. — Azìz-wahhàb: 38, 9. — Azìz-karìm: 44, 49.

86. "Allah has power [qadìr] over all things" (2, 20). Cf. 2, 106, 109, 148, 259, 284; 42, 9; 46, 33; 67, 1.

87. "Allah is the Powerful, the Dominator [jabbàr] " (59, 23).

88. "Had it been His will to take a son, He would have chosen whom He

Immanent (57, 3). He is all, and beside Him the whole universe is nothing.

His relations with men are "those of a slave-owner toward his subjects," even when there is question of clemency and pardon.[89] He is above all *rabb*,[90] Lord: of the universe,[91] of heaven and earth,[92] of the daybreak (113, 1), of the "throne,"[93] of the East and West.[94]

In his hands is the fate of all creation. He is creator of life and death (67, 2). He puts to life and to death.[95] He does what He will (2, 253). Chooses whom He will (39, 4). Forgives whom He will, and torments whom He pleases (2, 284).

God of men, king of men, He is the lord *[rabb]* of men (114, 1-3). His is the dominion of heaven and earth (4, 171). His is the most active, always creative

---

pleased out of His own creatures. He is the One, the Subduer *[qahhàr]* " (39, 4). Cf. 12, 39; 13, 16; 14, 48; 38, 65.

89. NAL. II, p. 607.

90. The epithet *rabb* occurs in the Koran more than 950 times, and is almost always attributed to God. Cf. BAQ., p. 285-299.

91. "*rabb al-alamìn*," Lord of the universe, is one of God's most common predicates in the Koran: 1, 1; 2, 131; 5, 28; 6, 71; 7, 54. In Sura 26, *The Poets*, it recurs at least five times: v. 23, 44, 77, 109, 127, 145, 164, 180, 192. — Concerning the cult of "*Rabb al alamìn*" in Arabia, cf. HAD. II, 125-26; MOUB. II, *Pent.* II, p. 102-103; NOL. I, p. 112; JEF., p. 136-137.

92. "Say: 'Who is the Lord *[rabb]* of heaven and earth?' " "Answer: 'Allah' " (13, 16). Cf. 17, 102; 18, 14; 19, 65; 37, 5; 44, 7. Elsewhere, *passim*, cf. BAQ., p. 285-289.

93. "He is the Lord of the Throne *[arsh]* " (21, 22). — "Of the glorious Throne" (9, 129; 23, 86; 27, 26). Cf. 23, 116; 43, 82.

94. "He is the Lord of the East *[màshriq]* and the West *[màghrib]* and of all that lies between them" (26, 28). Cf. 2, 115, 142; 37, 5; 55, 17; 70, 40; 73, 9.

95. "He ordains life and death and has power over all things" (57, 2). Cf. 2, 258; 9, 116; 10, 56; 45, 35; 53, 44.

(55, 29) rule of creation's vicissitudes in general (49, 18), and men's in particular.[96] His is to orient and guide the select group of forefathers,[97] by virtue of a bilateral covenant.[98]

As is obviously possible to verify from this list of attributes, forming with several others the so-called Moslem "rosary,"[99] one typically Christian epithet totally disappears — that of the *father*.

Allah is par excellence *rabb*, lord. But He is not, and cannot be called *abb*, father. He is not "father" in relation to men; nor "father" within the sphere of deity. In His intimate life, God did not generate Himself a son; neither in His providence did He regenerate children.

"Allah is one. And He is the eternal. He begot none, nor was He begotten. And none is equal to Him" (112, 1-4). "He is

---

96. "It was He who gave you ears, eyes, and hearts: yet you are seldom thankful. And it was He who placed you on the earth, and before Him you shall all be assembled. And it is He who ordains life and death, and He who controls the night and the day. Can you not understand?" (23, 78-80).

97. "He is your Lord and the Lord of your forefathers *[abà'ikum ul awwalìn]*" (26, 26).

98. "When We made a covenant *[mithàq]* with the Israelites, We said: 'Serve none but Allah. Show kindness to your parents, to your kinsfolk, to the orphans, and to the destitute'" (2, 83).

99. According to a *hadith* (cf. TABB., p. 123-124), the Moslem believer who at the end of each *salàt*, prayer, praises *[sàbbaha]* Allah 33 times, thanks *[hàmada]* Him 33 times, extols *[kàbbara]* Him 33 times, and then adds to these 99 glorifications the following profession of faith: "*There is no other god but Allah, who is with no associate. His is the dominion and praise, and He has the power over all things,*" shall obtain the forgiveness of all his sins (cf. TABB., p. 124, note).

By adding to the 99 divine attributes the supreme name, ALLAH, *[al ismu-l à'dham]*, one attains the number one hundred; one has then the *sùbha* or *tasbìh*, the "Moslem Rosary," which "was introduced as a pious practice a couple of centuries after Mohammad." NAL. II, p. 607.

all sufficient, and too high to need a son" (4, 171)."There is no other God but Him"(3, 18).

Fatherhood in fact implies necessarily a previous genitive act. And this genitive act in Mohammad's mind is conceivable only and exclusively in terms of flesh. In other words, it is essentially and totally the product of sexual relations between male and female, like a man generating a man, and a lion generating another lion: "He is the creator of the heavens and the earth. How should He have a son when He had no consort, and when, alone, He created all things?"(6, 101).

The lady "companion" [sàhibat], the woman lover, the female consort, the sexual relations, the carnal generation are obviously absurd things never to be tolerated with regard to God. "We ... shall serve none besides our Lord. He (glory and exaltation be to Him) has taken no companion [sàhibat]" (72, 2-3). "They say Allah has begotten a son. He is far higher than that! He is what the heavens and the earth contain; all things are obedient to Him" (2, 116). "No, Allah has taken no child [wàlad]" (72, 2).

The Koran is boldly explicit in this matter.

The crux of the problem lies in the fact that while meditating on God and thinking about His greatness, Mohammad kept himself outside the sphere of the life which is properly divine, at the margin of the supernatural experience. He never crossed that border to enter in God's intimacy and share His divine friendship. He simply halted at the threshold, not daring to venture into the mystery proper and reach at the strictly divine, "trinitarian" life.[100]

Now, without the Trinity, of which the Verb is the second person — and, of course, without the divinity of Christ, Mary's

---

100. The mysterious "mi'ràj," understood in its mystical sense, was according to Massignon reduced "à une sorte de circumambulation de Mohammad autour de l'Union." MASS. (Textes Musulmans pouvant concerner la nuit de l'espirit, 1938), II, 399.

Divine Motherhood in the Koran remains inconceivable; and any statement on it, just unthinkable.

D. Mary's Unity with Christ

Throughout the sacred Book of Islam, Mary is never depicted as severed from Christ but always closely tied to him, despite the repeated assertions to the contrary by Zakarias. The way they read in the Koran, the Marian Texts show a clear "Christological" setting. None of them favors an "anti-Christian" image for Mary; none tries to make of her an exclusively "Jewish" person (Zk. p. 160), despoiled, that is, of her typically "Christian" identity (p. 165, 195, 208, 212). If Mohammad spoke of her so personally and so eminently, he did it only because of her relation to Christ as his mother, and because of Christ's relation to her as her natural son [ibn Maryam], even if for polemic views he was denied God's natural and divine sonship.

Mary's unity with Christ is stated indirectly by the Koran's continuous pairing of her name with that of Jesus, as though they were an inseparable couple bound by the same destiny. She is united to a "Christian" Christ, to a prophet and a messenger of Allah to all those among the "People of the Book" who call themselves after the Gospel [Injeel]. This metronymic unity, i.e. the identification of the child by his mother, is quite rare in the Semitic world. It is rather exceptional. In tracking down their genealogical roots, Orientals are known to follow their paternal, not maternal, line.

Mary's name in the Koran emerges conspicuously and all by

itself eleven times.[101] Annexed to the name of Jesus, however, and always with the invariable apposition, *ibn Maryam*, son of Mary, it recurs twenty-three times.[102]

This reference to Jesus with the apposition *"ibn Maryam"* and no other additive, occurs twice (23, 50; 43, 57); by the same apposition and the addition of a proper epithet that blends with it, thus coining three different expressions enhancing each other, it occurs twenty-one times as follows: five times, *al Masih ibn Maryam*, the Christ, son of Mary;[103] thirteen times, *Issa ibn Maryam*, Jesus, the son of Mary;[104] three times, *al Masih Issa ibn Maryam*, the Christ Jesus, son of Mary.[105]

Thus so far is the Koranic thought as regards Mary and Jesus' unity by names.

The psychological solidarity is another factor by which Mary and Jesus are also tightly united.

The relationship between mother and son, and vice-versa, is a world of affections and sentiments all its own. Two people live it, each feeling to be an indivisible part of the other's dreams, hopes, and whereabouts. Neither claims it alone. Neither owns it exclusively. It belongs to them both, and both have in it an equal and correlative share.

This psychological world begins with time. And no sooner

---

101. Cf. 3, 36, 37, 42, 43, 44, 45; 4, 156, 171; 19, 16, 27; 66, 12.

102. In his computation, MASS. (I, p. 312) falls into a slight inaccuracy. Only 23, not 24 times, does Mary's name recur in the Koran related to that of Jesus. And the apposition "Son of Mary," with no further additive, recurs two times only, not three.

103. Cf. 5, 17 bis, 72, 75; 9, 31.

104. Cf. 2, 87, 253; 5, 46, 78, 110, 112, 114, 116; 19, 34; 33, 7; 57, 27; 61, 6, 14.

105. Cf. 3, 45; 4, 157, 171. — MASSON (*Jésus, homme parfait*), I, p. 197-201; (*Miracles attribués à Jésus par le Coran*), I, p. 211-214.

are mother and son aware that they are in it than they experience an affective and mysterious hunger for each other. Here begins the odyssey of their psychological solidarity. The mother is conscious that her child is hers, and the son admits that the mother is his. Their interests are mutual. And so is their life. And their destiny. They seem to live for each other. And by intuition they know each other. Sharing their world together, they're gratified. They're bored and feel empty when apart.

The need for being together increases also with time, and their starvation grows and evolves as all along both grow and evolve. They begin to realize they're necessary for each other, and each sees in the other a complement for self. Hungry for her son's affection, the mother sees in him a needy portion of hers. And starving for his mother's presence, a son feels the need for his helping mother.

Whether on the mother or the son's lips, the expression "I miss you" says a lot in this respect. It is the cry of the common blood starving to possess, or be possessed by, the one half running in the veins of the other. The knowledge that the other half of your rosy little world "does care," is the answer to that cry.

The need one party feels to love or be loved, to care and be cared for, to give and be given back, is clear evidence of either's psychological hunger after what fills it in the other. By caring, neither is favoring the other. Mother and son are just satisfying a reciprocal emotional need; and by so doing, both do not always realize they're just fulfilling in one another what each is missing, or starving for.

Psychological hunger, as we see it, is a clue to an impelling psychological solidarity. Or, the reverse of it if you want. Among normal humans, this solidarity attains its closest unity only in mother-son relationships, and vice-versa, due to common blood. In these human people, however, when to the link of flesh and blood a supernatural factor is added, this affective cohesion attains a sky-high level. That is exactly the case with Mary and Jesus.

Acting in this psychological solidarity, Mary cared for Jesus.

She availed her son of her services when he needed them. As the Koran witnesses to it, Allah made Mary His instrument to act as His *intermediary* and provide Jesus with his "first epiphany," exposing him publicly to the pagan world; and to introduce him to her skeptical people, the Jews, thus publicly proclaiming his mission and charisma. Both functions Mary fulfilled at the time with full consciousness and responsibility.

And acting in the same solidarity, Jesus responded to the maternal gesture.

He cared for his mother, and availed her of his intervention when she most needed it. Charged by her folks with a crime she did not commit, Mary resorted to silence and declined to justify herself. What she did was more eloquent than what was expected. She then needed some help not available for her except from Jesus, her son. Presently, he crossed the human limits in her eyes of faith. A cry sounded in the depths of her being, that Jesus, her other self, could do it. From under the swaddles her hand folds out, then curves back with the finger pointed at the infant. Simultaneously the eyes of those present fell on the child in her arms. Responsive to the mother's plea, the Baby spoke as a prophet and a messenger of salvation, saying: "I am the servant of Allah. He has given me the Gospel and ordained me a prophet. His blessing is upon me wherever I go, and He has ordered me to be steadfast in prayer and alms-giving as long as I shall live. He has exhorted me to honor my mother and has purged me of vanity and wickedness" (19, 30-32).

Mary's unity with Christ goes uninterrupted. It lasts for the span of life, rooted as it is in the closest possible natural communion — the consanguinity, or blood relationship. Mary is tied to Jesus as his mother; and for that reason she is forever a co-sharer of his destiny, of his intimate feelings, and of his sorrowful and joyful events.

A vigilant and sharp eye cannot but notice the fact that Mohammad looks at Mary always from a *relative* angle, that of her relation to Jesus.

There is no question that the Koran addresses Mary directly; in person, in her own prerogatives and private affairs. In ultimate analysis, however, the Koran honors her with a singular position and reserves for her a special kind of treatment, because of her connection with Jesus. They are kin. To him she is a mother; and to her he is a son. Were this Christological perspective to be ignored, or were Mary's person severed from that of Christ's, then the exceptional treatment which the Koran honors her with, by *"singling her out from, and extolling her above, all the women of the universe,"* would be enigmatic, let alone indeed defeated. But the opposite is true. Throughout the Koranic length, and particularly in the Marian paragraphs, the *relational* concept of motherhood, or better the function of *mother* that Mary carries out toward Jesus, involves such a prime importance that it alone justifies in full the singularity of regard reserved to her.

Also according to the Koran, the ultimate motive for Mary's greatness, not to say the ultimate *raison d'être* for her own existence, is Jesus as her *son*. And by correlative necessity, of course, is Mary as a *mother*.

With regard to Christ — not as Son of God, but as a simple creature that Allah might at will annihilate (5, 17) — Mary enters in Mohammad's polemic plan as a decisive deterrent against all infidels, polytheists be they or associators; and above all, against those who dare claim for Christ the condition and the dignity of the *"Son of God."*

E. *Mary's Eminent Dignity*

It follows as a logical consequence from the dignity of Jesus, since children's honor, glory and prestige redound by connatural reciprocity upon their parents. And vice-versa.

Mother of an illustrious personage *[wajih]*, noble in this world and in the other (3, 45); mother of a prophet *[nabi]*, full of God's wisdom and the science of the sacred Books (3, 48); mother of an apostle *[rasul]*, amply endowed with charismatic powers (3, 49) and adorned with such an integrity of character that it ranks him among the closest souls to God (3, 45), Mary claims for herself an unparalleled dignity. Her ascendency is such that no match can be found for it.

This eminent dignity is in fact clearly proclaimed by the Koran in the third section of the angelic announcement: *"Mary, Allah has chosen you. He had made you pure, and He had exalted you above all the women of the universe: 'àla nisà' el 'alam-ìn"* (3, 42).

The substantive *'alam-ìn* recurs in the Koran no less than seventy times, always carrying the same meaning. It denotes the ensemble of all realities existing, visible and invisible. Such realities are distinct from Allah who, alone, is the **Reality** subsisting[106] and immutable.[107] They are rather opposed to God

---

106. "There is no other god but Him, the Living, the Subsistent *[al qayùm]*. Neither slumber nor sleep overtakes Him" (2, 255). — *Qayùm* is a barbarism of Syriac origin; it means: he who never sleeps, who is always awake. CF. HAD. III, p. 143. — *Al-qayùm* (3, 2; 20, 111) means "He who subsists (exists) by himself and maintains the whole creation in existence." MAS., p. 800. Cf. JEF., p. 244-45.

107. "Say: 'Allah is One; Allah, the Immutable *[as samad]* ' " (112, 12). —

(3, 97), being his effects, his making. He is their creator, their molder, their modeller.[108] To borrow the trite etymology repeated by the exegetes, 'alam-ìn — [regular plural form of 'àlam, world], worlds, and consequently universe — has a collective sense and designates all the created beings: the angels, the "jinn,"[109] men, the animal kingdom, the vegetable kingdom, and the mineral kingdom. In the word *universe* as a whole, they're all included as parts.

The eulogistic expression 'àla l 'alam-ìn, above the universe, is by the Koran attributed also to the Israelites, chosen as a special people by Allah;[110] and to the messengers most quoted by Allah.[111]

As to Mary, her praise is not expressed in *absolutely* superlative and unconditional, but relatively superlative and restricted, terms. Mary is not located on top of the *whole* universe,

---

The predicate *sàmad* offers no sure meaning even for the Moslem exegetes themselves: "They interpret it with *unique*, or with *compact, homogeneous*, and, later, almost unanimously with *eternal*." BAUS., p. 736. *

(*). The exact sense of *sàmad* is *lasting*. The Arabic root *sàmada* means to stay, to endure, to continue to be. Therefore, *"Allah is One; Allah, the Everlasting,"* is the accurate version of the Koranic expression. (Fares)

108. "He is Allah, the Creator [al-khàliq], the Originator [al-bàri], the Modeller [al-musàwwir]" (59, 24). Cf. note 11, p. 119.

109. MASSON (*Les djins et les démons*), I, p. 175, 184. — The Jinn, a residue of pre-Islamic paganism, still persist in their spectral influence in the Near East. Created from purest flame (55, 15), not from clay as man was (15, 28), they form a medium category between angels and men. Some are good, and some evil. They organize in groups: "Inspirent les poètes, font vaticiner les devins, tourmentent les déments et malades et sont la terreur nocturne du voyageur." BL. IV, p. 20. For KELLERHALS the Jinn would be "Satyrn und Nymphen der Wüste." KEL., p. 51. — Some modern exegetes "ne fanno addirittura dei 'microbi' (salafìyya) o 'dei capi forti e potenti [ahmadìyya]'" BAUS., p. 544.

110. "Children of Israel, remember the blessing I have bestowed on you, and that I have preferred you to all nations [al-alamìn]" (2, 47, 122).

111. "Each of these We have favored above all Our creatures [ala-l-alamìn]" (6, 86).

but she is exalted above the *women* of this universe, "'àla nisà' *l'alam-ìn*."

Therefore, if we spare the Text any use of violence and extortion and interpret it in the obvious meaning it naturally offers, we will have to admit that the Koran, in the particular sector of women — which is a limited fraction of the universe, endows Mary not only with a high, but simply supreme, dignity. None among her peers is to be her superior.

Here we find ourselves at odds with a theory proposed by some commentators moved more by pious zeal than by scientific seriousness. "Mary," they think, "is superior only to the women who were her contemporaries,[112] but not to those who came before or after; especially she is not superior to the women — wives and daughters of the Prophet." Not at all! We reject this opinion as inconsistent and unsustainable. The Koranic enunciation is so clear and explicit that it will suffer no detour or short-cut interpretation — not even to favor Mohammad's blood relatives.

Mary is superior to all women. And she had thus been proclaimed not by man's will, but by God's own order, the Koran witnessing. Only man's ignorance, his short-mindedness, his fanaticism might sustain, but never justify, such a restricted inter-

---

112. TAB. VI, n. 7025-7027 (p. 393-94): *All women*, here, means the women of the time when Mary lived, n. 7036 (p. 400); the women of old. — GEL., p. 74: *All women* are those of Mary's own time, i.e. her contemporaries. — ZAM. I, 362: Mary's exaltation above all women must be understood in that, alone among all women, she had a son with no man's contribution; a singular privilege granted to no other woman of the universe.
   To the contrary the Orientalists. MONT. (p. 89): "Il t'a choisie parmi (toutes) les femmes du monde." — BL. IV (p. 81): "Il t'a choisie sur (toutes) les femmes de ce monde." — "Il t'a choisie de préférence à toutes les femmes de l'univers." MASS., p. 66. — "Und hat dich erwählt von den Weiben aller Welt." HEN., p. 70. — "Und bevorzugt vor allen Frauen der ganzen Welt." ULL., p. 57. — SAV. (p. 150): "Tu es élue entre toutes les femmes." — KAS. (p. 74): "il t'a élue parmi toutes les femmes de l'univers." — Likewise, PES. (p. 33). — And, long before, MARRACCI: "et elegit te super mulieres *omnium Mundorum*." MAR. II, p. 110.

pretation which, surely, is not intended by the Koran, nor anticipated. On my account, a shortened exegesis in this case ought to be rejected as foreign and spurious.

Standing by the Koran's very letter and not heeding the mental acrobatics of some commentators, we ought to retain as an authentic Koranic doctrine the fact that in the feminine sector, whether in paradise[113] or on earth, no woman[114] may challenge Mary, the mother of Jesus, in dignity. Absolutely no woman. Not Fatima,[115] the Prophet's beloved daughter.[116] Not his

---

113. Regarding Mary's glory in the other life, authors, based upon a hadith, maintain that Mary is queen of all women in paradise. Cf. IBN HANBAL, Musnad, III, 64, 80; TIRMIDHI, ABU NU'AIM (ap. HAY., p. 77). Mary is superior to the three most excellent women that have ever existed: Asiya, Khadija, and Fatima. Cf. TAB. VI, n. 7026-7097 (p. 394-397). — In another hadith, Mohammad had reportedly stated that his young wife, Aisha, is superior to all women of the paradise except Mary, Imran's daughter, who is superior to her in dignity. Cf. TAB. VI, n. 7032 (p. 398-399). On the other hand, Aisha herself, willing to emphasize her own prerogative, calls on Mary as a second term of comparison. Cf. GAUD., p. 113. — Mary, in fact, is "la plus honorable de ses Servantes auprès de Lui." DAMARI, (ap. HAY., p. 77).

114. According to a hadith, four are the ladies among the women of the universe: Mary, Imran's daughter; Asiya, Faraoh's wife; Khadija, the Prophet's wife; and Fatima, the Prophet's daughter. Cf. BOUKHARI, Traditions, II, 515; IBN HANBAL, Musnad, III, 135; TAYALISI, Musnad, n. 504 (ap. HAY., p. 77). At the first place appears Mary, as one sees. She is absolutely the first, since Allah has proclaimed her "Dame sur toutes ses servantes." TABARI (ap. HAY., p. 77).

115. By Aisha's confession, the dearest daughter to Mohammad was Fatima who was later married by Ali, the Prophet's cousin. Cf. FAD., p. 256. — Regarding the cult of Fatima by the Shiites, Massignon notes: "Il est extrêmement remarquable de constater le travail de la pensée des Musulmans qui les a amenés à envisager pour Fatima, graduellement, les privilèges de Marie [...]. Des Shiites pensent qu'elle n'a pas accouché par les voies normales, mais par le nombril. Et il y a même qui pensent qu'elle a conçu par l'oreille, comme Maryam." MASS. (La notion de voeu et la dévotion musulmane à Fatima, 1956), p. I, p.580. Italics are ours.

116. We observe, by the way, that Fatima was Mohammad's daughter, not wife, as was erroneously written (HIND., p. 271) and repeated (ROSCH.,

dearest wives, such as the aged Khadija,[117] or even the very young[118] and tender Aisha.

From this true and theoretical premise inevitably follows a practical corollary — which has potential for further vital developments.

By virtue of her eminent and rather supreme dignity, it is lawful, or even, right, to offer Mary a true and proper *cult*. This shall obviously respect the "bounds set by Allah,"[119] and thereby it shall not take on the form of adoration (latria) due exclusively to God.[120] It instead shall be an obsequious cult (dulia) — cult by veneration, or adoration in a large sense,[121] in tune with Mary's exceptional position in the salvation plan.

An undeniable fact is that Islam does not follow the tone and trend of its doctrine, so as to assign to Mary the right place

---

p. 243; TOD., p. 210). Besides, none among the ten legal wives of the Prophet appears to have borne the name: Fatima. Cf. SH., *op cit.* — There was a marriage project with a certain Fatima, bint ad-Dahhak; but it never took place. The proposed wife, aware of the feminine jealousies congesting the Prophet's Harem and worsening by the presence of the young Copte, Mary, preferred to return to her folks, "où elle gagna sa vie en ramassant des crottes de chameau." GAUD., p. 229.

117. Cf. SH., p. 27-50.

118. She was betrothed to Mohammad at six or seven years of age (SH., p. 63) while the Prophet was in his fifties; and was married three years later, at Medina, a few months after the Hegira. *Loc. cit.*, p. 78. Cf. ESS., p. 194.

119. "These are the bounds set by Allah [hudùd ul-lah]: do not come near them" (2, 187). Cf. note 44, p. 55.

120. "Do not prostrate yourselves [la tàsjudu] before the sun or the moon; rather prostrate yourselves [wàsjudu] before Allah, who created them both" (41, 37). Fifteen are the Koranic verses which reserve to Allah alone the prostration [sujùd], or the adoration in proper terms: 7, 206; 13, 15; 16, 49; 17, 107; 19, 58; 22, 18, 77; 25, 60; 27, 25; 32, 15; 38, 24; 41, 37; 53, 62; 84, 21; 96, 19. And they are commonly maintained to be Meccan.

121. "And when We said to the Angels: 'Prostrate yourselves [ùsjudu] before Adam,' they all prostrated themselves [sàjadu] except Iblis" (Satan) (2, 34). Cf. 7, 11; 17, 61; 20, 116.

she deserves in the practice of public worship.[122] The statement by some that, in Islam, the Virgin Mary appears "haloed by a veneration equal to that which is attributed to her by Christianity,"[123] may, and may not, be an exaggeration. What stands unquestionably true, nonetheless, is that the Koran does not forbid, but rather favors, at least implicitly, some public cultic exhibitions toward Mary.

What *these public cultic exhibitions* might, or should, be at the practical level, Mohammad does not spell out in clear-cut terms. With the Koran in hand, however, we can easily establish some less general cultic forms, following — as we shall do by analogy — the norms and suggestions prescribed as a guideline for similar cases.

a. — Cult by Veneration

This form of worship is a key to all the rest.

Ruling for his "household" — *ahl el bait* — Mohammad

---

122. Cf. MUL., p. 269. — BOUBAKEUR, notes in this regard: "Dans l'Islam, il n'y a pas de place pour la Vierge dans la liturgie." BOUB., p. 615. And as a justification of this flaw he adds: "Le Coran dans son intransigence monothéiste s'attaque à tout culte rapprochant la créature du Créateur quant à leur essence ou associant le créé au Créateur (hyperdulie mariale)." *Ib.*, p. 616.

123. "Marie, mère de Jésus, apparaît dans le Coran, dont une sourate porte son nom, auréolée d'une vénération presque égale à celle que lui consacre le christianisme." GAUD., p. 384. Italics are ours. — Cf. PEIR., p. 43.
The veneration tributed to Mary by Christians is immensly different from the one rendered to her by Moslems. Sufficient evidence of that are certainly the form of worship called "hyperdulia," which is inspired by the Divine Maternity — a dogma that Islam rejects, the theological developments of Mary's mediation, and the confident recourse of the faithful to her powerful intercession.

enjoins his wives and daughters not to show in public in a less dignified and respectful manner as their distinctive mark (33-59). By that respectful attitude they should be easily recognized from the rest of the people, and not molested. This injunction is also valid for the believers. Whether entering the Prophet's house or dealing with his Harem, they must show courtesy and self-restraint: "**If you ask his wives anything, speak to them from behind the curtain**" (35, 53). This respect due to his family derives from the nobility redounding on them from their closeness to the Prophet, i.e. from their relationship to him by consanguinity, affinity, or parenthood.

The Prophet's WIVES are not to be weighed by the same scale as are other women. They form a privileged caste (33, 32). Their eventual faults are doubly punished; likewise is their reward for being faithful to their commitments (33, 30-31). Any dealing with them should consequently be seasoned with a peculiar exhibition of filial devotion, of deferential respect. Besides, tender devotion and reverential respect are charged by the Koran on all born of women: "**Honor ye [ittaq-u] the bosoms who bore you**" (4, 1).

Because the Prophet relates to his subjects more than they do to one another, and because his wives are "mothers" to all believers,[124] reverential behavior and respect are a must in his presence (49, 2) and in that of his wives as well. None is to molest the Prophet's wives (33, 53), or bring them offense (33, 59). Offense and disturbance brought to the "household" — *ahl el bait* — will inevitably redound on the Prophet's person himself; and to offend or molest the Prophet constitutes in God's sight, who sent him, an enormous crime (33, 53).

---

124. "The Prophet has a greater claim on the faithful than they have on each other. His wives are their mothers *[ummahàt-uhum]* " (33, 6). — In this regard observe ZAMAKHSHARI (III, 523): All the faithful have become brothers, since the Prophet has become their common father in the new faith.

More so than other women, the Prophet's wives should be treated with kindness and civility. Even after the death of the Prophet, they have to be regarded as something holy, never to be touched, never to be profaned.

Due to the fact that the believers, men and women, are mutually helpers, protectors and patrons [àwliya'], Islam has from the beginning tolerated and, later, following the collectivity's unanimous consent,[125] recognized officially the veneration of the saints and friends of Allah.[126] In this particular category of àwliya' figure, as components, the members of the household (33, 33); the first emigrants [muhàdjirs] from Mecca to Medina (9, 100); the ansàr, Mohammad's auxiliaries who stood by him soon after the Hegira (9, 117; 61, 14); the shùhada (57, 19), martyrs of the faith in Allah, authentic believers, who died (jàhad-u) for Allah's cause[127] and won the greatest success;[128] the siddìq-un (righteous) and the sàlih-un (goodly, saintly) whom God overwhelmed with his favors (4, 69); and also

---

125. There are no sacraments in Islam, nor priesthood. And consequently there is in it no church hierarchically constituted, with a supreme head to decide in doctrinal matters. In conflicts of opinions, "the difference will be resolved only with the running of time, when among the doctors a prevalent opinion will materialize into what constitutes the ijmà (general consensus)." NAL. II, p. 605. Cf. GAR.- AN., p. 403-407.

126. "Believers, take neither Jews nor Christians for your allies [àwliya] " (5, 51). "Those that have embraced the faith and fled their homes, and fought for the cause of Allah with their wealth and their persons; and those that sheltered them and helped them, shall be allies [àwliya] to one another" (8, 72). — The word wàli (pl. àwliya) generally involves the sense of a pact rather than a mere friendship and has, in the Koran, according to Muqatil, ten different meanings at least. Cf. NWY., p. 114-115.

127. "Sabil Allah" (2, 8, 72) is an idiomatic expression for the new religion, Islam, its establishment and its triumph.

128. "It is they who shall triumph [fà'izun] " (9, 20). — 'Theirs is the supreme triumph [al fàuz ul adhìm] " (9, 72, 89, 100, 111; 57, 12; 61, 11, 14).

those who distinguished themselves by the remarkable and praiseworthy social undertakings they accomplished.[129]

Now, acting in the Koran's spirit, if not really in the very letter of it, why couldn't one have for Mary the same expressions of esteem and devotion required for Moslem women? Why can't one cultivate a tender veneration toward her, or nurture ostensibly some adequate forms of homage or worship toward her? Her motherly relation with Christ, the noble and great messenger among the great messengers of Allah, would surely justify such revering testimonials.

b. — *Cult by Invocation*

Two types of prayer are known in Islam: the *descending* and the *ascending* prayer. By the first, even God "prays," for instance, on the Prophet *[salla]* and on his "household" and says "peace be on him," or "on them," and showers on them His complacency, mercy and forgiveness. By the second, the faithful Moslem prays to God, asking him for help or a favor for himself or for others.

The latter form, prayer of petition *[du'à']*, may be tendered directly to Allah for a personal favor (40, 60), or

---

129. "Au Maghreb on vénéra surtout les hommes qui se levèrent contre l'envahisseur infidèle, lorsque l'Espagne voulut conquérir le Maroc après la prise de Grenade (1492); ce sont les "marabouts". SOURDEL D., *L'Islam* "Que sais-je?" 355 [Paris, Presses Univ., 1968,] p. 57.

Anyhow, despite the fierce opposition by the *Hanbalites*, the cult and veneration of the *àwliya* (saints, God's friends, benefactors) had an enormous growth in Islam.

indirectly by the means of a third person, v.g. a patron [walì], or an intercessor [shafi']. In the last case, the supplication is formulated by the intercessor and aims rather at someone else's good.

Here are a few examples taken from everyday life[130] and reported by the Koran itself.

The angels, we read there in fact, solicit of God forgiveness for the earth dwellers (42, 5). Noah prayed for forgiveness for his parents, for the believers, men and women, who would have sought refuge in his house (71, 28). Abraham implored mercy and forgiveness for his pagan father,[131] his own children, and all the believers on the Day of Reckoning (14, 41). Jacob implored of God pardon for his children guilty of sin (12, 97-98). Moses asked God forgiveness for him and for his brother Aaron (7, 151). Mohammad himself several times addressed God by pleas and prayers for the members of his community.[132]

---

130. For instance, in the funerary services (cf. TABB., p. 159-165), the petition for the deceased (ib., p. 161-163) is one of Islam's pillars [arkàn].

And with regard to the prayer to Fatima and her intercession, writes Massignon: "Il est certain que l'intercession de Fatima a été très fréquement invoquée comme celle d'une martyre, qui, de son vivant, 'ne priait pour elle,' mais pour les autres. L'histoire des Shiites est pleine de récits de grâces obtenues de Fatima." MASS. (La notion de voeu et la dévotion musulmane à Fatima, 1956), I, p. 575-76.

131. "The forgiveness that Abraham asked for his father was only to fulfill a promise he had made him" (9, 114). Cf. 19, 47; 26, 86; 60, 4.

132. "If, when they wronged themselves, they had come to you imploring Allah's pardon, and if you, the Apostle, had sought of Allah forgiveness for them, they would have found Him forgiving and merciful" (4, 64). "Un texte qui semble d'abord se référer aux anges, servit de base scripturaire pour affirmer l'intercession de Muhammad en faveur de sa Communauté, puis de chaque prophète-envoyé en faveur de son peuple [...]. Les hadith aiment à redire que 'les portes de bronze de l'intercession s'ouvrent à la prière du Prophète de l'Islam'." GAR., p. 86.

As a theoretical justification of this practice, we may adduce the Koranic teaching on *intercession*[133] and *intercessors*.[134]

Intercession is mentioned explicitly in at least thirteen verses. Added to others which contain the idea without the name, they give us the concept of its *modality*, its *subject*, and its *terminus*.

The *shafà'at's* (intercession's) fundamental requisite is Allah's complacency. Without his permission (53, 26), his acceptance (21, 28), his previous sanction (19, 87), there is no true and effective intercession.[135] Without God to begin with, none has power to act as an intercessor.[136] Allah's sanction is a must mainly on the Day of Reckoning (20, 109). Then, all depends categorically upon God's will,

---

133. "Guard yourselves against the day when every soul will stand alone: when neither intercession *(shafà'at)* nor ransom shall be accepted from it, nor any help given it" (2, 48). Cf. 2, 123, 254; 4, 85; 43, 86; 53, 26; 74, 48.

134. "They shall have no guardian or intercessor *[shafi']* besides Allah" (6, 51). Cf. 6, 70; 10, 3; 32, 4; 40, 18. — "Will there be intercessors *[shùfa'a]* to intercede *[yàshfa'u]* for us?" (7, 53). Cf. 6, 94; 10, 18; 30, 13; 39, 43. — "We have no intercessor *[shafi']* now" (26, 100). — "No intercessor's plea *[shafà'at u-sshàfi'in]* shall profit them" (74, 48).

135. "The gods to whom they pray besides Him have not the power to intercede for them" (43, 86). — "Numerous are the angels in heaven; yet their intercession shall avail nothing until Allah gives leave to whom He accepts and chooses" (53, 26).

136. With God's leave as a prerequisite, the intercession becomes good *[hàsanat]*, and is benevolently answered. Contrary to that is the bad intercession *[sàiy'at]*, whose subject is "accountable for its evils" (4, 85).
Therefore excluded from the privilege of interceding are all those who do not believe in Allah and His Prophet (26, 100): the unbelievers, the hypocrites, the wrong-doers. For those no intercession shall be profitable: neither in the other life (40, 18), nor in the present: "It is the same whether or not you beg forgiveness for them. If seventy times you beg forgiveness for them, Allah will not forgive them, for they have denied Allah and His Apostle. Allah does not guide the evil-doers" (9, 80).

who is free to grant or refuse the exercise of interceding.[137]

The *intercessor (shafi')* as a rule may be any person accepted to Allah and praying to Him for the sake of others
(2, 48, 123), an angel (42, 5), a devout servant of God like
Abraham (2, 126; 26, 86), and mainly Mohammad.[138]

The *ultimate terminus* at whom the intercession stops is
God in person (34, 23). Being such an absolute lord, he may
answer or reject a petition and make it void and sterile,[139]
even if it is addressed by Mohammad himself.[140]

There are Moslem authors who deny to Islam any possible form of mediation and, consequently, intercession. I
only quote Qerdàwi: In Islam there is no room for
priesthood,[141] no room for mediators,[142] because Islam

---

137. "Before that day arrives when there shall be neither trading nor friendship nor *intercession*" (9, 80). — "Numerous are the angels in heaven; yet their
intercession shall avail nothing until Allah gives leave to whom He accepts and
chooses" (53, 26).

138. Between the eschatological intercession (20, 109), mainly of Mohammad's, and Mary's intercession on the Last Day at the universal judgment, there
is, in Massignon's opinion, no dependence whatsoever nor an imitation properly
speaking. The analogy, or parallelism, are the product of an "autonomous activity" between Christians and Moslems, as well as of "un fonctionnement
analogue de réflexion collective sur des thèmes symétriquement disposés suivant
la structure du dogme, ici et là." MASS. (*Les Recherches d'Asin Palacios sur
Dante*. Le Problème des influences musulmanes sur la chrétienté médiévale et
les lois de l'imitation littéraire), I, p. 64.

139. In such case, the intercession will be, in the Koranic terms, *saiy'at*,
bad (4, 85), and it is attributed to the false divinities (10, 18; 36, 23).

140. "You shall not pray for their dead, nor shall you attend their burial.
For they denied Allah and His Apostle and remained sinners to the last"
(9, 84).

141. QER., p. 148-149.

142. *Loc. cit.*, p. 154-156.

means the emancipation of man's conscience from any mediatorial attitude.[143]

But Official Islam as a whole, under influence by Sufism and Shi'ism, has accepted and developed the cult of "saints" while ranking Mohammad as the greatest of them all.[144] Also, it has admitted in its dogma the doctrine of intercession "in which, for importance and efficacy, culminates Mohammad's mediation on the Last Day. Furthermore, influenced by the import of Christian ideology and practices, Islam accepted the intercession of other mediators: angels, martyrs, prophets and saints who — besides Mohammad — intercede in favor of the devout and repentant sinners."[145]

With these premises in mind, who would object to Mary's mediatory power? Who would exclude her from the list of countless intercessors with God? Wasn't she like them favored by Allah? And more than they exalted above all the women of the universe? Wasn't she chosen from among them all to be instrumental, by her consent, in actuating God's salvific plan? If the Moslem believer had recourse to her and implored her intervention, would he act perhaps against his Koran's teaching? Or betray the Prophet's genuine thought? Would he be charged with infidelity? With polytheist idolatry? Would he be blamed for so doing, and doomed as wrong?

We stand for the diametrically opposite opinion. Based

---

143. *Loc. cit.*, p. 151-152.

144. "La doctrine musulmane a développé le culte des saints comme un remplacement nécessaire des cultes locaux préislamiques, qui avaient conservé leur valeur dans l'esprit des convertis. Il est inévitable que le Prophète fut consideré comme le plus grand des saints et qu'on lui attribuât des qualités particulières de perfection, une incapacité de commettre le mal." GAUD., p. 218.

145. GOT., p. 25. Cf. NAL. II, p. 609.

on the Koran and the Islamic Tradition, we say that all who invoke Mary and appeal to her powerful intercession are adhering to the orthodoxy of the Koranic Message. Far from labelling them as renegades of Mohammad's thinking, we consider them as his faithful interpreters: *in theory*, in that they read in the depths of his mind the ineffable respect he implied for Mary; *and in practice*, in that they offered this "reverential bud" of his affection, which he bequeathed to them all, the favorable climate to see it grow and develop into a precious shoot of spiritual life.

c. — *Cult by Imitation*

This form of worship is unquestionably desired by the Koran. And the proof of it is the insistence by the Book on recommending the imitation of Mohammad, Allah's Apostle. "You have in Allah's Apostle a good example [usùwwat hàsanat] for those who look to Allah and the Last Day, and remember Allah always" (33, 21). This imitation should not remain a mere theory, but it ought to be translated into practice as a way of life, or an incentive to further develop in the soul of the believer a deeper sense of Allah's sovereignty.[146] "If you truly love Allah, follow me. And Allah will love you and forgive you your sins" (3, 31).

And then, again, if the Koran often calls to mind the "stories of the Prophets," it does it for a definite purpose, to stress the fidelity to God by enduring persecutions and hoping for the final triumph of Allah's cause.[147]

---

146. GAUD., p. 218.

147. Regarding the *historic* relations of the Koran and the so called "stories

Finally, as for Mary, Mohammad does not propose her only as a *Sign* for the world here and beyond to admire, but also as a *Model* to imitate.

2. Mary M a t h a l, a Model

Before going into this other Koranic element, I believe it is necessary to consider awhile *two premises* of historico-apologetic background.

They will help us to see in a fuller perspective and evaluate adequately Mohammad's exceptional gesture in proposing Mary, the mother of Jesus, as an example to follow, as an ideally human model to pattern one's behavior upon and imitate.

1. First Premise: *Islam "ante litteram."*

The Meccan Prophet used, right from the outset of his career, one of his most congenial and successful strategies: He fought the temptation to expose himself as a religious

---

of the prophets", notes NWYIA: "Quand la conscience musulmane reprend à son compte un fait emprunté, par exemple, à la Bible ou à l'agiographie judéo-chrétienne, *elle ne peut s'empêcher dans la plupart des cas d'y opérer une transposition, en lui mêlant des détails fabuleux ou en lui donnant une orientation qui en transforme le sens."* NWY., p. 74. Italics are ours.

innovator,[148] a revolutionary, a promoter selling a new type of religion or cult. In other words, he rightly understood that it was more in his own interest, at the time he was carrying out his plan, to keep himself on the track of an already established religious current, the "biblical monotheism" in this case, then more prevalent in the Hejaz than any other.

At first — that is during the whole Meccan Period (c. 612-622) — Mohammad recognized the validity of former revelations made respectively to the two communities,[149] Hebrew and Christian, through Abraham,[150] Moses,[151] and Christ.[152] Not only that, but he was intimately persuaded that he was in full accord with the "People of the Book."[153] With them, indeed, he constantly

---

148. "Say: 'I am not an innovator [bid'] among the apostles' " (46, 9). — "As Mohammad conceived it while he lived at Mecca, as was pointed out by Chr. Snouck Hurgronjie, there was no question of founding a new religion." NAL. I, p. 149.

Besides, speaking of religion in strict terms, the Koran offers nothing really new, nothing original; but only a re-thinking, a re-emphasizing, a re-proposing of this or other doctrinal or practical issues already known to the previous revelation, or which can easily be retraced in the Jahiliya's pre-Islamic institutions, Jewish or Christian sources.

149. "So that you may not say: 'The Scriptures were revealed only to two communities [ta'ifatàin] before us, and we have no knowledge of what they teach' " (6, 156). — For the revelation prior to Islam, made to the "People of the Book," cf. 3, 168; 4, 131; 5, 5.

150. "We gave Abraham's descendants the Book and the Wisdom" (4, 54). Cf. 29, 27; 57, 26. — Elsewhere are mentioned the "earlier scriptures" [assùhuf ul ùla] (87, 18; 20, 133); the sùhuf of Abraham and Moses, 87, 19; the sùhuf of Moses, 53, 36.

151. "We gave Moses the Book" (32, 23). Cf. 6, 91; 11, 17; 46, 12.

152. Allah will instruct Christ in "the Book, the Wisdom, the Torah, and the Gospel [injeel]" (3, 48). Cf. 5, 110; 19, 30.

153. "Ahl el Kitàb": Cf. also 2, 105; 3, 64; 4, 123; 5, 15; 57, 29; 98, 1. — "Mahomet crut dès le début que ses révélations provenaient de la même source que celles des Juifs et des Chrétiens." PAR., p. 598. — Cf. VAYDA G., Ahl-al-Kitàb, EI, t. I (new edition) p. 272-274.

Today we are able to state that Islam constitutes the summary of the final

maintained a spiritual connection which proved to have been most beneficial.

Later, on the heels of the historic rupture at Medina, he railed against both Jews and Christians *[nasàra]* charging them with having adulterated[154] the divine revelation. Then introducing himself as a restorer of the primitive religion, he connected himself directly with the community *[mìllat]* of Abraham, Allah's friend (4, 125), who in his opinion was neither a Jew nor a Christian (3, 67) but a *hànif*.[155] And stated explicitly his creed

---

outcome of a long process of monotheist ripening which slowly evolved in Hijaz and Mecca on the heels of a stubborn, yet effective, propaganda by both Jews and Judeo-Christians *[nasàra]*. Cf. HAD. II *(The Koran's Christian Era)*, p. 26-89; 396-438. — WATT also agrees that the monotheism of the Arabs ought to derive "principalement d'influences chrétiennes et juives." WAT. I, p. 51; cf. p. 210-207. Cf. MOUB. II, *Pent.* I *(Le monothéisme coranique et ses témoins)*, p. [99]-174.

154. "Some Jews take the words of the Scripture out of their context *[yuharri-fùna]* thus altering their meaning" (4, 46). Cf. 5, 13, 41.

According to recent Moslem authors, the Christians also have adulterated the Scriptures. Modern Christianity, they say, mainly with its dogmas on the Trinity, Incarnation and Redemption, is nothing else but a hybrid syncretism of pagan, Egyptian, Greek, and Roman legends. Cf. QER., p. 134; SAB., p. 61-63; 197-198, 218; SHAR., p. 214-241.

155. "Follow that faith of Abraham, *hànif* [upright] as he was, and no Associator" (3, 95). Cf. 6, 161; 16, 123. Concerning the use of *hànif*, cf. MOUB. I, p. 151-161, with relative bibliography (p. 161); WAT. I, p. 204-207; BL. VI, p. 55, 56; JEF., p. 112-115; and WATT MONTGOMERY, *Hànif*, in EI, t. III (n. ed.), p. 168-170.

"Le mot *hànif* est l'araméen *hunàpa* qui parait avoir le sens de 'hérétique', non conformiste'; il aurait été appliqué à des hommes qui renonçaient aux croyances des ancêtres." GAUD., p. 68-69. — Today they bring it closer to the type of *homines religiosi*; individuals, according to GABRIELI, "dalla viva e inquieta coscienza religiosa, non soddisfatta dal rozzo politeismo patrio, e al tempo stesso non trovante appagamento in nessuna delle due storiche forme di monoteismo che aveva attecchito nell'Arabia." GAB. I *(La culla dell'Islam)*, p. 18.

For the relationship between Islam and *Hanafism*, a movement with strong Judeo-Christian tendencies, cf. HAD. II, p. 150-159. — The theory heretofore describing the environment in which Mohammad was born, grew and received

that on a par with *"all who surrendered themselves to Allah before him"* (2, 137), i.e. the Moslems *"ante litteram,"* he believed in "Allah" and in all that Allah had revealed to "Abraham, Ismael, Isaac, Jacob, and the Twelve Tribes; in what was transmitted to Moses, Jesus, and the other Prophets" (2, 136).

But once this creed ripened into a personal persuasion that he was more than just a warner and a bearer of good news,[156] that he indeed was a prophet and a messenger of Allah,[157]

---

his first education as pagan and polytheist is far outdone; in my opinion it is already high time we discarded it as obsolete and non-historical. For further and more conclusive researches on the subject, the attention should rather focus on the Judeo-Christian penetration in the Hijaz, not on the pagan and associationist history of the *Jahiliya*. Cf. in SHAR., p. 85, the list of some followers of Hanafism. Among them is Waraka Ben Nawfal who, in Haddad's words, was "the Bishop of Mecca." Cf. note 466.

156. "We have sent you as an announcer *[bashìr]* and a warner *[nadhìr]* " (2, 119). — "Prophet, We have sent you as a witness, a bearer of good news *[mubàsshir]*, and a warner *[nadhìr]*; one who shall call men to Allah by His leave and guide them like a shining light" (33, 45-46). — *Nadhìr*: 11, 12; 25, 1; 35, 23; 74, 36. — *Nadhìr mubìn*: 7, 184; 15, 89; 22, 49; 26, 115; 29, 50; 38, 70; 46, 9; 51, 50-51; 67, 26. — *Mùndhir*: 13, 7, 38, 65; 79, 45. — *Nadhìr wa bashìr*: 17, 105; 25, 56; 33, 45; 48, 8.

According to Gaudefroy-Demombines, *nadhìr* is a Judeo-Aramaic term and it enhances Mohammad in the task of a warner of a material punishment, like the one which destroyed the old peoples. Cf. GAUD., p. 82. — According to MOUBARAC, Mohammad was a *nabì* (prophet) in its old Arabic use, i.e. one who "brings the news of the event imminent par excellence, the final judgment of God." MOUB., p. 16.

157. "Prophet *[nabì]*, you are well enough with Allah and with the faithful" (8, 64). Cf. 9, 73; 33, 1; 49, 2; 60, 12; 66, 1. — "We have sent forth to you an apostle *[rasùl]* to testify against you" (73, 15). Cf. 2, 285; 3, 132; 4, 59; 8, 27. — *Rasùl mubìn*: 43, 29; 44, 13. — *Rasùl karìm*: 68, 40. — *Rasùl Allàh*: 7, 158; 9, 61; 33, 53; 91, 13; 98, 2.

"Un auteur dit que *rasùl* est un *nabî* qui apporte une Écriture, tel Moïse; et que le *nabî* est celui qui prophétise, sans avoir d'Écriture, tel Josué. Suivant un autre auteur, le *rasùl* est celui auquel a été révélé une Écriture ou bien auquel est apparu un ange, et le *nabî* est celui qu'Allah charge de l'application des lois ou bien qui suit un *rasùl*. Tout *rasùl* est *nabî*, mais non l'inverse. Mohammed

Mohammad shifted to another audacious idea: he proposed himself not only as another link in the chain of the illustrious messengers of the Old and New Testament,[158] but as the crowning and the ultimate sealing[159] of all the Prophets.

These Prophets have become his forerunners (35, 25), to the extent that Christ himself is shown to be his herald.[160] In this new perspective the Koranic Message is not only "good news"

---

est, à la fois, Envoyé et Prophète. Il y a eu cent vingt-quatre mille *nabî* et trois cent treize *rasûl.*" GAUD., p. 83. — According to SABUNI, on the contrary, the prophets were 120,000; the apostles, instead, only 25. Cf. SAB., p. 14.

158. "You are indeed one of the apostles" (36, 3). Cf. MASSON *(Les Prophètes antérieurs de l'Islam mentionnés dans le Coran)*, I, p.310-335; GAUD. (ch. III, *Histoire universelle: les prophètes),* p. 337-400. — On the Koranic "prophetology" cf. MOUB. I, p. 15-25; and HOROVITZ, *Nabì,* in EI, III, p. 857-858.

159. "Mohammad is the apostle of Allah and the seal *[khàtam]* of the prophets" (33, 40). Exegetes are not unanimous about the meaning of *khàtam* in the present verse. For some it is the closing of the prophecy, in that the divine revelation had ended here. Consequently, in God's actual plan of salvation, there will be after Mohammad no true, but only false prophets. For others *khàtam* refers to the past, not the future, and would be a confirmation of what had previously been revealed.

160. "And of Jesus, who said to the Israelites: 'I am sent forth to you by Allah to confirm the Torah already revealed and to give news of an apostle that will come after me whose name is Ahmad" (61, 6). The promised One in the Gospel's announcement, as is known, is the Holy Spirit, the Paraclete (cf. Jo., 14, 16, 26; 16, 7). But the παράκλητος (the consoler) has been arbitrarily changed in περικλυτός (praised, i.e. Ahmad, Mohammad). Based upon the Koran (7, 157), some Moslem Exegetes pretend that Mohammad has been announced in the Old Testament also, v.g. in *Dt.,* 18, 15-18.*

(*). Childish also is the theory of some commentators linking the year 570, when Mohammad was born, to the *pentekoste hemera* (the fiftieth day after Jesus' resurrection), when the Paraclete came down on the Apostles. Some of those say they see an allusion to Mohammad in Habacuc's text: "*God will come from the South, and the holy one from Mount Pharan*" (Hab. 3, 3), not far from actual Mecca, the birthplace of the Prophet. (Fares)

and a "guide."[161] On an even level with the Torah[162] and the Gospel[163] in terms of light and guidance, it is proposed as a continuation and a confirmation[164] of the previous revelation. Torah, Gospel and Koran would then be three successive exhibits of the same divine communication, differing only by "form and language, not by substance."[165] But that is not all. In the actual plan of divine revelation the Koran would be a *Providential Correction Book* for whatever falsity or mutilation the Sacred Scriptures had suffered from Jews and Christians alike over the centuries.

Along with this line, Islam, aroused by Mohammad to new life and enforced by a sweep of renewed faith, is presented on the level of man's history as the religion par excellence: the religion of God *[dinù 'l lah]*; the guide of God; the path of

---

161. "For to you We have revealed the Book as a clear proof for all things, a guide *[hùda]*, a mercy, and a good news *[bùshra]* to all Moslems who surrender themselves to Allah" (16, 89). Cf. 2, 2, 120, 185; 3, 4, 97; 6, 35. — Hùda Allàh: 2, 12; 3, 73; 6, 71, 88; 28, 5. — Hùda wa màw'idhat: 3, 138: 5, 46. — Hùda wa bùshra: 2, 97; 16, 102; 27, 2. — Hùda wa nùr: 5, 44, 46. — Hùda wa shifà': 41, 44. — Hùda wa ràhmat: 6, 154, 157; 7, 52, 154, 203; 10, 57; 16, 64, 89; 27, 77; 31, 3; 45, 20.
The two terms hùda (guide) and ràhmat (mercy) are among the list of those Koranic words to which the exegetes attribute a plurality of meanings. Thus hùda would have 17 synonyms, and ràhmat a dozen. Cf. HAD. III, p. 149.

162. "We have revealed the Torah in which there is guide *[hùda]* and light" (5, 44). Cf. 2, 185; 6, 154; 47, 25; 48, 28; 61, 9.

163. "After those prophets We sent Jesus, the son of Mary, confirming the Torah already revealed; and We gave him the Gospel, in which there is guidance *[hùda]* and light, confirming *[musàddiq]* that which was revealed before it in the Torah, a guide and an admonition to *[Allah's]* fearing people" (5, 46). Cf. 3, 4.

164. "He has revealed to you the Book with the truth, confirming *[musàddiq]* the Scriptures that were revealed before" (3, 3).

165. NAL. II, p. 608.

God;[166] the authentic right path,[167] the only infallible guide[168] for all men (2, 185), mainly the *muttaqìn*, the devout, the God-fearing, who from the heart seek Allah (2, 2).

Islam is the typical form of religion Allah has chosen (2, 132). God's genuine adorers are the Moslems.[169] All believers in Allah, men and women, are "ipso facto" *muslimùn*. [170] And vice-versa. It was Allah Himself[171] who reserved the epithet

---

166. "And you shall surely guide men to the right path: the path of Allah *[Siràt Allah]* " (42, 53). — "Such is the path of your Lord *[siràt ràbbika]*, a straight path" (6, 126). — "Do not squat in every road, threatening believers and debarring them from the path of Allah *[sabil Allah]* " (7, 86). Cf. 14, 1; 34, 6.

167. "Know that this path of Mine is straight *[inna hàdha siràti mustaqìman]* Follow it, and do not follow other ways *[sùbul]*, for they will lead you away from His way *[sabil-ihi]*. Thus Allah exhorts you, in the hope that you may fear Him" (6, 153). — "Therefore hold fast to that which is revealed to you, because you are on the right path *[siràt-en mustaqìm]*" (43, 43). Cf. 1, 6; 2, 142; 3, 51; 16, 121; 23, 73; 24, 46; 43, 61; 48, 20; and elsewhere, *passim*. — "We have just been listening to a Book revealed after that of Moses, confirming the previous ones and guiding to the truth and to a straight path *[tarìq-en mustaqìm]* " (46, 30).

168. "The Koran was revealed, a book of guidance with proofs of guidance *[baiynàt]* distinguishing right from wrong" (2, 185).

169. "Not so are the loyal servers of the Lord *[ila ibàd-al 'lah il mùkhlisìn]* " (37, 40). Cf. 37, 74, 138, 160, 169.

170. "But you, My servants, who have believed in My signs and were Moslems *[muslimìn]*,... enter the garden" (43, 69). Cf. 2, 133; 46, 15; 49, 17; 51, 36. "Nor are you a guide to the blind out of their error if only you can make the believers in Our signs hear you; these are the Moslems *[muslimìn]* " (27, 81). Cf. 28, 53; 29, 46; 30, 53; 33, 35.

171. It is hard to understand why an expert, such as BOUBAKEUR, had translated the verse 78 of Sura 22 thus: "la religion de votre père Abraham qui vous a donné le nom de musulmans avant et en cette révélation" (BOUB., p. 696); and why MOUBARAC, had likewise attributed to Abraham the "terminological genesis" of Islam and of *muslimìn* MOUB. II, *Pent.* II, p. 4, 9, 55). *

(*). Accurately translated, the Koranic text in question should read thus: "Fight in the cause of Allah the battle which becomes Him. He has chosen you;

mùslim to the followers of the primitive religion already professed by Abraham,[172] the father of *muslimìn* (22, 78).

With that in mind, no one wonders why Mohammad was so anxious to make his followers believe that the *mùslim* (surrendered to God) and the *muslimùn* (the Moslems forming the community of believers) were all those who have, one way or another, over the centuries, adhered to the One and true God and adored Him.[173]

and, in the observance of your religion, the faith of your father Abraham, He laid on you no unbearable burdens. In this and in former Scriptures, He (Allah) has given you the name of Moslems" (22, 78). (Fares)

The Koran, in fact, leaves no doubts as to the direct attribution of revelation to Allah alone: He is the only author of the previous revelation and of the Koranic *tanzìl* as well, to which v. 78 alludes. Both exegetes and translators refer to God, not to Abraham, the pronoun *hùwa* (*He*, in italics) in Fares' note. Among exegetes cf. BAYD. II, p. 80; GEL., p. 450; TAB. and RAZ., quoted by BOUB. I, p. 697. Among translators cf. SAV., p. 353; KAS., p. 265; MONT. II, p. 16; BL. IV, p. 367; MAS., 418; HEN., p. 320; ULL., p. 275; BAUS., p. 264. PESLE then writes very simply: "*Dieu* vous a donné le nom de musulmans" (PES., p. 218). Italics are ours.

172. "He has chosen you; and, in the observance of your religion, the faith of your father Abraham, He laid on you no unbearable burdens. In this as in former Scriptures, He has given you the name of Moslems" (22, 78).
The predicative *mùslim* appears in the Koran since the first Meccan period (cf. 51, 36), but without bearing the "technical" character it later had: i.e. to belong juridically to the "Middlemost Community" which Mohammad had constituted upon the monotheistic faith of Abraham. The God of Abraham, in fact, is the God of Islam; and the faith of Abraham is the faith of Islam. Cf. MOUB. I, p. 103-118. — And DRAZ notes opportunely here that the Koran does not define Islam as a "Mohammedanism" rivaling Judaism or Christianity: "Être musulman, c'est appartenir en même temps à Moïse, à Jésus, et à tous les messagers divins depuis la création du genre humain." DR., p. 55.
Contemplated under this new light, Islam becomes a tremendously invaluable religious phenomenon! As a "heavenly" religion, i.e. "revealed," it would be the continuation of the heavenly religion already revealed to Abraham himself. Cf. MOUB. II, *Pent.* III [*L'Islam dans une nouvelle perspective chrétienne*]. p. [1]-78.

173. "Dès les premières années de son triomphe, l'Islam se présente à la fois

According to the Koran, consequently, there have been Moslems *ante litteram* long before Mohammad; there was an Islam *ante litteram*; [174] "Abraham's religion *ab antiquo*" (22, 78).

Real *muslimùn*, and considered as *muslimùn*, [175] were all those who had before Mohammad surrendered to Allah; who before and after the Hegira adhered to Mohammad; who after the rupture with "ahl el Kitàb" formed alone a new community, "middlemost"

---

comme une *religion* avec ses dogmes et ses lois, comme une *cité terrestre* qui s'organise en Empire mondial, comme une vie quitidienne qui commande *l'attitude sociale et culturelle de l'homme.*" GAR., p. 33. Italics are ours.

174. "Apostolos, quemdam Prophetas, imo et Sanctos omnes tum veteris tum novi testamenti, fuisse *Moslemos* [...], Mahumetani constanter tenent cum Alcorano. Hoc autem nomen Moslemus, proprie significat, *tradens*, quasi se totum tradat Deo." MAR. II, p. 238. — "Musulmano *(mùslim*, cioè arrendentesi senza restrizione ai voleri divini) e non soltanto Maometto e chi lo segue, ma anche ogni persona pia delle età passate o della presente che, nella forma cristiana o nella giudaica, abbia professato con sincerità, ardore e sottomissione profonda il culto del Dio vero ed unico." NALLINO C.A., *Nel tredicesimo centenario della morte di Maometto*, in *Gerarchia*, XII (1932), p. 501. in *Raccolta*, II, p. 68.

Too bad that BAUSANI did not give this instance the emphasis it deserves. A certain scruple holds him from translating *mùslim* and *muslimìn* into Moslem and *Moslems*, placing them perhaps between quotation marks, instead of resorting to circumlocutions like these: "eravamo prima tutti *dati a Dio*" (we were before all given to God) (28, 53); "a lui *noi tutti ci diamo*" (to Him, *we all give ourselves*) (29, 46); "credono nei nostri segni e *sono a Noi dedicati*" (they believe in Our signs and *are to Us dedicated*) (30, 53); "in verità tutti *i dati e le date a Dio*" (truly, *all women and men given to God*) (33, 35). And we bring this up only because we are, as he is, concerned about keeping the "original and Koranic spirit of the word." BAUS., p. 508.

175. The word *mùslim* seems to add to the word *mù'min* (faithful) the idea of a live, practical and operative faith. The *mùslim* not only adheres interiorly to Allah, as does the *mù'min*, but also subdues himself to Him exteriorly by observing the commandments transmitted by legitimate messengers, mainly Mohammad.

(2, 143), theocratic and opposed to the Jews and Christians [nasàra].

Moslem (41, 33), rather the first of all Moslems (6, 163), was Mohammad himself.[176] And he boasts of it. He is obviously first not for chronological order but for the importance of the task he was to perform: to be *"the Apostle sent by Allah with guidance and true religion, so that he may exalt it above any other religion"* (48, 28). Evidence of this successful performance are his psychological dispositions: he surrendered to Allah and complied with His command (10, 72; 27, 91); he believed in what had been revealed to him by the Lord (2, 185; 43, 43); he mouthed emphatically the path of Islam (6, 126); he fought to establish it and bring it to triumph.[177]

Chronologically, however, that is by order of successive generations, many more people have gone before Mohammad in practicing Allah's religion — Islam.

To prove that, the Koran furnishes us with such an abundance of important data that it makes the existence of *Islam ante litteram* an outstanding and irrefutable truth.

From the Koranic research results the fact that Noah, a believer in Allah and His worshipper (37, 81), wished himself no reward for his apostolate other than

---

176. "I am bidden to be the first [al-àwwal] of those who shall be Moslems [muslimìn] " (39, 12). BAUSANI translates: "mi è stato ordinato d'essere dei Dati a Dio il primo" (I was ordered to be, of those Given to God, the first) (39, 12). And in Sura. 6, 163: "e io sono il primo di quei che si son dati tutti a Lui" (And I am the first of those who gave themselves all to Him). Cf. 40, 66.

177. "Prophet, make war [jàhid] on the unfaithful [al-kafirìn] and the hypocrites [al-munafiqìn] and deal rigorously with them" (9, 73). Cf. 8, 75; 29, 29; 31, 15; 66, 9.

to be counted among the *muslimìn* (10, 72). —
Abraham, another among Allah's faithful adorers (37,
111), pleaded with God from the heart to make him a
mùslim, and to make his descendants a nation that will
submit to Him *[ùmmat mùslimat]* .[178] Because he re-
nounced the idols and embraced the true faith, Islam
(2, 131), and inculcated it in his descendants, he
became a true *mùslim* (3, 67), rather the father of all
muslimìn (22, 78). — Ismael, messenger and prophet
(19, 54; 4, 162), he also of the upright men (21,
85-86), shared with his father, Abraham, the prayer for
Islam's prosperity (2, 127-128). — Jacob never grew
tired of enjoining his children never to depart this life
except as men who surrendered to Allah (2, 132); and
while on his death-bed, he rejoiced hearing his sons
declare themselves unanimously *muslimìn* (2, 133). —
The chaste Joseph, Jacob's son, foreseeing and almost
anticipating Mohammad's exhortation (3, 102), sup-
plicated Allah to list him among the good and let him
die as a *mùslim* (12, 101). — Moses, apostle and
prophet (19, 51), messenger of the Lord of the universe
(43, 46), he also of the righteous and believing servants
(37, 122), was together with his brother Aaron guided
to the right path of Islam (37, 118). He professed
himself a *mùslim* and, as long as he lived, never
stopped stimulating his followers to keep up with him
in faith and trust in Allah, so that they may one day
unite in the one community of *muslimìn* (10, 84). —
Solomon declared to the Queen of Sheba that he was
given true knowledge the day he became a *mùslim*
(27, 42); and upon his example the Queen had surrendered to Allah as a *Moslem* (27, 44). — Jesus
himself, a noble, one of the closest to Allah and one of
the righteous (3, 46), had decidedly taken the right

---

178. "Lord, make us both Moslems; and make of our descendants a Moslem
nation *[ùmmat mùslimat]* " (2, 128). Prayer made by Abraham and Ismael
together.

path of the *muslimìn* (3, 51; 19, 36). The reason?
Because he acknowledged Allah as his Lord and God
(3, 51; 19, 36) by declaring himself expressly a slave,
not a son (19, 30). He foretold the coming of Mohammad, the Prophet of Islam (61, 6). He enjoined stead-
fastness in prayer[179] and almsgiving (19, 31), and
deliberately took the right path of the *muslimìn* (3,
51; 19, 36). — Likewise did his Apostles, the
"hawàriyùn." [180] Induced by the Master to stand and
vie for Allah, they responded proudly to the shame and
confusion of the arrogant unbelievers: "We are the
helpers of Allah. We believe in Him. And you yourself
bear witness that we are Moslems *[muslimùn]* " (3, 52;
5, 111).

These all were *muslimùn*, because Allah had bestowed on
them a favor (2, 122; 43, 13): He had introduced them to the
right path of the true religion, Islam.

According to these Koranic testimonies we have to conclude
that long before the properly called Moslems — i.e. before
Mohammad, Khadija, Abu Baker and the early adherents to the
Prophet's preaching,[181] there was a long and steady crowd of
muslimìn, whose most prominent exponents were Abraham and
his children, Moses and his brother Aaron, Jesus and his twelve
Apostles.

---

179. As Mohammad will later do. Cf. 2, 43; 5, 58; 22, 78; 24, 37; 27, 3.

180. "Believers, be Allah's helpers *[ansàr]*. When Jesus, the son of Mary,
said to his Apostles *[hawàriyun]*: 'Who will come with me to the help of Allah?'
they replied: 'We are the helpers of Allah!' " (61, 14).

181. For Abraham, cf. 2, 130; for Moses, 2, 53; for Jesus, 2, 87.

2. Second Premise: *The Rehabilitation of the Woman.*

Mohammad closed his days with a pain sharply aching in his heart. On Monday, June 8, 632, in the arms of his favorite Aisha, he died[182] a victim of a frustrated wish forever unsatisfied — the wish of leaving behind a son of his own to inherit and succeed him. Though usually able to contain his tears even in the face of cruel tragedies,[183] Mohammad failed to be strong on this one occasion which was the "most crushing misfortune of his earthly life": *the death of his sixteen-month-old child, Ibrahim.* After long years of anxious waiting,[184] the baby was born to him from a relation with a Coptic slave-girl, Maryam, sent to him in 629 by Maqàwkas, the governor of Egypt.

Thus bereaved, Mohammad had but one choice left to make. As a father in the flesh, he had to converge all his fatherly

---

182. "Il lunedi 8 giugno 632: unica data concernente la sua vita, che possa ritenersi sicura fino al mese e al giorno." NALLINO C. A., *Nel tredicesimo centenario della morte di Maometto,* in *Gerarchia,* XII, 6 (1932), p. 499. — GAUD. invece: "mais d'autres donnent la date du 2 rabî I" (p. 205).

183. The year 619-20 was called year of great sorrows, in which the Prophet's very dear wife, Khadija, the first of the faithful, died; and Abu Taleb, Mohammad's paternal uncle, who had tutored him since his sixth year of age, bereaved then of both father and mother. "Il convient, sans doute, de considérer comme un effet de sa maîtrise et de sa patience le fait que le Prophète ne pleurait pas; dans les grandes émotions, il se prenait la barbe." GAUD., p. 214.

184. Gaudefroy-Demombynes makes allusion to a "mystère familial" surrounding Mohammad (p. 90). To him, in fact, was addressed the insulting predicative àbtar, bereaved of a male off-spring. The tradition however has called the Prophet *Abu 'l Kàsim,* "par un enfant né de Khadija et mort en bas âge" (GAUD., p. 222). — For Ibrahim, deceased at the sixteenth month of age, Jan. 17, 632, Mohammad shed bitter tears (GAUD., 232). That day the sun was eclipsed, "et certains voulurent y voir un signe. Mais Mahomet qui se savait et ne se voulait qu'un homme, eut la noblesse de déclarer que 'les astres ne se voilent pour la mort d'aucune créature'. " DERM., p. 44.

affection particularly on Fatima — a woman.[185] And as a father of a spiritual family, i.e. as a politico-religious organizer of the new theocratic community, he at once conceived a compelling concern for all women, mainly those who have accepted his call and become his spiritual daughters. That is all the more true when one takes into account the new relationship binding the young Moslem community. It is not the ancestral link of tribe and race any more, but the "common religious faith," a revolutionary principle unheard of in Arabia till then.[186]

Conclusion: To this eager concern and that tactical congeniality we've mentioned in the last two premises, the sympathetic image of Mary, the mother of Jesus, cannot be an exception. Nor should it! Or else vain would be all the exceptional things the Arabian Prophet had done for her, that he did not do for any other woman. Vain his delight to treat of her at length and sing her praises and virtues so loudly throughout the Koran. Vain his reserving for her a special Sura and calling her alone by a proper name. Vain extolling her above all the women of the universe. Behind these rare tributes and testimonials, there was a special intent.

If in his successful strategy to incorporate into Islam the most prominent Jewish and Christian personages of the past Mohammad had a purpose, he most certainly also had one for Mary: He intended *to mark*[187] *her personality indelibly with the seal of Islam*. And if by affiliating the female believers into his

---

185. A Shiite tradition maintains that Fatima has realized in her person the prescript of Sura 33, 33. "Elle est devenue l'une des 'reines des femmes de paradis, au-dessous de Marie,' mère de Jésus [...]. Il est plus vraisemblable que son culte s'est développé parallèlement avec celui de la Vierge Marie dans la dévotion catholique et pour les mêmes raisons." GAUD., 235-36.

186. NAL. I, p. 603.

187. As a title of private property and exclusive ownership, people used the brand *[wàsm]* and with it they marked their livestock. Hence the *màwsim*, the seasonal fairs and periodic religious celebrations.

own "household" he meant to endow the fair sex with so tender a thoughtfulness as to rank them with his own family in dignity and honor, and make them co-sharers of his particular love and the veneration by all his followers, he certainly more so meant it for Mary: *to propose her as a living model to imitate by all believers, particularly by the Moslem woman.*

In this twin intent, we have to admit, Mohammad was as brilliant as successful.

A. Mary, the "M o s l e m"

We have to grant that nowhere does the Koran apply to Mary the adjective *"mùslimat"* as, by contrast, we have seen it do with regard to biblical figures, not excluding Jesus himself.

We notice however an implicit but convincing reference to that in the two concepts of *righteousness* and *devotion* the Koran explicitly attributes to Mary. Once it calls her *siddìqat*, an uprightly person; and another time it lists her among the qànitìn, the God-devout people. "The Messiah, the son of Mary, was no more than an apostle, other apostles before him having all passed away. His mother was a saintly woman *[siddìqat]"* (5, 75). "Mary, Imran's daughter, who preserved her chastity so We breathed into her womb of Our spirit; who believed in the words of her Lord and in His Scriptures and was one of the devout *[min al-qanitìn]"* (66, 12).

The term *siddìq* surfaces eight times in five different Suras in the Koran. Four times it is used as a substantive with a collective sense;[188] and four other times as an epithet for single individuals like Abraham (19, 41), Idris [Enoch] (19, 56), Joseph the chaste (12, 46), and Mary (5, 75).

The term qànit instead occurs some ten times with the meaning always identical and invariable: a person subdued and devout to God. Used most often collectively,[189] it was taken as an individual attribute only once, applied to Abraham and describing him as "a Nation devout to God" (16, 120).

Now, according to the rigorous Koranic teaching, the true righteousness and the genuine devotion imply necessarily the profession of that historic form of faith which renders to Allah the due worship without departing from the teaching of his messengers. Siddiqùn are precisely those who believe in God and his envoys: "Those that believe in Allah and His apostles [rusùli-hi] are the righteous [siddiqùn] who shall testify in their Lord's presence. They shall have their guerdon and their light" (57, 19).

As we have seen, the Koran acknowledges no religion acceptable to God other than Islam.[190] Islam alone embodies the

---

188. "He that obeys Allah and the Apostle shall dwell with the prophets and saints [siddiqìn], martyrs and righteous men [salihìn] whom Allah has favored" (4, 69). Cf. 57, 18-19.

189. "The Moslems, men and women; the faithful, men and women; the devout, men and women [qànitin wa qànitat]; the sincere, men and women" (33, 35). Cf. 2, 116; 3, 17; 66, 5. — The term qànit is one of the seven hundred words used by the Koran in a sense other than the original; it means basically: subdued, obedient. Cf. HAD. III, p. 135.

190. "This day I have perfected your religion for you and completed my favor to you. For you I have chosen Islam to be your faith [raditu làkum al Islàma dìnan]" (5, 3). — "He that chooses a religion other than Islam, it will not be accepted from him and in the world to come he will be one of the lost" (3, 85). — "You will please neither the Christians nor the Jews unless you follow their faith. Say: 'The guidance of Allah is the only guidance [hùda]'" (2, 120).

true and solid religion[191] that Allah himself imposes[192] and is pleased with.[193] This brings us to a logical conclusion: that *the faith in Allah* and *the profession of Islam* are two indispensable and essential components of the true *righteousness* and sincere *devotion.*

Furthermore, an evenly important inference flows from the preceding conclusion and lets us read Mohammad's mind with regard to Mary. His proclaiming her *siddìqat* (righteous) and counting her among the *qanitìn* (the devout) was unquestionably equal to asserting, implicitly but unequivocally, her incorporation to Islam "*ante litteram,*" and her membership in the community of "*muslimìn*" "*ante litteram.*"

In a few words: Was Mary *siddìqat?* And one of the *qanitìn?* Consequently she was "*mùslimat,*" and one of the "*muslimìn*" ante litteram.

And she was so on a par with Abraham, the *siddìq* (19, 41), the *qànit* (16, 120), and the father of *muslimìn* (22, 78).

---

191. "If Allah wills to guide a man, He opens his bosom to Islam" (6, 125). — The Koran was sent down to teach the true religion, the one intended by Allah (43, 78); the one revealed and confirmed by the previous Books (2, 101; 5, 51; 37, 37); the one which leads to the right path (46, 30). The religion of Islam has already been clearly recommended by Abraham and Jacob to their children: "*You shall not die except as Moslems*" (2, 132).

192. "Signs [*ayàt*] of the Wise Book [*kitàb*] " (10, 1). Cf. 3, 7; 4, 140; 12, 1; 13, 1; 15, 1. — "And this Book We revealed is blessed. Observe it" (6, 155).

193. "And whoever does have a better religion than the Moslem [*àhsanu dìnan mìn al-mùslim*], than he who surrendered [*àslama*] his face to Allah, who does right, and follows the faith [*mìllat*] of Abraham?" (4, 125). — In the Koranic language, *mìllat* (faith) and *ùmmat* (nation) involve always some religious meaning: "comunità religiosa, oggetto di un piano divino, dimenticando le moderne implicazioni di 'razza' e di 'popolo'." BAUS., p. 509.

B.   Mary, the "Model"

The Prophet of Mecca takes a further, more audacious step. He proposes Mary, the mother of Jesus, as an accomplished model to the Moslem woman who, through her faith in Allah and loyalty to His Apostle, has also become a *righteous* and *devout* person. Thus in fact the Koran has it: "To the believers Allah has set an example [. . .] in Mary, Imran's daughter" (66, 10-12).

"*To the believers*," i.e. those who sincerely and from the heart accepted the Koranic Message as opposed to those who refused to believe *[kafirùn]*, or those who said they believed with no internal adhesion *[munafiqùn,* hypocrites]. To those believers he proposes Mary as an example, *màthal.*

In a footnote to the verse concluding the romantic affair of Aisha[194] and reading: "We have sent you down revelations showing you the right path. We gave you an example *[màthal]* in the account of those who have gone before you, and an admonition to the God-fearing" (24, 34), Bonelli pretends that *màthal* here would coincide with the story of Joseph, the chaste (Sura 12), and with the calumny of which Mary was accused by her own people, the Jews (19, 27-29). "Both, like Aisha, were accused of incontinence; but their innocence, unlike hers, was proved true."[195]

---

194. Cf. the revelation concerning Aisha's affair, 24, 23. — In one of the military expeditions of the Prophet, his young wife, Aisha, was left behind after the caravan's departure. A young camel driver found her, wandering all alone by herself. When the night was over, the young cameleer took her to Mohammad. The incident brought against her not a few suspicions and criticisms. Cf. GAUD. (*L'affaire de Aicha*), p. 149-151; SH., p. 90-96; and WATT MONTGOMERY, *A'isha*, in EI, t. I (n. ed.), p. 317-318.

195. BON., p. 324, in note.

The fact that Mary was proved innocent to the scorn of her accusers is therefore in Bonelli's mind an "example" and an "admonition" by God, deterring his devout and fearing ones from suspicious and rash judgments. Mary's *màthal* consequently is to be strictly tied up with Aisha's love affair.

All pros and cons considered, Bonelli's interpretation seems to me quite short of the mark. It does not reap all the fertility of the Text, nor does it square with its historic context.

As for the Text, the structure of both Sura 19 in which Mary is proclaimed an *àyat*, sign, and Sura 66 in which she is proposed as a *màthal*, example, can ill combine with a reference to private individuals — say, the "harem" of the Prophet or his relationship with his wives. By such an interpretation, Mary's role as a sign and an example would be unreasonably restricted. Mary would then directly and almost exclusively be for the advantage of the Prophet's young wife, Aisha, i.e. *to salvage her lost honor and redeem her credibility in the eyes of the believers.*

Such a narrow prospect does not fit in with the majestic ring, style and setting of Sura 21, where Mary is projected as the last link in the series of the protagonists of salvation, the great prophets and messengers of God.[196] She appears as an *àyat* not for the benefit of one single person, although belonging to the "household," but of the whole universe: *"li-'l alamìn"* (21, 91). Likewise, in Sura 66, Mary is proposed as a *màthal* within a contour of broader dimensions. She is an *example* to imitate, not

---

196. Sura 21, *The Prophets*, is one of the very few whose title corresponds to its content. Along with Mohammad, scorned and persecuted, it offers the list of Allah's greatest messengers: Moses and Aaron (v. 78); Abraham (v. 51); Lot (v. 71); Isaac, Jacob (v. 72); Noah (v. 76); David (v. 78); Solomon (v. 79); Job (v. 83); Ismael, Idris, Dhu-l-Kifl (v. 85); Jonah (v. 87); Zachariah (v. 89); Yahia (v. 90). The quotation ends up with the remembrance of Christ and his mother, introducing, as a conclusion, the very beautiful verse: *"And remember the woman who kept her chastity, so in her We breathed of Our spirit, and made her and her son a sign [àyat] for the whole universe [li-l-alamìn]"* (v. 91).

only by a restricted category of people, but by everyone and all believers, men and women, with no limitations: "to those that believe" (66, 1).

Thus literally.

Historically also, it is certain that Aisha's love affair, which occurred during the Medinian period, is of later date than Sura 19, which is unquestionably *Meccan*. In this Sura the "monstrous falsehood" against Mary is mentioned (19, 27-28). Aisha's affair is subsequent to the other two Suras — 21 and 23, both Meccan — which describe Mary as *àyat*. Chronologically, it also comes after Sura 66 in which Mary is called *màthal*. This Sura, in fact, belongs to the first Medinian epoch,[197] while the Prophet's wife's affair dates back to the second — probably to the early days of 628.

With these positive data in hand, we therefore have to state that the three Marian Suras mentioned above cannot refer to Aisha's romantic affair. Consequently, far from Bonelli's restricted outlook, the twin terms [àyat] and [màthal] postulate general, extensive and universal dimensions for their meaning.

To stimulate man's reflection (59, 21) and invite him to call to mind some salutary truths (14, 25), God often loves to act as an artful pedagogue. He likes to talk to man by examples (2, 26), frequently explaining them to his slow mind (25, 33).

It has been noted that the word *màthal* — example, similitude, type — "is always being used in the Koran with the attribution of some similitude."[198] As a general rule that is true.

---

197. Cf. HAD. II, p. 403. — Haddad is rather skeptical about the young wife's innocence. Cf. *ibid.*, in note.

198. BAUS., 579. — Authors are not equally successful in determining the accurate meaning of *màthal*. BAUS. (p. 433) translates it with "*esempio*" (example); — KAS. (p. 443), PES. (p. 391), MONT. (II, p. 313), BL. (IV, p. 605), MAS. (p. 705) vert it into "*exemple*" (example). — ULL. (p. 495), into *Beispiel* (example). — HEN. (p. 539), into *Gleichnis* (image, comparison). — SAV.

The Koran uses *màthal* in more than eighty instances. And a close and accurate look at each instance indicates that the word takes on a particular nuance in each new instance. It means an example-*paragon*, or example-*similitude*, or example-*parable*, or example-*admonition*, or example-*model*.

Example-*paragon* is when two termini (persons or things) are confronted with each other for some comparative similitude.

Thus the example *[màthal]* of Jesus in the sight of Allah is compared *[ka-màthal]* to the example of Adam. God created Jesus of dust and then said to him: " 'Be,' and he was" (3, 59). — The large, dark eyes of the woman in paradise are compared *[ka-màthal]* to hidden pearls (56, 23). — Those to whom the burden of the Torah was entrusted and yet refused to bear it are compared *[màthal]* to the donkey laden with books (62, 5). — Those who took themselves allies besides Allah are compared *[màthal]* to the spider building a home. Surely her cobweb is the frailest of all dwellings (29, 41). — Those, that denied their Lord,[199] and their works are compared *[màthal]* to ashes the wind scatters on a stormy day (14, 18).

(p. 529): "Il propose à leur admiration Marie, fille d'Imran." — BOUB. (p. 1119), with regard to Noah and Lot's wives, writes: "Dieu cite comme exemple;" with regard to Faraoh's wife: "Dieu propose aux croyants, comme exemple;" with regard to Mary: "[Il leur propose aussi un *exemple*, Marie"]. — Far more accurate is, in my opinion, MARRACCI, who uses the term *exemplar*, (model), thus translating: "Et proposuit Deus in *exemplar* iis, qui crediderunt [...], Mariam, filiam Imran." MAR. II, p. 733.

199. "The *kafirùn* (unbelievers) may be compared *[màthal]* to a beast one talks to: all she hears is a sound and a cry. Deaf, dumb, blind, they understand nothing" (2, 171). "The *munafiqùn* (hypocrites) may be compared *[màthal]* to people who just kindled a fire; when everything around is lit, Allah puts it out leaving them in the darkness, nothing to see" (2, 17).

Example-*similitude* is when, without much development, one tries to clarify an assertion by another similar assertion for an easier and quicker understanding.

Thus he that gives his wealth for the cause of Allah is similar *[màthal]* to a grain of wheat which brings forth seven spikes, each bearing a hundred grains (2, 261). — He that spends his wealth for the sake of ostentation, not believing in Allah and the Last Day, is similar *[màthal]* to a rock covered with earth: a rainstorm hits it and leaves it hard and bare (2, 264). — A good word is similar *[màthal]* to a good tree with firm roots and branches spreading out in the sky. And an evil word is similar *[màthal]* to an evil tree torn out of the earth, with no roots to hold it steady (14, 24-26). — This worldly life is similar *[màthal]* to a summer shower[200] that germinated a growth and pleased the unbelievers. "Lush green at first, it soon turns yellow, then becomes a dry stubble" (57, 20). — Those who accompany the Prophet are similar *[màthal]* to the seed described in the Gospel: It puts forth its shoot and strengthens it so it rises stout and firm upon its stalk, delighting the sower (48, 29).

Example-*parable* is a prolonged allegorical narrative to illustrate a particular fact and make it more accessible to the understanding.

Such is the parable *[màthal]* of the owned slave and the free-born man, the helpless dumb one and the one who enjoins justice (16, 75-76). — The parable *[màthal]* of the man to whom Allah granted his signs

---

200. "This early life draws its similitude *[màthal]* from the rain We send down from heaven. It is absorbed by herbs and trees, and these, in turn, feed man and livestock" (10, 24).

(7, 175-177). — The parable *[màthal]* of the two messengers sent by Allah and strengthened by a third (36, 13-30). — The parable *[màthal]* of the false gods (22, 73).

Example-*admonition* is the quotation of a past event to unbelievers and those with a morbidity in the heart (14, 31), so they would learn a lesson for the future.

Such is the example *[màthal]* of Pharaoh and his army drowned in the Red Sea (43, 56). — The example *[màthal]* of Noah's wife and Lot's wife (66, 10). — The example *[màthal]* of the demons appointed to guard the "infernal fire" (74, 31).

Example-*model* is when the image or the behavioral way of life of an upright person is proposed to others as a pattern to inspire and stimulate them into a right living.

Such is the example *[màthal]* , even the supreme example *[al màthal 'ul à'la]* of God himself (16, 60; 30, 27). — Such is the example *[màthal]* of those who, before entering the paradise, give to the believers the pattern for righteous living and who suffered affliction and adversity (2, 214). — Such is the example *[màthal]* of Pharaoh's wife praised for her faith (66, 11).

And such for sure is the example *[màthal]* of Mary, Imran's daughter (66, 12).

In fact, in the Sura's paragraph relating to Mary, the word *màthal* is not taken only as a similitude, a parable, an admonition and more than a mere terminus of comparison. It is understood as an example-*ideal*, example-*type*, example-*model*. A live example that is pulsating, so rich with inner psychological feelings, so edifying by its exterior attitudes, so attractive by its charms that it stimulates in the seer the desire and the effort to pursue it, live it and assimilate it into his own self.

Needless to say that the above interpretation is far from being arbitrary or predetermined. The letter of the Text demands it, and so do the immediate and remote contexts of it.

While in fact *màthal* in the past verse relative to Noah and Lot's wives is taken for a "warning" or "admonition" calling for Allah's justice "severely punishing" (2, 211) and "severely tormenting" (2, 165), in our Marian Verse it bears a meaning altogether different; it means an example to follow, a model to imitate, an ideal to copy, by all who believed in God and had adhered to Him as Mary did.

Rather, the interpretation *example-model* here takes on ampler dimensions. The way the Koranic Text itself has it, Mohammad wants it projected through more magnifying lenses and upon a larger screen. Instead of narrowing it into one enunciation, he blows it into several remarkable perfections. He says in fact: **"Allah set an example [*màthal*] in Mary, Imran's daughter who preserved her chastity so We breathed in her womb of Our spirit; who put faith in the words of her Lord and His Scriptures and was one of the truly devout"** (66, 12).

Virgin, believer, devout. Very noble qualities of body and spirit that compel us to take the substantive *màthal*, not as a casual linguistic illustration, but as a brilliant model of an outstanding woman typically inviting her admirers to the pursuit of virginity, faith and devotion.

That is precisely the image that Mohammad had formed for himself of Mary since his early contacts with the Christians of Mecca. On the screen of his astonished mind, Mary was projected as a noble and dignifying model to imitate. That is how he envisioned her from the beginning. And that is how, in turn, he wanted her projected to the vision of the Arab woman, who was rehabilitated, or still yet to be rehabilitated, by Islam.

In the "actual Koranic reality," Mohammad's intent for Mary was tacitly present, never absent. He nurtured in his heart a wish: that all Moslem women believers look constantly to Mary for orientation and guidance, be inspired by her feelings and attitudes and imitate her virtues. In short, he bequeathed to them an explicit command: *"to see in Mary the suggestive example for the authentic and typical image of the Moslem female."*

One is indeed astonished at the purity of strokes with which the Arabic Prophet was pleased to draw the charming picture of Mary. The religious and moral profile he writes of her is unique in generosity and details. Without stint, he adorns her with the most exquisite religious dispositions: faith in God (66, 12); boundless trust in the divine providence (3, 37); instinctive recourse to Allah, the Merciful (19, 18); surrender to the divine will (3, 47; 19, 21); devotion (66, 12); saintliness (5, 75); virginal modesty (21, 91); piety and recollection (19, 17); silence (19, 26); prayer (3, 43); fasting (19, 26).

Of the above dispositions I shall willingly dwell on three which, in my opinion, give us a more accurate and extensive sketch of the genuine moral standard of the Moslem woman as featured by the Koran — *faith, religiosity* and *self-restraint.*

a. *Model of Faith*

First of all, Mary realizes in her own life the fundamental and indispensable requisite to become a *Moslem* and to be part of Islam: the *faith.*[201]

---

201. "Si Israël est enraciné dans l'espérance et la chrétienté vouée à la

To put trust in God, to believe in Him, to accept His salvific message delivered by special Apostles sent by Him: that is the psychological attitude the Koran demands of the Moslem before all else. Incredulity, an abominable crime *[rijs]* by unbelievers *[kafirìn]* and hypocrites *[munafiqìn]*, makes one an enemy of Allah (2, 98), an object of curse by Allah (2, 88), a cause for scorn by His angels (2, 101), and worthy of eternal fire.[202] Incredulity, unbelief, is a sin not to be forgiven by Allah (47, 34). No intercession shall be profitable to it (30, 13). It leads infallibly to hell (2, 7).

As for him who is considered a *siddìq* and a *qànit* — upright, obedient to God and devout — faith is an attitude-base. Without it, the whole structure of righteousness and devotion in a Moslem's life will fall to the ground.

Such condition attained its fullest in Mary. The Koran admits to no doubt in this regard: "Mary put her trust in the words of her Lord and believed in His Scriptures" (66, 12).

"She put her trust...believed!" Instead of the classical term *àmana* [to assent with the mind], Mohammad uses here the extensive *sàddaqa* [to assent by mind and heart, to trust] to insinuate that Mary's interior assent was psychologically total. Mary's assent was not shaky and hesitant, but it involved her whole being. Nor was it so fragile and tenuous as to be identified

---

charité, l'Islam est centré sur la foi." MASSIGNON L., *Les Trois prières d'Abraham* (La prière sur Ismael, Tours, 1935), p. 41. — "La foi que prêchait Mohammad est sèche et dominatrice comme le sable du désert. *Il n'en a pas exigé sur la terre de plus explicite.* Il n'en ait aucune, en outre, qui condense au même point en elle religion, conception du monde et droit." ESS., p. 74. The italic is ours. — For the elements, conditions, content, and value of the faith in Islam, cf. GARDET L., *Imàn*, in EI, t. III (n. ed.) p. 1199-1203. GAR.-AN., p. 347-349.

202. "But those that disbelieve and give the lie to Our signs shall be the heirs of Hellfire where they shall burn forever. Evil shall be their fate" (64, 10). Cf. 3, 12; 24, 39; 58, 4; 67, 6.

with the faith of a "fool" (2, 13), or an unbeliever.[203] Mary's faith was a mature adult's faith. It prompted her being completely, mind and heart, to cling firmly to God's veracity and believe the truths He revealed.

She believed in the "words of her Lord." These were delivered to her by the angel, Gabriel, on the annunciation day. And she received them with a total surrender and submission — so total indeed that no faith could be found superior to hers in the most believing Moslem woman. Not so was the attitude of Abraham's wife (51, 29), or even of Zachariah's (19, 8). By contrast with Mary in analogous circumstances, these two allowed themselves to bring forward their doubts and mental reservations. Abraham's wife, for instance, upon hearing that she was going to have a son, "came out crying and beating her face and saying, 'I'm but an old, barren woman' " (51, 29).

Mary's question, "How shall I bear a child," (19, 20), expressed maturity of judgment and prudence rather than doubt and hesitation. Her motherhood as announced by the divine envoy was to be actuated in an altogether unusual way. Unlike Mary, Sara was to follow in hers the normal course of Nature's laws.[204]

Once her fears and apprehensions were cleared to the satisfaction of what her own psychological and physiological terms demanded, Mary gave her consent with the simplicity of a child: She resigned to Allah Almighty; and trusted Him and let Him do in her His will. The proof of that is in the fact that, unlike Zachariah, she does not incur in the punishment inflicted

---

203. Not few are the Koranic verses in which the opposition is so clear between faith *[imàn]* and infidelity *[kùfr]*, and between believers *[mu'minùn]* and infidel or unfaithful *[kafirùn]* as well. Cf. 2, 91; 48, 13; 109, 1-6. — Cf. W. BJORKMANN, *Kafir*, in EI, II, p. 658-660.

204. "Elle ne posa cette question que parce qu'elle reçut de l'ordre d'Allah ce qui était absolument inhabituel aux créatures, tandisque, en ce qui concerne Sara, le cas n'était nullement étrange." TIRMIDHI (ap. HAY., p. 74).

upon him who dared not to believe: "For three days and three nights you shall be bereft of speech" (19, 10).

Finally, Mary's faith as described by the Koran takes on all the characteristics of an authentic *Moslem* faith, which are: total surrender to Allah's sovereign might and the unconditional gift of self, i.e. in body and soul, for the realization of His divine designs. Nothing keeps Mary from a quick and ready answer to God's advances. She believes what humanly speaking is impossible because she is convinced that Allah can do what He wants (19, 9, 21), and "He has power over all things" (64, 1). She entertains no doubt that Allah can cause a true and physical maternity to blossom and come to maturity without the usual sexual relations, without any male's previous contributions:[205] "The angel said to her, 'Thus it shall be. For the Lord has said: "That is no difficult thing for Me" ' " (19, 21a). The way it sounds, this reassurance by Gabriel is but a confirmation of Mary's intimate conviction.

In terms of faith, Mary competes with Abraham himself, the classical model of faith.[206] He believed in Allah Almighty and, with no hesitation of sorts, complied with His command; he agreed to sacrifice his only son (37, 102-109), never forgetting that according to God's promise he would be the father of many generations.

---

205. Cf. the dialogue that Moslem authors believe has taken place between Mary and Joseph when this latter "s'aperçut de la grossesse de Marie." A delicate dialogue, emphasizing Allah's almightiness. Is reported by TABARI, IBN ATHIR, THA'LABI, and KISA'I (ap. HAY., p. 71-72). — Cf. JAL. I, p. 28-29.

206. "You have a good example [usùwat hàsanat] in Abraham" (60, 4). Cf. 60, 6. — "Abraham est le premier parmi les personnages bibliques à jouir d'une présentation qui tende non plus à la seule menace, mais à l'édification et à l'instruction." MOUB. I, p. 25. Italics are ours. — Cf. PARET R., Ibrahim, in EI, t. III (n. ed.), p. 1004-1006.

b. Model of Religiosity

Like Jesus, Mary also was chosen by Allah to be the recipient of a particular *ni'mat*, grace or choice favor, that God bestows on His favorites to stimulate their gratitude and remind them of His generosity. Addressing Himself to Christ, Allah thus in fact says: "**Jesus, son of Mary, remember the favor** [ni'mat] **I have bestowed on you and on your mother**" (5, 110).

An analogous call to keep in mind, the bestowal of God's favor, also occurs in other Suras. It is addressed to men in general, so they would bear in mind Allah's goodness toward them by being their creator and provider (35, 3); to the children of Israel in particular, so they remember that they have been chosen among all peoples of the earth (2, 47, 122), freed from the slavery of Egypt (14, 6), and that they have received in the Koran a confirmation to their own Scriptures (2, 40); and finally to the Prophet's followers, the Moslem believers, so they would remember Allah's Covenant (5, 7) and His help against those who sought to harm them (5, 11).

While throughout the Koran such call is always and exclusively used collectively, here, in the case of Jesus and Mary, is the only instance where it is used individually. That spotlights better how much God is pleased with them both who, in His sight, are so close to Him, so favored, that He prefers them above all others.

This gentle call or reminder, fixed as it is in one of the chronologically last Suras, if not indeed *the* ultimate,[207] brings to us, as though in a capsule, Mohammad's latest thought on two privileged Koranic figures — Jesus and Mary.

---

207. It is still under controversy whether Sura Five, *The Table*, or Sura Nine, *Repentance*, ought to be considered as the very last in the line of the Koranic revelations.

Both constitute, according to him, the *terminus ad quem* of a special grace, *ni'mat:* God's particular benevolence and predilection.

Never has this last testimonial of esteem by Mohammad suffered alteration as to quality, or gone down in degree, despite the tragic ups and downs of his prophetic career. It was so much a part of his theological thinking and religious belief. Right up to the last moment of his life, his creed was that Jesus and Mary were bound together and inseparably by Allah's preventive love.

Mary surely tasted the flavor of this gratuitous love by Allah, transmitted to her in explicit terms by the angel (3, 42). Sensitive as she was to God's voice, she responded to it with all the momentum of her soul. She proved herself to be always and everywhere *religious*, always and everywhere *obedient* and *devout to God*. She consciously made true what has previously been pledged by her mother, without her knowing it: to live as a consecrated soul *[muhàrra-rat]* totally intent on Allah's service (3, 35).

An index of faith and its normal growth is *religiosity*. It is brought into effect, according to the Koran, by the practice of the tàqwa: the fear of God, the reverence of God, the piety toward God.

The incitement to tàqwa is frequent in the Koran.[208] And the categorical imperative "Ìttaqu 'llàh," "fear ye God," ap-

---

208. "Righteousness *[al-bìrr]* does not consist in entering your homes from the back. The righteous man is he who fears *[ittaqa]* Allah. Enter your homes by their doors and fear Allah *[ittaqu 'llàh]*, so that you may prosper" (2, 189). Cf. 2, 1, 2, 212; 3, 172, 198; 5, 93; 7, 96; 12, 109; 16, 128; 39, 20. — Regarding the value of *muttaqùn*, remarks MARRACCI: "Est una ex illis dictionibus quae saepe occurrunt in Alcorano, et significat *timentes*, vel *caventes*, saepe autem subauditur vel Deum, vel Gehennam, vel peccatum, praesertim idololatriae, vel hiusmodi. Latine dicemus *Piis*." MAR. II, p. 11.*

pears there as the "leitmotiv"[209] in the exhortation by Allah's messengers since the second epoch of the Meccan period.[210] It becomes impellent later, in Sura 5, *The Table*, where it occurs no less than twelve times.[211]

The command to fear Allah is addressed to all men in general (4, 1); and in particular, to Christ's Apostles (5, 112) and Mohammad's followers.

We are allowed to think, not without cause, that such an imperative had splendidly been actuated in Mary's life long before it had in Mohammad's. In a constantly pious and reverential attitude, Mary feared Allah at every moment of her life. Through both her sorrowful and joyous events she walked confidently in the light of the Lord.

One is indeed tempted to believe that Mohammad could not find a better way to project Mary to mankind than by casting her image through this divine perspective.

Before she is born, her parents vow her to God so that, free *[muhàrra-rat]* from whatever earthly impediments, she might devote herself totally to His service. Soon after birth, Allah favors her with His special assistance. An infant, a child, an adolescent,

---

(*). The entry into the homes through their back, not the front, doors, was an old Arab custom after returning from pilgrimage. Superstitiously, it was considered a good deed. (Fares)

209. "Have fear of Allah *[ittaqu 'llàh]*, and know that Allah is with those who fear Him *[al muttaqìn]*" (2, 194). — *Ittaqu 'llàh*: 2, 196, 203, 223, 231, 233, 278, 282; 3, 50, 102, 123, 130, 131, 200; 4, 1, 131; 49, 1, 10, 12; 57, 28; 58, 9; 59, 7, 18; 60, 11; 64, 16; 65, 1, 10; 71, 3. — *Ittaqu ràbbakum*: 39, 10, 16, 20, 73; 43, 63.

210. Through Lot: 11, 78; 15, 69. — Through Noah: 26, 108, 110, 163. — Through Hud: 26, 126, 131, 132. — Through Salih: 26, 144, 150. — Through Shu'ayb: 26, 179, 184.

211. "Help one another in the practice of good deeds *[al-bìrr]* and piety *[tàqwa]*; and do not help one another in what is wicked and sinful. Have fear of Allah *[ittaqu 'llàh]*, for He is severe when punishing" (5, 2). — In same Sura 5, *The Table*: v. 4, 7, 8, 11, 35, 57, 88, 96, 100, 108, 112.

she spends the years of her prime age in the vicinity of God, all anxious to do His will.

The Koranic stimulus to learn how to put oneself in God's presence and live in His remembrance (33, 41) must have been put literally into practice by Mary, motivated by her religious instincts before she could have been by her faith and piety. The recommendation "to remember Allah as one remembers his own parents — and with deeper reverence still" (2, 200), "and to praise Him morning and evening" (33, 41; 76, 25), must have been for Mary a program of life, even her main daily occupation. Tirmidhi writes beautifully in this regard: "Mary was asked to live in the state of an interior prayer, or 'prayer of recollection,' during which her heart should have been turned totally to God so He would fill it with love; and her soul completely overshadowed by Him so He would cover it and prevent its holy desires from leaking out and dissipating. Mary was ordered to live 'in a state of mental prayer and quietude,' seeking constantly the glory of Allah and making every effort to persevere in it."[212]

The remembrance [dhìkr] of God,[213] the remembrance [dhìkr] of the Lord,[214] the remembrance [dhìkr] of the Merciful[215] never abandoned her for one moment. All the more that, unlike other mortals, there was nothing inside or outside her that could divert her mind and heart from this continuous memory of God: not the feverish greed for earthly goods (24, 37), not the familial hardships and problems (63, 9), nor the snares of Satan (58, 19). From the very first moments of her human existence,

---

212. TIRMIDHI, Nawadir, 415 (ap. HAY., p. 75-76).

213. "I am Allah. There is no god but Me. Serve Me, and in the remembrance of Me [li dhìkri] offer your prayers" (20, 14). — "Remember Allah as you would remember your fathers, and more often still" (2, 200). Cf. 2, 152, 203, 239; 5, 91; 13, 28; 29, 45; 33, 41; 39, 22; 57, 16; 62, 9; 72, 17; 73, 8; 76, 25.

214. Remembrance of ràbb: 21, 42; 38, 32; 72, 17.

215. Remembrance of ràhman: 21, 36; 43, 36.

Mary was well provided with God's particular assistance (3, 36b).

To Allah, this Munificent Giver of every good thing (62, 11), Mary owes the provision of her food (3, 37b), and with a grateful heart she extols His generosity (3, 37c). Whenever she faced a danger (19, 18) and during the inevitable anxieties of life (19, 23), she almost by instinct took refuge in the Lord. Confident in His loving care, she abandoned herself to His unconditional disposition (19, 20-21).

Prayer, the personal prayer sustained by *fasting*, was unquestionably Mary's most eloquent expression of religiosity.

Over and over again the Koran insists on prayer for two main purposes: to recognize Allah's sovereignty and to be a bond tying the believers to one another.[216] Moslems, wherever they may be, shall gather for public or social prayer *[salàt]* to be held every Friday,[217] normally inside the Mosques[218] — or houses of God (72, 18). Individual and private prayers also are to be recited regularly within the family (10, 87) morning and eve-

---

216. The *qìbla*, a geographic point toward which the Moslem turns when praying, is unquestionably the strongest and most efficient bond tying all Arabs spiritually to one another the world over. Up to February 624, the *qìbla* was the same as that of the Jews: Jerusalem. But since then, on the heels of a particular revelation to Mohammad, Mecca, and more exactly, the *Ka'ba*, became *The Holiest of Holies* (2, 144) and the "brand" of the New Nation that follows the "middlemost way" (2, 143). — On the construction of the Ka'ba cf. MOUB. I, p. 73-80; A. J. WENSINCK, *Ka'ba*, in EI, II, p. 622-630; and in margin, note 466. — On the Kibla cf. C. SCHOY, in EI, II, p. 1043, 1047; and WAT. II, p. 239, 243-244.

217. "When you are summoned to *Friday* prayers, hasten to the remembrance of Allah and cease your trading" (62, 9). Cf. TABB. *(La preghiera del venerdì)*, p. 153-158; NAD. *(Il venerdì, bilancia della settimana)*, (59-61).

218. "But stay at your prayers in the mosques *[masàjid]*" (2, 187). Cf. 2, 144; 9, 17; 22, 40. — The mosque, "luogo ordinato a una più commoda esecuzione della (preghiera,) specie quella in comune, non un luogo sacrale." BAUS., p. 547.

ning, and in the night-time too (11, 114). While fulfilling his prayer, the faithful Moslem should "stand up with all devotion before Allah" (2, 238) and observe certain exterior modalities and postures.[219]

As for fasting, *siyàm*, or *sàum*, the Koran holds it very beneficial to the *muslim* and prescribes its observance as an integral portion of prayer.[220]

Even in this particular field of prayer and fasting, Mary must show herself as a stimulating and encouraging model.

Mohammad wishes and hopes that Mary would attend her prayer with such inner fervor and outward devotion as to draw to her following the praying Moslem woman. He says, "O Mary, be obedient to your Lord. Prostrate, and adore, bending your knees with those who bend them" (3, 43).

This recommendation, so pathetic and concise, betrays the Prophet's wish to see Mary pray as a "Moslem woman," doesn't it? It contains the three successive, categorical and imperious feminine imperatives, *ùqnuti, ùsjudi, ìrkai*.

By the first, "*ùqnut-i*," — be devout, i.e. subdue yourself to God, surrender — he wants her to "*bend her mind to a worshipful assent*" — an interior attitude that pleases Allah and without which the act of adoration or worship of Him is nothing.

By the second, "*ùsjud-i*," — prostrate, i.e. fall on both knees and touch the floor with your forehead — and the third, "*ìrka-i*" — bend your knees — he wants her to externalize her inner devotion or surrender by two liturgical motions considered as typical characteristics of a true Moslem worshipper:[221] prostra-

---

219. Cf. 4, 103; 5, 6. — TABB., p. 65-100.

220. Cf. 2, 183, 187, 196; 4, 92; 5, 89; 33, 35; 58, 4.

221. Among the 12 fundamental pillars [arkàn] of the Islamic prayer —

tion with the head touching the floor and genuflection. To his followers, in fact, Mohammad had ordered: "You, who have believed! Genuflect, prostrate and adore your Lord."[222] But Mohammad's imperatives to Mary, though direct and peremptory, include at the same time a message to all Moslem women. They should look at Mary and imitate her *inner* and *outer* religious attitudes, whenever they stand in Allah's presence to pray or offer Him their share of due worship.

Fasting was immensely dear to Mohammad's heart — so dear indeed that he made it one of the five pillars, *arkàn*, of the new religion:[223] "Believers, fasting is decreed for you as it was decreed for those before you; it hopefully may help you fear God" (2, 183). During a whole lunar month, *Ramadàn* (2, 185), Moslems have to starve their stomachs from food so they can obtain from Allah the forgiveness of their sins and a bountiful

listed by TABB. (p. 115-118) before the 19 complementary ones (p. 118-123) — *rukù* (folding of the knees) and *sujùd* (prostration to the ground in sign of adoration) are two typical motions of the Moslem worshipper. Cf. TABB., p. 116-117.
    Concerning the value of the term *ùqnuti*, used by the Koran (3, 43), BOUB. notes (p. 119) that the verb *qànata* "implique en arabe une idée d'ascèse: être en oraison, prier longuement dans un total abandon de soi à Dieu, s'imposer une sévère abstinence."

    222. 22, 77. — "Prostrate yourselves with the others in prayers" (2, 43). — At the beginning of Islam, the "prostration" was so common that it left visible marks on people's faces: "You may see them *kneeling* and *prostrating*, seeking the grace of Allah and His good will. *Their marks* (from dust) *are on their faces, the traces of their prostrations*" (48, 29).

    223. Five are the fundamental pillars [*arkàn*] of Islam: the *shahàdat*, profession of faith; the *salàt*, canonical prayer; the *sàum*, fasting of the month Ramadan; the *zakàt*, the alm-tax; the *hàjj*, pilgrimage to Mecca. — For details on these fundamentals, cf. NAD., p.13-19 (prayer); p. 95-159 (alm-tax); p. 163-217 (fasting); p. 221-274 (pilgrimage). — GAND., p. 130-189 (prayer); p. 191-230 (alm-tax; p. 231-235 (fasting); p. 255-293 (pilgrimage). — QER., p. 210-234 (prayer); p. 235-270 (alm-tax); p. 271-280 (fasting); p. 281-295 (pilgrimage).

reward (33, 35); and their throats from anything not wholesome (2, 173), and from beverages — mostly alcoholic (2, 219); and their tongues[224] from any incorrect and superfluous talk, from any speech not dignifying and edifying (33, 32).

To Mary also the Prophet recommends fasting when he tells her: "And should you meet any mortal say to him: 'I have vowed a fast to the Merciful... I will not speak with any man today' " (19, 26).

Precious lesson indeed! Given so timely to the Moslem woman, it teaches her also, as it does all the daughters of Eve, to refrain from gossip, loquacity and pettiness.[225]

Before long this lesson was learned. A choice group of young Moslem girls put it into practice, open as they were to truth and goodness. Following the example of Mary, these Shiite young ladies in some towns of Lebanon and Syria observe faithfully even today what is called *"The mute fasting"* — or the "virgin's fasting"; they perform it in silent recollection in imitation of

---

224. "Pour l'Islam, comme pour le christianisme primitif, *jeûne* (siyàm) n'est pas s'abstenir d'aliments et de rapports sexuels, mais dans le cas, précisément visé par le Qur'an (19, 27) de la Vierge Marie, s'abstenir de parler: par *un voeu de silence (siyàman*: var. d'Ibn Mas'ud: *sàmtan*) permettant à la Parole divine d'être conçue en elle, à ce prix; et c'est l'amorce de toute la mystique: celle du 'fiat'." MASS., *(Mystique et Continence)* en Islam, 1951, II. p. 434. — Cf. also NAG., p. 374-384; and AMEL., p. 470-478.

225. Enough proof of that, without going too far, are the quarrels among the "Prophet's own Household" *[Ahl et Bait]*. Famous are the jealousies between Aisha, Mohammad's very young wife, and Fatima, his beloved daughter. As Aisha once complained to Mohammad about his uncontrolled passion for Fatima, the Prophet answered her that he would experience a flavor of paradise whenever he dealt with Fatima: "Quotiescumque ergo subit mihi desiderium Paradisi, osculor illam *[Fatima]* et ingero linguam meam in os eius et sentio ex ea auram Paradisi" *(Whenever the desire for paradise wells up within me, I kiss her [Fatima] and insert my tongue in her mouth, and a paradisiac fragrance from her assails me).* MAR. I, *[Mahumeti Auctoris Alcorani vitae rerumque gestarum Synopsis]*, p. 31. This paradisiac fragrance is due to the fact that Fatima was born after the Prophet had eaten the apple, offered to him by angel Gabriel, during his famous nocturnal journey.

Mary while, secluded in the *mihràb,* she conceived Issa, the Word of God.[226]

c. Model of Self-restraint

A vital message refusing and abhorring the "Cross"[227] and, along with the "Cross," any form of renunciation and self-denial; a message positively stimulating the exploitation of the goods of this earth and encouraging the enjoyment of all the pleasures it may afford;[228] a message endearing a fruitful conjugal life, permitting polygamy,[229] and so indulgent in terms of women[230] that

---

226. "Des témoignages directs m'ont été fournis récemment sur la survivance à Bagdad, à Tehéran, et à Mérida (Méxique: émigrés du Liban Sud) d'une coûtume mariale, immémoriale, observée par les jeunes filles shi'ites encore vierges: un jeûne, de voeu privé, pendant un, deux ou trois jours précédant le 15 Rajab: 'pour imiter Marie jeûnant en silence au Mihrab de Zacharie; et recevoir, comme elle, en elles, la parole de Dieu.' " MASS. *(L'oratoire de Marie à l'Aqça, vu sous le voile de deuil de Fatima,* [1956]. III. *Pratique dévotionnelles dédiées à Marie et à Fâtima),* I, p. 603.

227. It is known that the Koran denies the crucifixion of Jesus: the Jews did not crucify Christ, according to the Koran, but his double only. Cf. 4, 157-158.

228. "Eat of what is lawful and wholesome on the earth" (2, 168). — "Eat and drink, but avoid excess" (7, 31). — And one of the Koran's moral norms, chronologically the last, is an exhortation to enjoy, yet with moderation, the good things of the earth: "You, who have believed! Do not forbid yourselves, as unlawful, the good things that Allah has made lawful to you, provided you do not exceed" (5, 87). Cf. 2, 172; 20, 81; 52, 19.

229. "Then marry other women who seem good to you: two, three, or four of them" (4, 3).

230. "Your wives are a clothing to you, as you are a clothing to them"

it makes them a substantial requisite for heaven's bliss;[231] a message of mediocre morality conceived and tailored upon the needs of a new, "middlemost" society (2, 143), should shut the doors against any implicit or indirect desire for voluntary sterility, virginity and sexual continence.

But it is not so with the Koran. Surprisingly indeed, and yet not without pleasure, one has to admit the impact of Mary's personality on the Arabian Prophet. Won over by the fascinating charms of her spotless character, he felt elated enough to sing of her as the "one who knew how, and wanted, to keep her purity intact." Although he does not call her explicitly "The Virgin," on two different occasions and in two different epochs[232] he praises her for keeping undefiled her virginal sanctuary (66, 22). But Mohammad went further still. He thoughtfully framed Mary within an all-pure, ascetical and reserved atmosphere — the

---

(2, 187). — "Your wives are your fields: go then into your fields as you please" (2, 223). Cf. 4, 3; 33, 49. — Cf. DRAZ M. A., La morale du Coran, Paris, 1930; — BOUSQUET G. H., La morale de l'Islam et son étique sexuelle. Paris, 1953. — And Mohammad had no second thoughts in setting the pattern. As to the exact number of his wives, obviously after Khadija's death, authors have no unanimous opinion. MARRACCI ascribes to him, "juxta communiorem sententiam," 23 legal wives, "et, praeter uxores legitimas, quatuor etiam pellices ancillas nabuit." MAR., loc. cit., p. 32. — DIN. (p. 268): "épousa vingt-trois femmes." — ESS. (p. 194): "a eu quatorze épouses, qui ont été appelées les 'Mères des croyants'. Mais le nombre de femmes qui on sollicité l'amour de Mohammad est incalculable [...]. Jusqu'à la fin de sa vie, il n'a cessé d'accorder ses faveurs aux belles femmes, de les admirer, de les caresser, et de les étreindre."

231. "Reclined on couches ranged in rows, to dark-eyed houris We shall wed them" (52, 20). Cf. 3, 15; 36, 56; 55, 70-72. — ZAKARIAS remarks that the Rabbi of Mecca here does not speak "en parabole et en figure. Les musulmans ont toujours pris à la lettre ses fallacieuses promesses. Allez donc dire aux musulmans de 1956 qu'au Paradis ils n'auront pas de femmes! Aucun d'eux ne vous croira. Il leur est plus facile de concevoir un Paradis sans Dieu." Zk., p. 69.

232. Sura 21, The Prophets, belongs to the second epoch of the Meccan period. Sura 66, Prohibition, belongs to the first epoch of the Medinian period.

same atmosphere in which he envisioned she should live, operate and be the ideal image for the Moslem woman in displaying her familial and social duties.

By locking Mary within her *mihràb*, her face covered with a *hijàb* and with no one to talk to except her relative and tutor — Zachariah, Mohammad had apparently an intentional design for the mother of Jesus: he wanted to see her move and act in the same confined ambience he later imposed on the Moslem woman, a sort of a "recluse" in her own *hàrem*. Similar at least to Mary's, if not exactly the same, shall also be the exterior exposure and the style and the fashion of dressing he dictated to "his household," wives and daughters.

"To stay home and not display one's finery as women used to do in the pre-Islamic Ignorance Era" (33, 33); "to live separately in private quarters" (33, 55); "not to appear in public with the face 'unveiled'[233] and the mantel un-wrapped around their body" (33, 59); "to entertain freely with one's relatives (33, 54), but with the foreigners to avoid familiarity and converse only from behind the curtain, the *hijàb*" (33, 53) — are all cautions given by the Koran in order to protect the believers' honesty in their mutual relationship. Textually it reads: **"This is more chaste for your hearts and their hearts"** (33, 53).

The open recognition of Mary's singular virginity and the vociferous praise for it by the Koran must be, if we read Mohammad's mind correctly, the equivalent of an implicit but candid exhortation to shyness, self-restraint and modesty.

In between the lines, however, more is offered in this Koranic exhortation. The way its Text reads and sounds, it seems to be a theoretical correction of a morality all too often indulgent with the lures of the senses. Like a voice crying out from the

---

233. Mohammad did not impose the use of the veil [*hijàb*] on his wives until after his marriage to Zainab bint Khuzaima, and following a revelation with regard to that marriage. Cf. SH., p.151. — The *hijàb*, however, was already in use in pre-Islamic Arabia, as a protection of modesty. Cf. AQQ., p. 52-68; FAD., p. 245-248.

depths of the spirit to those who know how to capture the subtle call of the spirit, it invites the Moslem woman to refrain from the impulses of her sensuality so that she won't be swept away by the impure waves of the flesh and blood.

Whatever the outcome, Mary's "Koranic Fact" remains as significant as it is edifying. Despite her clear knowledge of the mystery of the human life and the laws regulating its transmission (3, 47; 19, 20), she chooses to keep her virginity: the bodily virginity (66, 12), and the mental virginity (21, 91). If this example of hers rings the same indiscriminately for every individual believer, it does more so for the Moslem female as such. Like Mary, she should earnestly raise her spirit above this muddy earth, to the realm where the Spirit of Allah more freely floats.[234]

Let Zakarias still declare himself bewildered: *"C'est vraiement ahurissant!"* (Zk. p. 191). He owes this bewilderment to his own self, to his inept and lame theory which does not recognize for the Koran other sources than the Jewish Torah. After we've proved it with material that is strictly Koranic, it is our conviction that the Holy Book of Islam not only extols Mary above all creation, but proposes her as a model that every believer ought to imitate if he or she wants to surrender to Allah in a true Moslem spirit. And it is right in the Koran that this "imitatio Mariae," so tenaciously opposed by Zakarias (*ibid.*), finds its most valid justification.

Far more objective is Boubakeur. Mary's full confidence in God and her unconditional surrender to His will according to

---

234. Following the Koran, and by virtue of the Koran, Mary's image in the most authoritative Islamic tradition is always projected against a background of purity and candor. We quote a recent author, SABUNI. Mary is portrayed by Islam as "the virgin, pure and chaste, who kept undefiled her virginity" (p. 196); "virgin pure, who grew up in an atmosphere of virtue and lived a life all pure and innocent" (p. 198). She lived, in fact, in the annexes of the temple, away from sin and under Allah's providential care (p. 199-200); and for life companion she had Joseph, an honest and upright youth who, like her, grew up in a pure and wholesome atmosphere (p. 197).

him, constitute precisely *"le symbole même de ce tawàkkul*
(abandon) dont l'Islam a fait le fondemment primordial de sa
doctrine, fondemment sans lequel la dévotion est vidée do son
contenu et devient une grossière entreprise de 'bons placements'
pour la vie future" (Boub. p. 612).*

I personally believe it is perfectly consonant with the
Koran's letter and spirit that, by proposing Mary as a *màthal,*
Mohammad had in mind not only a religious but a social purpose for the Moslem woman. He intended to raise her from the
downtrodden condition in which she was living and give her
back her former dignity and prestige. He wanted to guarantee
her better moral, spiritual and familial standards. He wanted to
heal the stigma that had long scarred her image. He wanted to
remove her for good from the abjection that had for centuries
crushed her in the pre-Islamic Ignorance Era, the *Jahilìya,* when
she lived as a mere instrument for domestic service and
hedonistic exploitation.[235]

And in this our modern era in which the woman's emancipation is promoted beyond the reasonable limits, how much
would Islam gain if the Religion of Allah would step back
courageously to its own sources and propose to the modern
Moslem woman the noble and attractive example of Mary,
daughter of Imran and mother of Jesus!

(*). "The very symbol of that surrender to God *[tawàkkul]* which Islam took
as its indispensable doctrinal foundation, without which devotion becomes void
of its content and turns into a senseless enterprise of 'good arrangements' for the
future life."

235. In that deadly obscurantist era, the social condition of the woman was
more than miserable. Cf. FAD., p. 25-241; AQQ., p. 68-75. — More a thing
than a person, the woman was "une sorte de bien de famille que son chef cède
à un mari contre paiement d'une dot. Elle passait en la possession de celui-ci,
qui pouvait la répudier." GAUD., p. 28. — "La espressione di *al-atyabàni* (le
due cose migliori), con le varie spiegazioni che ne danno i lessicologi, ma tutte
di ordine crudamente materiale, non basta a simboleggiare quell'attegiamento
verso la donna tutt'altro che idealistico e cavalleresco del più antico spirito be-
duino." GAB. II *(La società beduina e la poesia preislamica),* p. 24.

A PRODIGIOUS SIGN, *à y a t,* of eternal predestination realized in the time by exceptional prerogatives reserved to Mary and resulting in an unparalleled interior purification; an undefiled virginity in conjunction with a happy maternity; an intimate and familiar unity with Christ; excellence, rather supreme dignity, above all the women of the universe.

A SHINING EXAMPLE, *m à t h a l,* of the most desirable religious and moral attitudes in a Moslem female believer; example mostly of faith, of religiosity and self-restraint.

There it is in a capsule, the Koranic Message on Mary.

This synthesis is structured with material gleaned exclusively from the Koran — the Moslem Holy Book of Revelation. Far from being said or thought of as a genial lucubration of a hot-minded panegyrist, it must be retained as a rigorous conclusion of an accurate and passion-free research. A research conducted with love, I agree. But accompanied all along by the utmost scientific diligence that the work demands, and which the respect for others pretends.

It states a reality challenging any doubt or negation. An objective reality consigned by Mohammad to the Seventy Verses of the 13 Koranic Suras mentioning explicitly, and more or less extensively, Mary.

Chapter Three

CONCLUSION

To complete the preceding analytico-synthetical exposition, a word remains to be added on the historic origins of the Koranic Message before we conclude with two remarks — one dogmatic, and the other ecumenical, or pastoral.

I. *Historic Origins*

The Moslem tolerates no talk of *sources* for his Koran as a rule. A questioning of this sort hurts his religious sensitivity and

211

is incompatible with the orthodoxy of his conscience. To submit his sacred Book to a literary critique trying to establish its dependence on outside sources is just as impossible for him to conceive as scandalous to do.[1] In his firm belief, the Koran is Allah's word transmitted in Arabic tongue. Its source can be no other than divine. By Allah Himself it was "downed" onto Mohammad by straight "descent," or revelation. This theory is not the creed of the average Moslem only. It is the official teaching imparted at all Moslem theological schools and centers even today.

Hand in hand and in solid line with this theory are the Moslem Theology and Tradition. For both, the Koran is nothing but a partial, yet faithful, transcription of an Eternal Code, a heavenly prototype called the "Matrix of the Book" — Umm 'ul Kitàb (43, 3). This original Code is arcane [maknùn] and mysterious (56, 78), inscribed on special tablets well preserved from all eternity (85, 22) and which none may touch but the "purified" [almutahharùn] (56, 79). This Eternal Code is the source from which came forth the Koran and, before the Koran, the Torah and the Gospel (3, 3). Outside of it there is no other source.

The process by which the Eternal Code is transcribed or transmitted is called revelation. This is God's exclusive action, and it is taken not in its Jewish or Christian sense but in the version of it adjusted to the pre-Islamic mentality on the monotheistic type of God-man relationship. In other words, in this type of revelation God does not prompt the celestial concepts of the Hagiographer so he can elaborate them and express them in a human way. Nor does God elevate the Holy Writer's mind to conceive and grasp those concepts and record them infallibly under the divine inspiration. Rather, Allah acts as an absolute and formal dictator. Vocally, mechanically and materially He

---

1. "Étant donné la notion en jeu de révélation, le problème de possibles filières historiques ne se pose pas, ne peut pas se poser." GAR., p. 64. — "Il est évident que la question des sources du Coran ne se pose aucunement dans les cercles musulmans." PAR., p. 598.

dictates to man His word and helps him to put it down for his fellow men in a readable form — hence the *Koran*. And Allah usually does that in three different ways: by direct revelation, wàhi;[2] or talking from behind a veil, hijàb; or through a messenger, rasùl, sent and authorized by Him to make known His will (42, 51).

Despite its basic Judeo-Christian extraction, the Koranic version of revelation takes on a slightly different nuance. In all the divine religions, Mohammedanism included, God's excellence and man's lowliness have always traditionally been related in a vertical, up-and-down motion. Likewise, the divine communications to man were imagined as "descensional" while man's acts of prayer to and worship of God were called "ascensional." This elemental concept prevails in the Koranic notion of revelation. In ultimate analysis, therefore, God's revealing action is a *dictation*[3] coming down, a "descent" or **tanzìl**[4] of the word of Allah; it is

---

2. "È da rilevare che la rivelazione e ispirazione furono concepite da Maometto sotto forma di adattamento del concetto ebraico e cristinao a quello arabo preislamico dell'ispirazione testuale, meccanica, parola per parola, che i ginn o shaytan facevano a indovini e a poeti." NAL. II, p. 608. Cf. HAD. II, p. 196-200.

3. "Le texte du Coran se présente comme une dictée surnaturelle, enrégistrée par le Prophète inspiré; simple messager chargé de la transmission de ce dépôt, il en a toujours considéré la forme *littéraire* comme la preuve souveraine de son inspiration prophétique personnelle, miracle de *style* supérieur à tous les miracles physiques." MAS. *(Situation de l'Islam*, 1939), I, p. 16. Italics are ours. Cf. MASSON *(La vénération monothéiste)*, I, p. 215-284.

WATT remarks: "Le nom *wahy* et le verbe *awhâ* interviennent fréquemment dans le Qorân au milieu des contextes, où le sens de 'révéler par communication verbale directe est inapproprié.' Richard Bell a étudié ces usages et conclut 'qu'en tout cas dans les premiers morceaux du Qorân, *wahy* ne veut pas dire communication *verbale* du texte d'une révélation, mais est: 'suggestion', 'souffle', ou 'inspiration' survenant à l'esprit de quelqu'un et venant du dehors'." WAT. I, p. 82. Italics are ours.

4. "The Book that Allah has revealed *[nàzzala]* to His apostle, and the Book He formerly revealed *[ànzala]*" (4, 136). — Nàzzala: 2, 176; 3, 3; 4, 140; 7, 196; 76, 23. — Ànzala: 2, 90, 91, 99, 174, 231; 3, 4, 7; 4, 113; 9, 97; 39, 41. And elsewhere.

Allah's action by which He causes the word of His truth to "descend" [ànzala, nàzzala] on His prophet.[5]

In Mohammad's case,[6] the divine word or Koran was "descended" to him on different occasions,[7] in sections of two, three,

---

Based on the Koran (42, 51), Moslem authors ascribe to the divine revelation four modalities: *colloquy; inspiration*, or suggestions without words; *vision*, or allusive dreams; *oral and direct locution* through an angel. This last type was used with Mohammad. Cf. other analogous ways in *Num.*, 12, 6-8; and WAT. I, p. 82-85.

5. "Allah caused His tranquillity to descend upon him [...], and the word of Allah [kàlimat Allah] was exalted" (9, 40). — *Kàlimat ràbbika*: 6, 115; 7, 137; 10, 33; 11, 119; 40, 6. — "His word is the truth [qàuluhu 'l hàqq] " (6, 73). — *Nàzzala bil-hàqq*: 2, 176. — *Ànzala bil-hàqq*: 4, 105; 5, 48; 39, 2, 41; 42, 17. — "This is a revelation [tanzìl] from the Compassionate, the Merciful: a Book [kitàb] with clear and well defined signs [ayàt] " (41, 2-3). — *Tanzìl*: 32, 2; 39, 1; 40, 2; 56, 80; 69, 43.

The concept of *truth*, here, means "qualcosa che non è pensato dall'uomo, bensì elaborato da Dio e *dato all'uomo* da Lui per rivelazione. Il linguaggio coranico sembra ricordi a ogni istante la sovranità di Dio e l'inguaribile impotenza e incapacità dell'uomo in tutti e nei più minuti sensei." BAUS., 566.

6. Impressive were the phenomena that usually occurred along with the *tanzìl*, or the "downing," of the revelations. When Mohammad sensed their imminence, "Il frissonnait et tremblait, se faisait généralement couvrir d'un voile ou d'un menteau ("O toi, qui es couvert d'un menteau" S. 73 and S. 74), sous lequel on l'entendit souffler, gémir, pousser des cris rauques. Il en sortait en sueur avec lourdeur de tête qu'il soignait par des cataplasmes. Une tension musculaire intense est aussi signalée." DERM., p. 29. Cf. BL. IV, p.41; ESS., p. 77.

As for the great figures of history, so for Mohammad, the criteria of evaluation are so different that they often become contradictory. Here is a sample by KELLERHALS, from his paragraph *Wer war Mohammed?*: «Weil erklärt ihn als Epileptiker, Sprenger als Hysteriker, Koelle als Betrüger, Muir als ein Werkzeug des Teufels, de Goeje als Ipfer eines Brockengespensts, Andrae als Inspirierten, Houtsmal als echten Propheten». KEL., p. 79-84.

7. Cf. SAL., p. 49; HAD. II, p. 324. — To solve the problem that the Koran has been revealed *in its entirety* during the "qàdr" night (97, 1), including some *occasional portions* which were downed on different occasions, exegetes theorize that pursuant to the Koran's first revelation, "the Book would have been taken up back by Allah and revealed again later in portions." BAUS., p. 271. Cf. BL. IV, p. 42.

four and even up to ten ayàt at a time, depending on his
psychological attitudes and environmental needs.[8] It was
descended during the night of Qàdr (97, 1), one of those blessed
nights in which glorious and fateful things are decreed, and in
which "Allah's angels and His Spirit, by their Lord's leave, come
down with His decrees" (97, 3). The tongue in which the revelations were made was the clear and classical Arabic idiom of
Quraish,[9] the Prophet's ruling and most influential tribe of the
time. The purpose of the revelations was "to be an admonition to
you (Mohammad) and to your people" (43, 44) so he could lead
them from the darkness into the light — the ultimate dazzling
light of Allah Himself.[10]

---

8. "Allah sent down His tranquillity *[sakìnat]* on His apostle and the
faithful" (9, 40; 48, 4, 18, 26). It is peculiarly interesting that *sakìnat* appears
only in the "Medinian Suras." BAUS., p. 559. Therefore in the period of the
Prophet's major religious political hardships.

Cf. for instance the problem of *the wine and the màysir* (2, 219); of the orphans (2, 220); of the menstruation (2, 222); of the division of inheritance after
the defeat of Uhud (4, 7-11), and on occasion of Hudaibìya truce (5, 94); of
Aisha (24, 11-26); of Zaid and of the divorce of his wife on account of Mohammad (33, 37); of the Prophet's wedding to Zainab (33, 53); and of the secret
confided to, but not kept by, Hafsa (66, 3-5). — Cf. SH., p. 150-151; GAND.,
p. 24, 28; HAD. II, p. 23.

"Mahomet reçoit donc durant son Apostolat à Médine des révélations où
l'emportent les préoccupations d'ordre pratique. L'obsession du réel, de
l'immédiat, coupe les ailes au lyrisme." BL. VI, p. 225-226.

9. "It is an admonition to you and to your people *[li-qàumika]* " (43, 44).
Cf. 6, 66; 7, 145; 11, 49. — "In plain Arabic speech *[bi-lisànen arabìyen]* " (26,
195). — "In your tongue *[bilisànika]* " (19, 97; 44, 58). — "An Arabic Koran
[kur'ànan arabìyan] " (12, 2). Cf. 20, 113; 39, 28; 41, 3; 42, 7; 43, 3; 46, 12.

10. "It is He who brings down clear revelations to His servant (Mohammad)
so that he may lead you out of darkness into the light" (57, 9). Cf. 2, 257; 65,
11. — The Koran is the "light *[nùr]* which We have revealed" (64, 8); "light
from the Lord" (39, 22) for him who opens his bosom to Islam; "light," guiding
to the right path (42, 52; 57, 28).

"Allah is the light of the heavens and the earth. His light may be compared
to a niche that enshrines a lamp, the lamp within a crystal of star-like
brilliance. It is lit from a blessed olive tree neither eastern nor western. Its very
oil would almost shine forth, though no fire touched it. Light upon light; Allah
guides to His light whom He will" (24, 35).

With these intransigent notions in mind, who would then wonder why every attempt to set up a critical research is paralyzed, why every way to investigate some hypothetical "human source" for the Koran is precluded? Such an attitude, needless to say, dooms man's intelligence to a sort of a stagnant, humiliating immobilism.

According to Fr. Moubarak, the Moslem belief in the Koran as "inspired" and a "word of God" does not necessarily contradict scientific research on its "sources."[11] But then the term "inspiration" should be understood as it is defined by the Catholic Theology. God's inspiratory action in this case does not exclude the personal contribution of the Hagiographer; nor, consequently, the efficiency of an instrument or a secondary cause, or the use of some eventual marginal "sources."

A legitimate question however rises here: "Is the Ulema's, the Koranic Doctors', opinion and the average Moslem's belief oriented in this direction?" In an effort to be closer to the Islamic tradition, the Scottish Episcopalian W. Watt states that the influence of "sources" in the Koran's elaboration is "contrary to the belief of the Orthodox Moslems and must therefore be discarded."[12]

On the other hand the distinction forwarded by Moubarak between "*ressourcement*" and "*conditionnement*" of the Koranic Message[13] does not, in my opinion, hit the core of the problem.

This is the famous Koranic Verse of the Light [àyat an-nùr] which "amplissima eco ha trovato nella poesia e nelle speculazioni dei mistici." BAUS., p. 605. — Cf. CLERMONT-GANNEAU, La Lampe et l'Olivier dans le Coran, in Rev. de l'hist. des Religions, 81 (1920), p. 213-259.

11. For the sources of the Koran cf. NOL. I [Muhammad als Prophet. Die Quellen seiner Lehre], p. 1-20; II, p. 123-192; MOUB. I, p. 163-175.

12. "Or cette conception [des "sources"] serait contraire aux croyances des musulmans orthodoxes et dès lors à écarter." WAT. I, p.144.

13. "Si donc nous préférons parler de conditionnement du message coranique plutôt que de son 'ressourcement', quelle est dans cette ligne de recherches,

The *"conditionnement"* in fact refers to the *circumstances* of the revelation; in ultimate analysis it may coincide with the Koranic Discipline trying to determine the motives (psychological, environmental) of revelation *[asbàb an-nuzùl]*. The *"resourcement,"* by contrast, deals with the *content* of revelation and its immediate sources.

While dealing with the relations between the Koran and the Judeo-Christian Revealed Books in order to find a way out of this dead-end road, Watt proposes to the problem of the Koranic "sources" a solution that I would call "oblique," aiming at reconciling at least "pro forma" the traditional Islamic belief with the historical critique. Here succinctly is his thought:

> To the Koran, a "creative irruption" in the Meccan religious life of the seventh century, one may assign "sources" analogous to those of Shakespeare's *Hamlet.* Despite the many similarities in intrigues and plots and approaches to foreign elements, the question will always remain how to explain Shakespeare's "creative ingenuity." According to the Moslem doctors themselves, the Koran is not Mohammad's own work, nor a display of his intimate, religious conscience. Its relations and eventual parallelisms should therefore preferably be referred not to a particular "source," but to the doctrinal atmosphere prevailing in the historic ambience in which the Koranic recipients lived — I mean Mohammad first, his early followers next, and finally the Meccan and Medinian tribes. Only this ambience can tell us how closely were the Koran and the Judeo-Christian assertions tied to each other on one hand, and on the other, how solid was the identity between the Koranic teaching and its creed in the mass of the people at the

---

la nature exacte des correspondances entre la Bible et le Coran?" MOUB. II, *Pent.* II. p. 34. Italics are ours.

time. The proposed solution presents itself as an open road to the Western critic. It will allow him to investigate freely the Koran's eventual "source," to compare its main doctrinal "fiber" with the "basic" Judeo-Christian ideology of the epoch, to recognize the possible pagan import — if any, and to corroborate one's conclusions with positive and scientific proofs and examples without contradicting in any of them Islam's faith in its divine "descent." Consequently, coming to the sector of biblical or extra-biblical stories, a clear distinction is to be made between the "story" itself and the "message" conveyed by it. As such, the "stories," whatever their characteristics or details, may well originate from a human "source." Not so however their "message" or teaching. Whether implicitly or explicitly expressed, their "meaning" comes down uniquely from above — fruit of a divine "descent" or revelation. In short, the problem of the Koranic "sources" must in the end be reduced to this one dimension: "to know how and to what extent have the Judeo-Christian (and eventually pagan) ideologies settled in the Hijaz."[14]

Whatever the result, history is history. Faith does not contradict science, nor is it prohibitive of scientific research. On the other hand, hypotheses built on positive and undeniable data

---

14. WAT. I, p. 114-116. The dogmatic concepts (God, final judgment, etc.) were more or less the same as those in Judaism or Christianity. The originality, or the "creative irruption," consisted in that Mohammad delivered them with a marked stress and emphasis: "les présenta avec plus de force et, en mettant l'accent sur telle ou telle chose, en fit une synthèse plus ou moins cohérente." *Ib.*, p. 115. The creeds that were professed in Mohammad's time, or historical environment, were therefore materially *revealed truths*: i.e. by a divine and authentic revelation.

Sauvaget remarks: "On tend aujourd'hui cependant moins à rechercher des emprunts caractérisés, textuels, qu'à reconstituer l'*atmosphère idéologique*, l'évolution religieuse générale dans le contact avec les confessions juives et chrétiennes qui pénétraient en Arabie, qui caractérisent les conditions dans lesquelles s'est formé le Prophète de l'Islam." SAUV., p. 124. Italics are ours.

cannot arbitrarily be discarded, ignored or eliminated by fanaticism, obscurantism or any personal prejudices. The historian's task in that case is to dig out and determine their possible "sources."

Now, the similarity, or scriptural identity, between the Marian "material" in the Koran and the Christian documents prior to the Koran, is an undeniable and positive fact. Already noticed several centuries later, this situation gave birth to the necessity of a "critical research" demanding, in turn, an adequate and satisfactory answer. It is a real problem, and involves seeking the right solution; and to solve it, scholars have come up with different attempts, but none of them complete.

Indeed, I have no intention of facing the problem in all its magnitude. More by outlining than by extensively developing the subject, I shall then briefly indicate first, the solution that may be called *general*, that is regarding the Koranic content as a whole bloc; and secondly, the *partial* solution which deals with the Koranic Marian "material", or "facts."

1. *General Solution*

Experts here have fundamentally followed two more or less opposite directions, accentuating the influence of either Jews or Christians in the Koran. Thus two solutions have come up respectively: one *Jewish* and one *Christian*.

A. Jewish Solution

The Jewish influence in the Koran, as an almost solid theory, was pioneered by Fr. Marracci beginning in the second half of the seventeenth century. "*Magnam Alcorani partem fabulae Talmudicae et Rabbinorum deliria occupant.*"* And anticipating the Ps.-Zakarias, he asserted that the Koran's redaction dates back to Jewish writers, mainly to Abdallah, son of Salam: "*Certum fere habeo Judeos, et preasertim Abdallah Ebno-Salam eorumdem primo antesignanum ac deinde Mahumeti asseclam et discipulum, seu fere potius magistrum, Alcorani si non unicos, saltem praecipuos, auctores fuisse.*"** Abdallah, "*inter Judeos doctissimus,*"*** would have been the main source for the Koran.[15]

As has also been noted by Sauvaget (p. 124), the thesis favoring the Judaic imprint on Mohammad was sponsored also by Abr. Geiger, *Was hat Muhammad aus dem Judentum aufgenommen?*, 1893; Ch. Torey, *The Jewish of Islam*, 1933; S. Katsh, *Judaism und Islam*, Biblical and Talmudic

---

(*). "A large portion of the Koran is made of Talmudic tales and delirious hallucinations of some Rabbis." (Fares)

(**). "The Jews, I am nearly positive, namely Abdallah Ebno-Salam — once their prominent Leader and then a follower and a disciple of Mohammad, if not indeed his teacher — were, if not exclusively, at least partially, the authors of the Koran." (Fares)

(***). "Abdallah, the most erudite among the Jews." (Fares)

15. "Pour répondre à Monsieur le curé, le rabbin ne prend pas les Évangile; il relit les Apocryphes." ZK., p. 160.
    In a note published in *Études*, 94 (1961), under the title: *Les idées de Hanna Zacharias*, p. 82-92, the Dominican Fr. P.J. JOMIER, confrère of the pseudo-Zakarias, does not regret to point out that his colleague's thesis, rather than a recent discovery in the Islamic field, is a disastrous blunder — "une erreur désastreuse" (p. 82), with no solid foundation whatsoever (p. 83).

backgrounds of the Koran and its commentaries, 1945; and by
Wensink, *Mohammed en de Joden te Medina*, 1908.

Hanna Zakarias, a pseudonym, resumed this thesis on his
own in two volumes with the title: *De Moïse à Mohammad.*
Here briefly is the main thread of his opinion:

> The Koran is born of a suggestion, or better of a
> redaction of its material by an erudite Rabbi from Mec-
> ca. This Rabbi conceived the genial idea of using
> Mohammad as a docile instrument to promote among
> the polytheist Arabs the faith in the one, true God.
> From the beginning, Mohammad played the game. But
> later, pressed by his ever-growing desire to present
> himself to his tribesmen as a prophet and a messenger,
> he turned his back on the Rabbi and began his acrimo-
> nious polemic against the Jews and the *Nasàra*, accusing
> them of having adulterated the former revelation made
> by Allah to Abraham, Moses, and Jesus.
>
> As a general rule, therefore, one is not allowed to
> speak of a true Koranic derivation from the Gospel.
> That is valid not only with regard to Mohammad, but
> to the Meccan Rabbi also (Zk., p. 156, 160). The
> Koran's original sources would then be the Bible and
> the Talmud on one hand, and on the other, the Apoc-
> ryphal Gospels — particularly "the Infancy gospel,
> written in Arabic; the Gospel of Pseudo-Matthew, in
> Hebrew; and probably the Proto-evangelium of James
> in its Hebraic version." This complex of sources gave
> material birth to the Koran, or rather to the *Acts of
> Islam.* Redacted by a Jew, the famous Book contains
> the origin and evolution of the new religion. The core
> of the problem consequently is not Mohammad per-
> sonally; he has nothing to do with it. The problem must
> converge totally on the Rabbi of Mecca,[16] an individual
> of a staunch Jewish mentality.

16. "Et de ce fait les problèmes se trouvent complètement déplacés [...].

Speaking of Mary, one should call her properly "anti-Christian." The reason for that is the maternity attributed to her by the Christians hailing her "Mother of God." No! Although she was a virgin and, according to Isaiah, she conceived and bore through the breathing of the Spirit, yet she is no mother to a Christ-God; she is mother of Christ, a mere creature, from the lineage of the great prophets of Israel.[17]

As to the Koranic "facts" on Mary, the reported Rabbi would have hauled them by the handfuls from the Ps.-Matthew. Better yet, the "stories" of Sura 19, Maryam, are unquestionably extracted from the Apocryphal Scripts.[18]

The Ps.-Zakarias' solution is extremist, revolutionary, "explosive," and suffering from lack of adequate proofs. Audacious and hazardous as it is, it contradicts several historical data and is furthermore poor in the necessary documentation. If it had a milder tone and sounder reasoning, it probably would have

---

Tout le problème est concentré sur le rabbin de la Mecque" (II, p. 293). — "Le rabbin raisonne en Juif et fait consciemment oeuvre anti-chrétienne. Marie est vierge et mère de Jésus; mais soeur de Moïse et d'Aaron, elle n'est pas vierge et ne peut pas être mère du Christ-Dieu. Ce serait renier le monothéisme d'Israël." Loc. cit.

17. "La Vierge Marie, pour le rabbin, bien que dotée de dons exceptionnels, ne pouvait être qu'anti-chrétienne. Nous assistons ici à une large manoeuvre de la part du rabbin: Marie est vierge, comme l'affirment les documents hébreux; mais son fils ne sera qu'un Prophète de la lignée des grands Prophètes d'Israël. Il s'appellera Jésus et n'aura jamais la fonction de Christ que lui donnent les Chrétiens, contrairement aux grandes déclarations de Moïse sur l'Unité divine" (II, p. 299). Italics are ours.

18. "Il ne s'agit pas plus de savoir si Mohammed a connu lui-même l'Évangile de l'Enfance, le Protoévangile de saint Jacques, l'Évangile du Pseudo-Matthieu. Mohammed n'entre plus en ligne de compte" (II, p. 293).
"Les histoires de la sourate 19, 16-21 [...] sont incontestablement empruntées à cet apocryphe [Ps.-Matthew]" (II, 294).

marked, as has been said, "the psychological end at least of the Islamic phenomenon."[19]

My intent was to go no further in this hypothesis. But then Zakarias left me no choice. Time and again in his promotional book *Vrai Mohammad et faux Coran*, he brags of having accomplished a work of a "brutal objectivity" (p. 59) piping complacently that his conclusions — "absolutely revolutionary in Koranic matters" (p. 58) — were favorably received and labelled by critics as "rigorous and accurate" (p. 9). In the bind of tutoring the truth in defense of a historic reality, I felt it was my duty to confront the Ps.-Zakarias in an open and honest scientific challenge.

One cannot deny Zakarias a substantial dose of courage and daring. Particularly remarkable is his frankness in voicing out so unscrupulously his opinions. Too bad that he laid to waste so much time and so many resources to sustain a hypothesis that, in the eyes of all responsible critics, is absolutely untenable. But worst of all, he shows he is not slightly influenced by political stands; derailed by an open contempt for the Arabs (p. 44, 59, 130, 161, 200, 212, 225) and by an unrestrained fanaticism for the Jews (p. 45), he broke loose in an unreal world of whimsical imaginations, away from the honest textual analysis and strict historical control.

First, and in Zakarias' own words, the speeches reported in the *Acts of Islam* (that is the Koran) "contain absolutely nothing that is not characteristically 'spécifiquement' Jewish" (p. 28). In

---

19. PEIR., p. 29. — Besides, the Ps.-Zakarias himself recognizes he is accomplishing a "revolutionary" work: "Les résultats de notre travail constituent même une *véritable révolution* en matière islamique" [I, p. 7]. He goes on even further, as to state that his book is "le premier livre de vérité sur le Coran, Mohammed et l'Islam" in thirteen centuries; and that all the studies that were previously attempted had been "ouvrage de labeur, d'un labeur faussement orienté." *Loc. cit.* Italics are ours.

other words, they are "essentially and exclusively" biblical speeches (*ibid*).

What logical conclusion does this statement lead to?

Here is what Zakarias thinks he is authorized to say: "Such speeches can't consequently have but a Jewish author who knows the Bible, the Talmud and the Jewish literature. This erudite Jew can't be other than the Rabbi of Mecca — the head of the Synagogue" (p. 28, 29).

Thus Zakarias.

Would an unprejudiced reader by chance subscribe to this premise?

I, for one, can say this much: I would as long as there was question of *an author* well versed supposedly in both Bible and Talmud. But that this individual should *necessarily* (p. 28) be a "*Jew*," even a "*Rabbi*," and none other than "*the head of the Meccan Synagogue*" — one ought to have the guts to make and sustain such an assertion.

But let me here ask Zakarias a logical question that surfaces spontaneously in the mind: What if, instead of a Jew, the supposed author were a *Judeo-Christian* or one of those mysterious *hànifs* such as Bishop Waraka Ben Nawfal, the famed expert in Biblical and Talmudic matters? To say the truth, nothing prohibits the latter supposition from being objectively and historically possible and probable. And then? What would happen to Zakarias' colossal structure? It would just crumble down to ashes like the iron and clay statue mentioned by Daniel, struck as it was by a minuscule stone flying from the mountain (2, 34, 35)! In any case, Zakarias could not but assert with surprising temerity that all his conclusions were absolutely unquestionable: "Tout cela est d'une clarté irréfragable!" (p. 29)

Secondly, apart from the unfounded assumption that "Mohammad was a Jewish convert" (p. 26, 35) and from the chimerical evangelization project by the Synagogue Leader to "judaise" the Arabian Peninsula (p. 9, 61) by using Mohammad as a "spokesman" (p. 43), an "auxiliary" (p. 75), rather a mere channel or a loud-speaker ["tuyau"] to transmit the Rabbinic teaching, Zakarias never seems to tire of stressing the peculiarly Jewish character of Islam and the Koran's exclusive Judaic content.

At the origins of Islam there must have been one individual — not an Arab, but a Jew (p. 42). So the boasted Arabic Islam was nothing more than Judaism — in other words, the cult of Yahweh explained to the Arabs in Arabic by a Rabbi (p. 9-58). Islam therefore is not a new religion (p. 129), since without Judaism "it never would have existed" (ibid.). Per se, Arabic Islam has "no specific identity" (p. 193), "no autonomy" (p. 60), "no self-existence" (p. 63). In reality, it is nothing else but a version in Arabic of the Judaic religion (p. 61), a marginal development of it ["un à côté"] (p. 193). The Arabic Islam is the "triumph of Israel" (p. 59). Furthermore, during its shaping, the Koran was under no influence either by Allah or by Mohammad (p. 87). The Rabbi, Mohammad's instructor — and he alone — wrote and redacted the Koran, or better the Acts of Islam (p. 58), thus becoming the "creator of the Arabic religious idiom" (p. 10).

Now, from within the scope of a hypothesis so radical and so abrasive, I don't know how to explain reasonably and adequately the following facts, all ascertained, deposing against it:

1. How to explain, for instance, that the initial impulse to the apostolate came to Mohammad not from the zeal to promote the creed in a One and true God, Yahweh, but from a heart-felt and intensive eschatological piety? In other words: How to ex-

plain that the first and explicit subject that Mohammad preached about was a typically Christian theme, the "parousia," and not a theme exclusively Jewish, the monotheism? It is known, in fact, that the Hebraic name Yahweh never occurs once throughout the whole Koranic texture. Long before adopting the supreme name, Allah, the epithet *Ar-Rahmàn* was used from the very early days of Mohammad's mission — a one hundred per cent Arabic epithet, I mean, not Judaic.

2. How to explain again the line of demarcation (22, 17), the distinction and real antagonism (5, 57) decidedly established by the Koran between "Moslems" (followers of Mohammad) and "Jews" (members of the Synagogue)? Mohammad was, in Zakarias' hypothesis, a convert brought into the Jewish faith by the diligent care of the Rabbi (p. 31) and under the pressure by his wife, Khadija, purportedly a "Jewish-born," "juive de naissance" (p. 9, 73). If all that were true, why then the open Koranic distrust of the Jews? If they and Mohammad were co-sharers of the same religion, should he not have fared well with them? Should he not have loved them, supported them, and stood for them above any other community? How to explain his illogical and often blameworthy attitude against them, members of his own faith? Why did he crash down on them with ruder and cruder humiliations (2, 65; 5, 42; 7, 166; 62, 5), maledictions (5, 60, 64, 78) and reproaches (7, 163, 168) than he dealt the Christians *[nasàra]* (5, 82; 6, 52)?

3. Coming finally down from the chimerical world of theory to the practical, Zakarias' thesis can hardly find an answer for the merciless and drastic extermination by Mohammad of all the Jewish groups of the Hijaz — such as Banu Qainuqa, Banu Nadir, and Banu Quraiza. Such cruelty should never have happened were the Koranic Message, in substance, nothing but a derivation or an extension of the same religion, the Jewish. If the Arabic Islam were indeed a historic continuation of Jewish Islam (p. 147), then instead of putting to the sword the followers of the new faith, Mohammad should have by all means given them his favor, protection and unconditional support.

Thirdly, if Islam were exclusively Judaism and the Koran a "radically anti-Christian" book (p. 11), then how can one explain and justify the sympathetic and benevolent attitude Mohammad took toward those who profess themselves by saying, "We are Christians *[nasara]* "? Why in the Koran is so much sympathy and warmth shown the Christians and not the Jews (5, 82; 24, 36-38)?

Concerning the Christian religion, Mohammad reserves for Jesus, the son of Mary, an exceptionally unique praise. In his words Jesus is the Word of Allah, the Breathing of His Spirit, a Noble in this world and the next, and one of the most favored by God, even if he is not called properly son of God (3, 45). Now how to reconcile these laudatory expressions with the statement that the Koran is an "anti-Christian" book? How to explain Mohammad's esteem for the Apostles of Jesus, described by him as God's fervent "auxiliaries" *[ansàr]* (3, 52; 61, 64)?

And with regard to Mary, the mother of Issa, if Mohammad had it in mind to "cut her off from her Christian community" (p. 165), to portray her as an "anti-Christian person" (p. 139) and thus "relegate her to her Jewish past" (p. 160), then why did he bother to defend her against the Jews themselves, people of her own tribe and religion, from the "monstrous falsity" they were uttering against her (19, 27-33)? Why did the Arabian Prophet work out her defense in a Christian perspective by resorting to Christian documents, the Apocrypha (p. 189), and not in a Judaic perspective by taking from sources authentically Judaic? And, finally, why did he ascribe to her so much dignity and credit that in terms of moral guilt and shame he equated the "monstrous falsehood" by the Jews against her character (4, 156) with their "denial of truth" while stating how Christ died (4, 157), with their crime of "infidelity to the Covenant," with their "rejection of Allah's revelation," and with their "iniquitous slaying of His holy prophets" (4, 155)?

Weighing all this, I cannot but confirm that Zakarias' book on Mohammad is, contrary to his explicit statement (p. 9), an absurd and ridiculous "farce."

It is sad indeed to realize that by dwelling obstinately on one fixed idea, the exclusive Judaic origin of Islam and the Koran, the author has failed to reach at the "noumenon" of them both. In other words, he did not understand the "soul" of Islam, the fruit of Mohammad's religious experience; nor the meaning of the Koran, a typical account of the "creative irruption" mentioned by Montgomery Watt (I. p. 114). From the peripheral point of view where he placed himself, Zakarias saw nothing in Mohammedanism but a complex phenomenon of religion, community, and civilization. Toward it, therefore, he could nurture only misunderstanding breeding in turn contempt and hatred. Of himself alone, and not of Mohammad, he can indeed repeat his own disgraceful words: "He has failed at his own test" — "il a échoué à son brevet."[20]

B. Christian Solution

This comes in a twin dress: one of a thorough *Christian* tailoring, and the other *Judeo-Christian*.

---

20. "Si ce livre a été écrit par Mohammed, de sa propre initiative, il faut carrément conclure qu'il était bien ignorant. Il aurait même échoué a son brevet. Si ce livre a été inspiré par Allah, il faut encore conclure qu'Allah a besoin de reviser son histoire, vu qu'il a oublié bien de notions élémentaires." ZK., p. 165.

Besides St. John Damascene, for whom Islam is a Christian sect,[21] the pioneers of the Christian solution are as quoted by Sauvaget (p. 124): Tor Andrae, *Der Ursprung des Islam und das Christentum*, 1926; R. Bell, *The Origin of Islam in its Christian Environment*, 1925. To these I may add A. Sprenger, *Das Leben und die Lehre des Mohammad*, 1961-65; and Fr. Casanova, *Mohammad et la fin du monde*, 1911.

The Judeo-Christian solution was also sponsored among others by G. Sacco, *The Religious Beliefs of Mohammad, Their Source and Rapport with the Judeo-Christian Traditions* [Rome, 1922].

Recently, Fr. Yussuf Haddad dealt with this thesis in a book entitled *Al-Qur'an wa-l-Kitàb* (The Koran and the Book), but without delving too deeply into the subject (p. 304-335; 985-989).

Later, however, he took it up again and more diligently and "ex professo" developed it in a book entitled *Al-Qur'àn, dà'wat nasranìyat* [The Koran, a Judeo-Christian Call]. It is one volume in a series by the same author, entitled *In View of the Islamo-Christian Dialogue*. As to its publication there is no mention of time and place. But, as it comes in the second place in the mentioned series, it must surely date from 1969. That year, in fact, several publications on the matter saw light at Junieh, Lebanon; the first of them was an introduction to the Islamo-Christian dialogue [Feb., 1969]; and the third dealt with the relations between Islam and Christianity "tout court" [December, 1969]. Here in a summary are the main thoughts:

---

21. JOA. DAMASCENUS, *De haeresibus liber*, n. 101, "Ismaelitarum supersitio." MG. 94, col. 762-773. — Cf. KHOURY, PAUL, *Jean Damascène et l'Islam*, in *Proche-Orient Chrétien*, t. VII (1957), p.44-63; t. VIII (1958), p. 313-339 ..from p. 317-320, in what sense, according to the Damascene, the term αἵρεσις should be understood with regard to Islam; cf. nonetheless ABEL, ARMAND, *Le chapitre CI du livre des Hérésies de Jean Damascène: son inauthenticité*, in *Studia Islamica*, (p. 1963), p. 5-25.

a.) The orthodox and official Christianity had no impact on Islam. Its proper name, *masihìyat* (hence: *masìhi* [Christian] and *masihiyùn* [Christians]), is totally absent from the Koran and never mentioned by any Sura (p. 6). What left a marked imprint, however, was the *nasraniyat* (hence: *nasàra* [Judeo-Christians]), a sect born quite early in the bosom of Christianity (p. 23-54). It had a gospel (p. 95-108), a doctrinal system (p. 109-135), a method (p. 136-147), a faith (p. 147-178) and a legal code (p. 178-197) all its own. This was the Judeo-Christian sect.

To escape persecution (p. 56-68), these sectarians *[nasàra]* took refuge in Arabia, Hijaz and Mecca (p. 68-95) and they had prospered (p. 202-270). During the first decade of the seventh century they had in Mecca their own Bishop *[qass]* in the person of Waraka Ben Nawfal, the uncle to the noble and wealthy Quraishi woman, Khadija, who will later become Mohammad's first wife through the mediation and good arrangements of Waraka himself (p. 285-288). They had their own Church *[bì'at — kà'bat —* sacred place for worship] in the Ka'ba itself,[22] where the famous "black stone"[23] was kept by them no less than as a "symbol" of Christ — and this before the conquest of Mecca in 631, and

---

22. Cf. Haddad's two articles in the magazine *Al-Maçarrat: The Ka'ba of the Mecca, Christian Church,* 58 (1972), p.361-369; and *"The Black Stone of Mecca, Type of Christ,"* 58 (1972) p. 219-224.

23. Here is how DIN. (p. 11) describes the story of the "black stone": It fell down from Paradise. Angel Gabriel picked it up and gave it to Abraham and to his son, Ismael, at the moment they were building the Temple of Ka'ba. By their hands it was located where it stands today, to tell the pilgrim the point of departure for his ritual roundabouts. Snow white at the beginning, it then became black "à la souillure des péchés commis par les pélerins qui vinrent la toucher et la baiser."

before the "purification" of the Sanctuary[24] performed
by Mohammad in person.**

    b.) Mohammad grew up in an environment quite
familiar to him (p. 651-652) and saturated with Judeo-
Christian spirit (p. 271-289). Bishop Waraka baptized
him[25] with the water from Zemzem well (p. 278) and

---

24. Delicate and quite significant was Mohammad's gesture on the day his
victorious followers proceeded to the "purification" of the Ka'ba. Paintings of
all sorts decorated the Temple's walls inside: trees, angels, prophets, Jesus and
Mary. The Prophet ordered that with a cloth, soaked in water from Zemzem
well, they cancelled everything except what his hands would cover; and at once
his arms opened and stretched over the images of Jesus and Mary. Cf. HAD. II,
p. 985; and in *Al-Maçarrat, loc. cit.*, p. 367.

(**). Ka'ba, from Ka'b — stump, fixed to the ground, cubic — is actually a
square and cubic building rising in the center of Mecca, about 48 feet high. In
one of its corners stands the famous square and cubic "black stone," reportedly
dropped from heaven to Abraham by angel Gabriel. During the Jahiliya, the
pre-Islamic Ignorance Era, Ka'ba was a pagan Sanctuary wherein all divinities
were worshipped. Among these were mainly the pagan god Hobal, and Al-Làt,
Al-Uzzàt and Al-Manàt, claimed by pagan Arabians to be Allah's daughters.
The Prophet purified it from the idols, thus becoming, since, the Islamic Kìblat
(from koubàlat, opposite), the point toward which Moslems all over the world
turn to pray. In the Ka'ba square, not far from the building, is the well
Zemzem, nearly seventy feet deep. Pilgrims drink its water as a blessing.
Moslem tradition believes that the angel Gabriel was the first to dig it, to provide the thirsty Egyptian Hagar and her baby, Ismael, then both stranded in
the torrid desert, with a drink. Therefore, it is also called "Ismael's Well." Lost
thereafter, Abdu-l Muttalib, the Prophet's grandfather, found it centuries later.
(Fares)

25. To Mohammad's baptism Fr. Haddad relates (p. 278-279) both the
"guidance" Allah gave him (93, 6) when he was found "erring" (93, 7), and the
"opening of the chest" to relieve him from the burden which "weighed down
his back" (94, 1-3).
    With regard to the "opening of the chest" notes Blachère: "L'expression
ouvrir la poitrine est métaphorique; le sens en est élucidé par trois autres
passages. Ces versets signifient simplement: "N'avons-nous pas ouvert ton âme à
la foi et ne t'avons-nous pas délivré du crime d'idolatrie?" BL. IV, p. 11. Consequently, there is no question here at all of opening of chest, of extraction of
heart, and of washing it with immaculately white snow by the angels. Cf.
WAT. I, p. 82-85.

lavished on him his support and protection during the
early calls of his religious and prophetic career
(p. 294-324). Before starting his own mission, Mohammad, along with some of his relatives and tribesmen,
devoted himself to exercises typical of the *Hànifite*
religious movement (p. 273-275) — such as rising to
prayer at night as Monks were in the habit of doing;
taking ritual ablutions; fasting during the month of
Ramadan; circumambulating, or touring around the
Ka'ba seven times. This Judeo-Christian, monotheist,
Hànifite religious movement left in Mohammad's soul a
deep, indelible and decisive mark (p. 270-531; 652-671).

c.) Even the Koran is deeply imbued with Judeo-
Christian material. This pervades the substance of its
message (p. 533-551), its various forms of expression
(p. 551-569), its method (p. 570-596), its religious formulas (p. 597-615) and its creeds (p. 616-682).

Once instituted and established (p. 197-210; 640-
641), this new "middlemost" community, Islam —
understood in its proper and most rigorous expression
(p. 680-683) — absorbed into its system the old Judeo-
Christian sect (p. 681-682) and gradually kept
assimilating it until the sect disappeared forever.

These facts hitherto are positive and historically
ascertained. Taken therefore into account, they compel
us to admit that Islam, as stressed by Mohammad and
deposited in the 114 Suras, is substantially a pressing
Judeo-Christian call, a continuation of the message fundamentally transmitted by the Judeo-Christian sect;
dà'wat nasraniyat.

Haddad is well aware that he is opening an altogether new
road and, by that, that he is running counter to positions that
have thus far been peacefully taken for granted, mainly with
regard to the Islamic "cradle." His thesis is developed with an as-
tounding accuracy. And as such, no doubt it will raise storms of

opposition in some intellectual circles known for their stone-hard immobilism. But it is destined to make its way through and, eventually in time, impose itself on the acceptance of Scholars. As a response to the author's more than legitimate wish (p. 705-707), it will constitute the indispensable platform for any Islamo-Christian brotherly encounter. Further yet, like a blueprint in the hand emphasizing the main lines of creeds in common, it will invite Moslems and Christians and Jews to an honest and fruitful dialogue, around the ecumenical table of mutual respect and understanding.

If from the thematic and doctrinal points of view it may seem of a lesser value, greater by far will be its beneficial impact from a psychological stand. As a priceless "ecumenical" tool, mainly in the pastoral approach, it will help break the ice between the two monotheistic blocs and bring them together.

Along with it, it will be enough to point out that the outspoken antagonism by the Koran to Christianity did not aim at the Christian religion in its genuine and orthodox expressions, because they were unknown as such to the Koran; but rather at some private and well-defined Christian sects condemned, at least partly, and rejected by the official Christianity. Legitimately then we can conclude that the confusion between *nasraniyat* (Judeo-Christian sect) and *masihìyat* (Christianity) had in the past no use other than to have poisoned the relationship between Christians and Moslems — not excluding the Jews; it threw confusion into the already over-intricate atmosphere, provoking retaliatory vendettas from apologists on either side.

2. Partial Solution

As a norm in determining accurately the "sources" for the

Marian facts in the Koran, we shall follow the orientation suggested by Haddad in the solution above. Our research, therefore, will zero in on *Christian* documents, and prevalently on the *Apocryphal Gospels*.

This same pattern was in 1933 followed by Sidersky,[26] although in a quite elementary form; and in 1950, with more depth and seriousness, by A. Belli, in the magazine *Aevum*; but, victim of a setback, he gave up on it right after the start, thus leaving behind a truncated work.[27]

By limiting himself to a simple comparison between the Koranic and Christian texts whether canonical or apocryphal, Sidersky says in substance that much of the Koranic material relative to Christ and Mary was in blocs taken out of the *Protoevangelium of James* and the *Gospel of the Nativity* of the Ps.-Matthew. Thus the *"histoire de la Vierge Marie"*[28] was "extracted" from the Proto-evangelium from which he also quotes some passages;[29] the *"miracle du palmier"* was instead "borrowed" from the Ps.-Matthew,[30] insinuating that the textual

---

26. SIDERSKY D., *Les origines des Légendes musulmanes dans le Coran et dans la vie des Prophètes*. Paris, Geuthner, 1933.

27. Cf. *Aevum*, 24 (1950), p. 442-446. Despite the author's note: "to follow," on page 466, it seems to me that there has been, at least in the last twenty years, no *continuation* of the magazine for which I searched in vain. Besides, after the publication in 1958 by M. TESTUZ of the "Papyrus Bodmer V," *Nativité de Marie* (Cologny-Genève, Bibliotheca Bodmeriana), and after the publication of Fr. STRYCKER, Belli remains surpassed in the second part of his study (p. 443-466).
Like Sidersky and Belli, other authors also depend on the Apocrypha for the respective references: v.g. ZAK. II, p. 292-293; WENS. (p. 359): "Un grand nombre de traits racontés concordent en partie ou entièrement avec les histoires des Évangiles apocryphes." And others otherwise.

28. "Toute cette légende est tirée du *Protoévangile de Jacques*, dont M. Charles Michel a donné une excellente édition." SID., p. 137.

29. SID., p. 137-138.

30. "Le miracle du palmier est emprunté à l'*Évangile du Pseudo-Matthieu*

dependence of the Koran upon the Apocrypha here is rather literal: "est *tirée*" (extracted); "est *emprunté*" (borrowed).[31]

In my opinion, three facts can be stated as positive and ascertained:

a.) That Mohammad had a vast, if not indeed accurate, knowledge of the Christian stories and legends around the infancy of Jesus and Mary.

b.) That in the Marian sector the Koran depends predominantly on the Apocrypha — that is, the *Proto-evangelium of James*, the *Ps.-Matthew*, and the *Arabic Gospel of the Infancy*, although more on some than others.

I would not however dare assert a script-from-script dependence, textual or literal. What today seems to me more in tune with the historic truth, is an *oral, objective dependence; one of content, not of form.*

In other words, the inter-exchange in the matter between Koran and Apocrypha ought to be explained not by the fact that Mohammad had access to written documents which he could directly consult and study, but rather by what he could have gleaned from his social contacts with the Christian environment. It is proven that in Mecca Mohammad had built close ties with many Christians, laymen or monks, and especially with Bishop Waraka Ben Nawfal,[32] as we have seen earlier. He also travelled

---

(chapitre 20), lequel le place à l'époque de la fuite en Égypte de la Sainte Famille." SID., p. 142.

On the speech of the baby Jesus from the cradle (19, 30-31), SIDERSKY notes: "Il est emprunté au premier chapitre de l'Évangile arabe de l'enfance, où il est dit textuellement: 'Jésus parla, étant au berceau, et dit à sa mère: Je suis le Fils de Dieu, le Verbe, que vous avez enfanté etc., et mon Père m'a envoyé pour sauver le monde'." SID., p. 143.

31. SID., 137, 142, 143. Cf. notes 28, 30, above. (Fares)

32. Cf. HAD. IV, p. 279-283.

periodically to neighboring foreign countries while attending to the business of his future wife, Khadija, herself quite open to doctrines relative to Christ and Mary. Contacts like these, inside and outside Hijaz, must have prompted him to engage frequently in religious discussions motivated all too often by the inner urge, so natural to the Orientals, to be curious about, or interested in, their interlocutor's creed and religious practices.

Thus, by talking and listening rather than by direct reading of scripts, Mohammad could have memorized some biblical history including the "stories of the prophets" in general, and then some Christian history part of which were the "stories" referring to Jesus and Mary in particular.

Pareja writes well indeed in this respect: "It is really fair to think of an *oral transmission*, Arabo-phonetic, by Christians and Jews who were living in the same environment in which Mohammad was, to explain the source of several religious notions contained in the Koran."[33]

And also Quadri: "It is not likely that Mohammad had had *direct* knowledge of the sacred Jewish and Christian books. The more or less accurate notions from these books and the apocryphal literature, pertaining mainly to the New Testament, he must have gleaned from *caravaneers, merchants, slaves* and *monks*, and particularly from two Christian monks, Bohaira and Nestur, whom, according to the legend, he met in Syria."[34]

Regardless of what exactly the Koranic adjective *ùmmi*[35] — illiterate, or national — does mean, there is no indication

---

33. PAR., p. 598. — Italics are ours.

34. QUAD., p. 278. — Italics are ours. — Cf. BL. VI, p. 33.

35. "Those that shall follow the Apostle — the Unlettered Prophet *[an nabì-ya'l ùmmi]* " (7, 157). Cf. 7, 158. — "Non vi è dubbio che il vocabolo si collega con *ùmmat*; e allora sorge la domanda: che cosa è *ùmmat?*" NALLINO C. A., *Il significato del vocabolo coranico* Ùmmi, *applicato a Maometto, e quello di* 'al-Ummiyyùn'. In *Raccolta di scritti editi e inediti*, II, p. 62. — "Malgrado la grande autorità del Nallino, ci sembra meno probabile la sua identificazione assoluta di *ùmmi* con 'nazionale,' 'arabo'." BAUS., p. 506. — "Il existe donc

whether Mohammad knew the Greek, Syriac, Armenian, or Latin languages in which the Apocrypha were either written, or redacted, or translated, or manipulated.[36] Nor is there any evidence that they had, in the Prophet's time, existed in an Arabic version so as to suppose he could have read them and made use of them. Therefore I say that the opinion stating that there is in Sura 3, *The Imrans*, "a complete and *nonetheless ver-bal* parallelism with the apocryphal *Proto-evangelium Jacobi*," is false and over-exaggerated.[37]

c.) Finally — and this is the point I am coming at and on which I intend purposely to dwell — that, while the "Marian events" common to both Koran and Apocrypha present a sub-stantial *accord*, their narrative however is so different and *diverging* in many details that it suggests caution, restricting by that their dependence to an *oral* rather than *written* source.

To demonstrate that adequately, more time and paper is needed. Nonetheless, and by way of illustration only, I shall

---

une quasi-certitude que Mahomet n'a pas été analphabète." BL. IV, p. 32. — DR. (p. 109): "Mohammed savait-il lire et écrire? Le Koran nous répond par la négative, et il donne cet état d'analphabétisme comme l'une des preuves de la divinité de son instruction." — MOUB. I, p. 167: "Or cette question reste pen-dante." — MOUB. II, *Pent.* II, p. 54, in note: "Le Prophète se dit 'ummi,' ce qui veut dire plutôt qu'il ne connait pas d'Écritures révélées et qu'il a été en-voyé à ceux qui n'en possédaient point jusque-là. Mais quand même le Prophète aurait su lire, il aura sans doute beaucoup plus *entendu lire.*" — Cf. R. PARET, Ummi, in EI, IV, p. 1070-1071; NOL. I, p. 14-18; WEIL G., *Mahomet savait-il lire et écrire? In Atti del VI Congresso Internazionale degli Orientalisti,* (Firenze, 1880), I, p. 359-360.

36. "Laissant de côté la question de l'analphabétisme, tous admettent que Mahomet ignorait les langues dans lesquelles étaient rédigés les livres sacrés des autres religions." PAR., p. 589. And that, despite generic and not sure informa-tions by some Moslem authors. Cf. HAD. II, p. 69.—"Mahomet, on l'a dit, n'a connu aucune langue autre que l'arabe. C'est donc par la seule voie orale qu'il a pu avoir quelque connaissance des religions monothéistes. Cette connaissance superficielle et lacuneuse se complètera avec le temps, au hazard des circon-stances." BL. V, p. 36.

37. PEIR., p. 44. Italics are ours.

reduce my observations to the *Proto-evangelium of James* alone, the most famous, authoritative, and also the oldest among all Apocryphal Gospels.[38]

Here again I pass over Mary's visit to Elizabeth (c. 12), the hardships Joseph went through,[39] the visit by the Magi (c. 21), the killing of the Innocents (c. 22), the assassination of Zachariah "in the vestibule of the temple of the Lord" (13, 3) — all events of which there is no trace in the Koran. And I shall limit myself to pointing out from both texts, Koran and Proto-evangelium, the respective *agreements* and *disagreements* concerning four "historic" events expressly recorded in the Koran: *Mary's birth, her presentation in the temple, her annunciation, and Christ's birth.*

A. Mary's Nativity

a.) The two Texts agree on the following:

—That the newborn is a baby girl and not a boy.[40]

---

38. Concerning the *time* of the Proto-evangelium: "Nous estimerons raisonnable de placer la composition du Protoévangile dans la seconde moitié du IIe siècle." STR., p. 418. Therefore the Proto-evangelium is "le plus ancien et le plus célèbre des évangiles apocryphes de l'Enfence." *Ib.*, p. [V]. — And concerning the *place:* "Nous concluons que le Protoévangile n'a été écrit ni en Grèce, ni en Asie Mineure, ni en Syrie-Palestine, mais très vraisemblablement en Égypte." *Ib.*, p. 423.

39. His shock upon recognizing Mary pregnant (c. 13); the revelation by the angel (c. 14); the charges brought against him and his cross-examination (c. 15); the test of bitter waters (happily) undergone (c. 16).

40. *Proto-ev.*, 5, 2 (STR., p. 88); *Cor.*, 3, 36.

—That her name was given her by the mother and not by the father.[41]

—That her name is Mary.

b.) Beside these few points in common, however, there are several important *differences* in the details. Here are the main ones:

—The Koran does not mention Mary's mother by her own name, maybe not knowing it, while the Proto-evangelium says explicitly that her name was "Anna."[42]

—The Koran contradicts the Proto-evangelium openly by calling Imran Mary's father (66, 12); his real name instead according to the Proto-evangelium is "Joachim."[43]

—The Koran makes no mention whatsoever of Mary's virginal conception in Anna's womb. Mary's virginal, but not immaculate,[44] conception is on the contrary explicitly

---

41. "Anna washed herself of her impurity, suckled the baby and gave her the name of Mary: καὶ ὠνόμασεν τὸ ὄνομα αὐτῆς Μαρία." (5, 2—STR., p. 88). — "And have called her Mary: *sammaìtuha Maryam*" (3, 36).

42. "His wife, Anna — Ἡ δὲ γυνὴ αὐτοῦ ῎Αννα — was weeping" (II, 1 — STR., p. 68). Cf. 2, 3, 4; 4, 1; 5, 2; 6, 3; 7, 1. For textual variants of the name, cf. STR., p. 309.

43. "A very wealthy man, Joachim: ἦν ᾿Ιωακείμ " (1, 1 — STR., p. 64). Cf. 1, 3, 4; 4, 2, 3, 4; 5, 1; 5, 2; 7, 1, 2. For editorial variants, cf. STR., p. 313.
   Note that Mary's descent from her father Imran is stated by the Koran not only directly (66, 12), but also indirectly, i.e. by saying that her mother was Imran's wife: "Imran's wife said." (3, 35).

44. "El Protoevangelio supone sin duda la concepción *virginal* de Maria. Pero otra cosa es que esté ahí implicita la persuasión de una concepción *inmaculada*, como después de Jugie quiere Perler." ALDAMA J. A. de, *El Protoevangelio de Santiago y sus problemas*. In regard to a recent publication [P. Stryker], in Ephem. Mariolog., 12 (1962), 114. — "Con i dati forniti dal

stated by the Proto-evangelium,[45] and twice.[46]

—The Koran reports no details as to the social condition of Mary's parents. The Proto-evangelium describes them instead as a wealthy couple: Joachim was rich with livestock (4, 4); he offered his gifts to the Lord "in twofold quantity;"[47] and had at his service a handmaid (2, 2) and several shepherds (4, 3).

Protovangelo e tenute presenti le acute osservazioni del Prof. Perler, ci pare di non poter credere che l'A. abbia insegnato la dottrina dell'Immacolato Concepimento di Maria." PERETO L. M., La "Natività di Maria," in Marian., 22 (1960), p. 190.

45. With the Papyrus Bodmer V published, the reading of the perfect tense εἴληφε rather than the future λήψεται ought to be considered already sure and mandatory. And likewise, consequently, the old belief in the virginal conception by St. Anna.

We note that the edition of the N.T. Apocrypha, published in 1963 by E. Hennecke and W. Schneemelcher, carries the verb in the future, though between brackets, thus translating: "Go down; behold, your wife Anna has conceived (shall conceive)." EDGAR HENNECKE, New Testament Apocrypha, edited by WILHELM SCHNEEMELCHER, vol I. Gospel and related writings (The Westminster Press, Philadelphia, [1963], p. 376.

46. "Your wife has conceived in her womb [εἴληφα]" (4,2). — "Behold, barren though I am, have conceived [εἴληφα] in my womb (4, 4).

Like that of Tischendorf, Amman's edition (p. 194) carries in the two instances quoted above, the future: λήψεται, λήψομαι.

Fr. PERRETTO, loc. cit., wants that the aorist εἴληφα be referred to a conception of Mary according to the normal ways, and, therefore before the departure of Joachim into the desert. But that is in disagreement with the Proto-evangelium's text. Fr. STRYKER, in fact, notes: "C'est après le départ de son mari qu'Anne se met à prier pour obtenir une descendance (5, 8-15). Ensuite l'ange qui apparaît et lui dit: 'Anne, Anne, le Seigneur Dieu a exaucé ta prière. Tu concevras [συλλήμψεις] et tu enfanteras [γεννήσεις] et on parlera de ta posterité dans le monde entier." STR., p. 83, n. 3.

It must be remembered, incidentally, that St. EPIPHANIUS, panar., 79, 5-7 (MG., 42, 748), and ANDREA DA CRETA, Canon in B. Annae Conceptionem (MG., 97, 1313), have known and fought the sentence of the virginal conception.

47. "He offered the Lord twofold quantity [διπλᾶ] of what he owned, saying within himself: 'The additional quantity I'm paying shall be for the whole people.' " (1, 1 — STR., p. 64).

—The Koran ignores the joyful and sad events of Joachim's life: no word on the bitterness (1, 4) and the scorn he experienced in the Temple (1, 2) for not having given an offspring to Israel (1, 3); no word on his retreat to the desert, his fasting for forty days and forty nights (1, 4); no word on the angelic annunciation to console and comfort him (4, 2); no word on his return home (4, 3), on his embrace (4, 4) of Anna, his wife, who was waiting for him by the Golden Door.[48]

—The Koran, furthermore, in contrast to the Proto-evangelium, makes no mention of the detail that Anna gave birth to Mary "in the seventh month" (5, 2); nor of the presence of a midwife who, to Anna's question: "*What did I bring forth?*" answered, "*A baby girl!*" (5, 2). Again disagreeing with the Proto-evangelium which describes Anna's heart as thrilled with joy over hearing the midwife's reply (2, 2), the Koran pictures the poor mother in such a state of surprise, frustration and bitterness that she speaks her grievance to the Lord (3, 36a).

—In return though, the Koran, not the Proto-evangelium, relates the good mother's pious gesture when, right from the beginning, she consigned her baby and her future descendant to God's protection from the wicked Satan (3, 36b).

To conclude, if the Koran's author had under his eyes the Proto-evangelium script from which he could quote, the above differences would not have taken place. Their evidence, therefore, excludes any possible direct dependence

---

48. "And Anna waited by the door: πρὸς τῇ πύλη " (4, 4 — STR., p. 82). Notes Fr. Stryker opportunely: "Le mot grec πύλη désigne une porte monumentale (de ville, de temple, etc.), non la porte d'une maison θύρα ." *Ib.*, p. 83, note 4.
The Ps.-MATTHEW has Joachim and Anna meet "ad portam, quae aurea vocatur" (3, 5 — AM., p. 292).

between the Koran and the Proto-evangelium, and favors the minimum that can be retained: the presence of a fragmented and inaccurate information obtained by hearsay.

B. Presentation in the Temple

To this theme the Proto-evangelium devotes four chapters[49] and relates a plethora of particulars. The Koran deals with it, instead, in three or four short verses in Sura 3.

a.) The points on which both convene are:

—The benevolent welcome by the Lord.[50]

—The stay in a sacred place, the Temple,[51] in the "Sancta Sanctorum,"[52] according to Proto-evangelium; in the Sanctuary [mihràb] of Zachariah, according to the Koran (3, 37).

—The miraculous provision of food.[53]

---

49. They are the chapters 7, 8, 9, 10.

50. Proto-ev., 7, 3 (STR., p. 100); Cor. 3, 44.

51. "Mary dwelt in the Temple of the Lord like a dove" (8, 1 — STR., p. 100). Cf. note 80, Chapter One, p. 69.

52. "You have forgotten the Lord your God, you, who were raised in the Holy of Holies [εἰς τὰ ἅγια τῶν ἁγίων.] and have received the food from the hands of the angels" (15, 3 — STR., p. 134).

53. Proto-ev., 8, 1. — Cor. 3, 44b.

—The perplexity and the subsequent miracle which decides who should be Mary's tutor or guardian.[54]

b.) The *divergences*, however, are noted mainly in the following seven cases:

—In the *preparatory circumstances*. Joachim provides his daughter with a bevy of "immaculate girls" to escort her, each with a torch in hand, so that Baby Mary won't turn back[55] nor her heart stray out of the Temple of the Lord (7, 2). Of this cortege there is not the slightest mention in the Koran.

—In the *reception*. The Koran reserves Mary's reception to Allah alone, her Lord (3, 37). The Proto-evangelium wants her received instead not only by the Priest in charge of the Temple at the time[56] but also by the whole house of Israel (7, 3).

—In the *chronology of facts*. While totally ignored by the Koran, these facts are accurately recorded by Proto-evangelium: Mary was presented in the Temple at three years of age exactly (7, 2); and her sojourn in the Temple

---

54. *Proto-ev.*, 8, 2-3; 9, 1-3. — *Cor.*, 3, 44b.

55. "When she stood in front of the Temple of the Lord, hurriedly she climbed the fifteen steps, without turning back *[ita cursim ascendit, ut penitus non aspiceret retrorsum]*, and without calling her parents." Ps.-MATTHEW, *Gospel of the Nativity*, 4.
"Il volgersi indietro avrebbe, qui, valore di presagio funesto e di rinuncia al servizio divino cui Maria era stata votata dalla nascita. Si veda [...] per il probabile modello veterotestamentario, *Gen.*, 19, 26, a proposito della moglie di Lot, che, per essersi voltata indietro, è trasformata in statua di sale." DI NOLA A. M., *Protovangelo di Giacomo* (La Natività di Maria). Premessa, traduzione e note. Coll. "Piccola Fenice," 32 [Parma, Guanda], p. 60.

56. "*The Priest welcomed her*, and, after kissing her, he blessed her and said: 'The Lord has exalted your name above all generations. In you, in the last days, the Lord shall show redemption to the children of Israel'" (7, 2).

lasted for nine years, until she reached her puberty at twelve years of age.[57]

—With regard to the *mysterious food*. According to the Koran, it was provided by Allah with no other intermediary (3, 37); according to the Proto-evangelium, instead, Mary received it from the hands of the angel (8, 1).

—With regard to the *tutor*. The Koran knows none other than Zachariah (3, 37); in the Proto-evangelium instead, Mary's tutor and guardian was the aged[58] Joseph. Following advice from heaven (9, 1), hearing the threats uttered to her by the Priest (9, 2) and struck with fear (9, 3), Joseph decided to take Mary under his custody and brought her over to his house (9, 3).

—With regard to the *controversy* on who the tutor should be. The Koran alludes, but distinctly enough, to the throwing of quills or pen feathers in the river (Jordan), with only Zachariah's quill staying afloat. The Proto-evangelium on the contrary speaks of a dove which came out of Joseph's staff, flew, circling over his head, and finally rested on it (9, 1).

—Finally, while on one hand the Proto-evangelium (alone) mentions the *weaving of a veil* for the Temple of the Lord (9, 1), a project in which the lot drawn to spin the scarlet yarn fell to Mary (10, 2), the Koran (alone), on the other, provides us with the fascinating traits revealed by the angel to Mary concerning her eminent place in Allah's

---

57. "As she reached her *twelve years*, a decision took place by the Priests, who said: 'Behold, Mary has reached the age of twelve in the Temple of the Lord. What shall we do with her, so that she will not contaminate the Sanctuary of the Lord our God" (8, 2 — STR., p. 100).

58. "Joseph protested saying: 'I have children and I am old, while she is but a young girl: may I not become a laughing stock for the children of Israel!'" (9, 2). — Another "chronistic safeguard of Mary's virginity is Joseph's old age, which supposes his impotence." DI NOLA, *loc. cit.*, p. 63.

designs (3, 42) and the invitation to practice piety and prayer (3, 43).

C. The Annunciation

a.) The two Texts, Koran and Proto-evangelium, agree here on five points:

—On stating Mary's virginity.[59]

—On attributing to God alone the virginal conception of Jesus, outside of any sexual relationship.[60]

—On having an angel announce to Mary the good news.[61]

—On reporting Mary's psychological reaction, caught by surprise as she was, by the angel; her fear,[62] and perplexity.[63]

---

59. "Joseph, the lot fell to you to be in charge of tutoring Mary, the virgin of the Lord" (4, 1 — STR., p. 108). To receive someone in one's home for tutorship is quite different from contracting marriage, or being engaged. It is therefore another proof of the concern about emphasizing Mary's *virginity*: "The Priest remembered the young girl, Mary, who was from the tribe of David. She was *immaculate* before the lord" (10, 1 — STR., 110). Cf. *Cor.*, 19, 20.

60. *Proto-ev.*, 11, 3. — *Cor.*, 3, 47; 19, 20.

61. "And behold, the angel [ἄγγελος] appeared in front of her" (11, 2 — STR., p. 114). "The *angels* said: 'O Mary' " (3, 45).

62. Feeling of fear: "Have no fear, Mary." *Proto-ev.* (11, 2 — STR., p. 114). Cf. *Cor.*, 19, 18.

63. Perplexity: "Upon hearing (those words), Mary was perplexed." *Proto-ev.* (1, 2). Cf. *Cor.*, 19, 20.

—On relating the reassuring answer by the angel, God's messenger.[64]

b.) On all the rest they *disagree* with regard to the place, content and modality of the apparition:

—*Place.* In the Proto-evangelium the episode occurs in two successive phases. First outside the house, at the fountain, where Mary had gone with the jar to haul some water (9, 1); then inside the house, while she was spinning wool (1, 1-3). — The Koran instead says that the whole episode took place inside "a place to the east" (19, 16) to which Mary withdrew, or in the "*mihràb*" of Zachariah (3, 37), with no mention whatsoever of the fountain.

—*Objective.* While the Koran, in contradiction with the Oriental customs, neglects entirely the previous greeting, the Proto-evangelium has it as the first thing and then reports it in the same formula used by the Canonical Gospel (Lk. 1, 28). — With the evangelist Luke the Proto-evangelium agrees substantially on spelling out the qualities of the future newborn.[65] The Koran instead dwells willingly on promoting him as a "messenger to the children of Israel" (3, 49); it extolls his miraculous charisma, of which he will

---

64. *Proto-ev.*, 11, 2-3. *Cor.*, 19, 19. — Worth noting is the use by both sources, Proto-evangelium and Koran, of the term *Word* [Verb, Kalimat]. In the *Proto-evangelium*, the conception takes place by virtue of the Word [ἐκ λόγου]; in the Koran, the angel announces to Mary "a Word" [kàlimat] coming from ALLAH. (3, 45).

With regard to the formula: συνλήψῃ ἐκ λόγου αὐτοῦ, different from the way *Matthew* (1, 20) and *Luke* (1, 35) express themselves, thus writes De Aldama: "*Concebiras de su Verbo* (Protoevangelio 11, 2). El autor del Protoevangelio conoce bien Mt. 1, 20 (cf. 14, 2), como lo conoce también S. Justino (cf. Dialogo, 78,3). Pero al hacer la equivalencia: ek pnéumatos = ek lógou está copiando a S. Justino, que precisamente allí explica ese mismo diciendo: 'Ahora bien, el Espiritu y la virtud, que de Dios proceden, no pueden entenderse de otro modo que del Verbo' (33, 6)." ALDAMA, *loc. cit.*, p. 126-127.

65. *Proto-ev.*, 11, 3. — STR., 116. Lk. 1, 31-32.

make use only with "Allah's leave,"[66] and excludes any possible reference to his divine filiation.[67]

—*Modality*. At the beginning, that is in the phase around the fountain, the Proto-evangelium mentions only a "voice" without determining its source (9, 1); only later, in the subsequent phase, it speaks of "an angel" who appeared to Mary while spinning (11, 2). The Koran, on the contrary, ignores the spinning detail altogether and suddenly brings into appearance in perfect human semblance, the Spirit of Allah — the angel (19, 17). — The Proto-evangelium refers the conception of Jesus to God's Word — the *Verb*,[68]

---

66. "From clay I will make for you the likeness of a bird. I shall breathe into it and, by Allah's leave, it shall become a living bird" (3, 49). — The animation of the clay figurines is also quoted by *Ps.-Matthew*, c. 27, and by the *Arabic Infancy Gospel*, c. 36, but with notable difference in the details.

The *Koran* speaks of "likeness of birds" which Jesus brought to life with a "breath," and after the unconditioned "leave of Allah."

The *Ps.-Matthew* mentions explicitly "twelve" sparrows moulded of clay "on a sabbath day" (which triggered Jesus' playmates to denounce him to his father, Joseph, who reprimanded him), and with "mud from puddles." They were not animated by a "blow", or "breath", but "when Jesus slapped one hand against the other and said: 'Fly!' "

The *Arabic Infancy Gospel*, to the contrary, points out that Jesus was *seven*, and from clay had moulded several statuettes of donkeys, oxen, birds and other animals. They became alive at a command of his, after which they immediately began to move and bounce about. Whenever Jesus "gave his orders," the birds and sparrows darted off and came to rest on his hands. According to GEL., (p. 75), the bird to which Jesus gave life and motion is the "bat", considered the most perfect of all winged animals.

As one can see, contrary to the Koran, there is in the two Apocrypha no mention of a *vivifying breath* like that of Allah while creating Adam.

67. "I am the servant of God *[abd Allah]* " (19, 30). In the *Arabic Infancy Gospel*, to the contrary, the Baby Jesus "laying still in the cradle," had, right from the beginning of his existence, proclaimed himself *"son of God, the Verb"* (cf. note 475).

It seems inaccurate, therefore, to pretend that the Christ of the Apocrypha is "more of a man than a God," and closer to the Islamic Christ than to that of the Canonical Gospels. Cf. PEIR., p. 29.

68. Cf. *Proto-ev.*, 11, 2. As we have already pointed out (note 64, above),

Who, together with the power of God, overshadowed Mary when she was sixteen years of age (12, 3). The Koran, instead, without mentioning Mary's age, ascribes the conception of Jesus to a *word by Allah* — an order emanating from Him through a "fiat," according to some; and attributes the actual taking place of the conception to a "breathing" of Allah's Spirit into Mary (21, 91).

—The Proto-evangelium mentions expressly Mary's consent and reports it in almost identical terms as does the Gospel: *"Behold the handmaid of the Lord. Let it be done to me according to your word."*[69] Of this instance there is no mention at all in the Koran.

—The Proto-evangelium shows itself very concerned about stating Mary's virginity during childbirth,[70] a particular not mentioned clearly in the Koranic narrative.

D. *The Birth of Jesus*

a.) The two Texts *convene* on the substance of the fact: Mary gave birth to Jesus.[71]

---

the text has that Mary shall conceive "of the Verb": ἐκ λόγου. The affirmation, however, is not exclusive because in c.19, 1, Mary is said to be bearing in her womb a fruit "conceived of the *Holy Spirit*": ἐκ πνεύματος ἁγίου (AM., p. 250).

69. *Proto-ev.*, 19, 2 — Str., p. 154. — *Cor.*, 19, 23.

70. "Salome, Salome! A wonder have I to tell you about! A virgin gave birth [παρθένος ἐγέννεσεν]: something that nature cannot do" (19, 3) — 8 AM., p. 254.

71. *Proto-ev.*, 19, 2. — *Cor.*, 19, 23.

b.) They *disagree* on the circumstances of how, when and where.

According to Proto-evangelium, in fact, Jesus was born in the surroundings of Bethlehem (18, 1), in a desert and solitary place (17, 3), and in a "grotto."[72] The Koran, on the contrary, has him born by a palm tree (19, 22-26) the trunk of which served as a support, as a hard back rest of a "delivery chair."[73]

The Proto-evangelium shows us Joseph first on his way to Bethlehem accompanied by a son of his (17, 2) leading the donkey Mary was riding, and then later anxiously in search of a midwife (19, 1). Next, passing over in silence the evangelic episode of the shepherds and angelic choirs, the same Apocryphum multiplies the prodigies at the moment of Christ's birth: silence and wonder strike the whole creation; paralysis of the universe from any activity (18, 2): above the grotto, while an obscure cloud fades slowly away, a dazzling light bursts inside the grotto and, as it does, the Baby Jesus appears wrapped in it (19, 2); the midwife Salome is punished for not believing in Mary's virginity as still intact after childbirth (20, 1); the same midwife is healed at merely touching the newborn Baby (20, 4).

Of all these particulars there is no trace in the Koranic narrative.

Those are the concordant and discordant data surfacing

---

72. "And there he found a grotto [σπήλαιον] and he took her in" (18, 1 — STR., p. 146). Contrary to an assumed dependence of the *Proto-evangelium* from the story of Dionisius' birth in a "grotto," sponsored by Testuz (p. 19-21). — Cf. PERRETTO, *loc. cit.*, p. 183, in note.

73. "Il tronco della palma avrebbe avuto la funzione del duro schienale della 'sedia del parto,' come crede anche Muhammad Aly *["She* (Mariam) *may have had recourse to the trunk of a palm tree to find a support in the throes of Childbirth"].*" BEL., p. 454.

from an accurate confrontation between the Marian narratives in the *Koran* and the *Proto-evangelium of James*, the most authoritative among Apocryphal Gospels. They are positive data, within everybody's reach, and undeniable. They ought not to be neglected, nor ignored.

Whenever the Koran's authenticity is brought into question, it is not hard to understand what discomfort the average Moslem, mostly intellectual, goes through. In front of a serious and pressing difficulty, he feels urged almost by instinct not to argue about it, but to let go and barricade himself behind the "revelation" rather than face freely and relaxedly a Koranic evaluation. Frequently, however, he does surrender himself to the *ghàyb*, the arcane and occult, the knowledge of which is God's own prerogative.

Open-mindedness in the case cannot be a one-sided attitude. Any orthodox Moslem, mainly a scholar, must feel bound to abide by it. He also should be aware that his interlocutor, when a Christian opponent, is likewise going through a difficult and embarrassing mental hardship. He should show him understanding just as he wants to be understood, and both should sit down and approach the problem of concordances and discordances between Koran and Proto-evangelium in an honestly ecumenical and scientific spirit.

For a satisfactory solution in the matter there is no use in taking as a second term of comparison the Canonical Gospel — and particularly the portion of it usually called the *Infancy Gospel*.

That will only widen the gap between the two documents as they confront each other in terms of Marian and Christological "data."

I would not like to report here all the evident discrepancies between the Koran and the Gospel in their narratives on Christ's annunciation and birth — the only twin events common to both sources. It will be enough to mention briefly all the other episodes about the infancy of Jesus that were entirely omitted by the Koran, and which by contrast were duly recorded by the Gospel and, at least in part, by the Proto-evangelium: Mary's visit to Elizabeth (*Lk.* 1, 39-56); the angel's apparition to Joseph (*Mt.* 1, 18-15); the Baby's circumcision (*Lk.* 2, 1-21); His presentation in the Temple (*Lk.* 2, 22, 38); the Magi's coming (*Mt.* 2, 1-12); the killing of the Innocents (*Mt.* 2, 16-18); the flight into Egypt (*Mt.* 2, 23; *Lk.* 2, 39, 51-52); the loss of Jesus and his finding in the Temple (*Lk.* 2, 41-50).

One thing then remains for us to do: to confront the Koran with the *Apocrypha*.

The Koran's objective agreement with them is, as we have seen, quite relevant. The formal one instead, the accord in the wording, is still more relevantly deficient, which leaves us with no other alternative than to conclude that the *Marian facts* in the Koran depend materially, not formally, on the Apocrypha; *orally*, not *scripturally*.

Our present stand, we believe, is in line with the modern trend followed by contemporary Scholars. Rather than struggling for a dependence as of a text from text, which is just as hard to sustain as to prove, they resort to the environment in which Mohammad lived and operated — a religious atmosphere dense with "Judeo-Christian ideology." For years, the Arabian Prophet shuttled between these two major monotheistic currents. Of one of them he was at one time a part. With them he argued, and from them he learned. Much of the things he heard at the time, he memorized, mulling them over for a while.[74] Later, in a style

---

74. MARRACCI had already noted: "Cum per emporia Syriae cum Mercatoribus Christianis et Judaeis, inter quos plures erant haeretici, praesertim Ariani, et Nestoriani, assidue versaretur: interrogabat eos de rebus Religionis eorum: et Judaei quidem fabulas Talmudicas, quibus Alcoranus totus refertus est; Christiani vero historias apocryphas illi venditabant." MAR. I [De Alcorano], p.41. — ESS. (p. 53): "Au Yémen comme en Syrie, la caravane de Mohammed rencontrait en premier plan de l'actualité le problème de Dieu. Dans les bazars, parmi les fonctionnaires, dans les églises, les jardins, aux bains, on ne discutait pas autre chose." — NAL. I (P. 194): "I suoi primi informatori

and wording proper to his own tribe, his "creative irruption" would give them the version suitable to the purposes he had in mind. That materialized in the "facts" about Issa and his mother, Maryam.

II. Dogmatic Remark

What is the theological value of the Marian facts of the Koran?

To answer this question a distinction is necessary between the Koranic data deriving from a common source — which we shall call "historic," and those elaborated by Mohammad's own meditation and reflection — which we shall call "prophetic."

As we have said earlier, the Marian literature in the Koran came into it from Christian sources — the Apocryphal Gospels, mainly the *Proto-evangelium of James*. From this as a premise,

---

furono quasi certamente cristiani appartenenti alla categoria di commercianti non arabi di passaggio per la Mecca, oppure schiavi d'origine abissina o siro-palestinese o mesopotamica; in ogni caso, cristiani di fede ardente, ma non molto versati nelle dottrine della loro religione, imbevuti di eresie, in un certo senso giudaizzanti." — DERM. (p. 12): "Il connut des chrétiens, mais sans doute assez ignorants et fort éloignés des centres d'orthodoxie. Il entendait sans doute oralement divers récits de l'Ancien et du Nouveau Testament, du Talmud et des Apocryphes, mais sans avoir accès aux textes." — And for the "Stories of the old Prophets," IDEM (p. 27): "Ces histoires [...] *ne semblent pas tirées des textes écrits*, mais évoquent des *oraux* d'après la Bible, le Talmud, et les Apocryphes." Italics are ours. Regarding the entry of Christianity in Arabia, see bibliography in BL. VI, p. 58; cf. also WAT. I, p. 190-192.

the conclusion logically follows: the "historic" elements relative to Mary in the Koran reflect *Christian beliefs* which were alive and circulating throughout the distant Arabian Peninsula in the first decades of the 6th century A.D. They were Christian, or Judeo-Christian, items of faith; not always clear in terms of technical formulas, but always orthodox. It is known, in fact, that Christianity in the Arabian Peninsula was as a whole superficial and contaminated with two major heresies: the Nestorian, dominating in the North and seeping through from Persia; and the Monophysite, ruling in the South and coming across from Abyssinia.[75]

Whichever the case, the Marian "historic" dogmas or literature in the Koran, once established in their Christian origin, can consequently in no way be called a Moslem product, but are rather a result of *Christian* traditions. In other words, they are derivatives of a Christian faith and, at the same time, developments of a Christian literature both prior to the first decades of the seventh century of our actual era. They're effluents running with turbid waters, if you want to call them that, but nonetheless witnessing unquestionably to the purity of their Christian mother-river.

Whatever in the Koran is the result of Mohammad's own ingenuity and evaluation should be welcome instead as a typically *Moslem* contribution.

However, because all Marian "historic" and "prophetic" elements are inserted in the Koran and adopted by it, they

---

75. If the information of St. Epiphanius (Panar., 19, 3; 30, 2) referred to the Arabian Peninsula, properly called, then Arabia ought to be considered a hatchery of many heresies. All in all, however, the Arabia meant by the Bishop of Salamina: "*in Palestinae finibus*" (*Haeres.* 66, 1 — MG. 42, 30 C), must have rather been the Petran Arabia (Petra: an old city to the east of modern Jordan), one of the fifteen provinces forming the *Diocesis Orientis*, which, in turn, was one of the five "dioceses" of which the *Praefectura Orientis* was constituted. It is quite known that the *Praefectura Orientis* and *Praefectura Illyrici* formed together the whole of the *Oriental Roman Empire* after the death of Theodosius the Great (+ 395).

indeed ought to be taken as an *indivisible portion of the Koranic Message*.

This theoretical conclusion determines a practical consequence that can be duly appreciated only by those who well know what the Koran does represent for Islam.

Taken in its threefold current use of a religion, a community, and a civilization,[76] all in Islam has to part from the Koran and finally come back to the Koran. All, including grammatical and literary branches — such as morphology, syntax and rhetoric. Whatever comes up as opposed to the Koran should with no hesitation be regarded as suspicious and discarded as an opening to error and unorthodoxy.[77] Far from being the fruit of Mohammad's ingenuity, the Koran for the average orthodox Moslem is the word of Allah; it is the infallible truth that *"falsity cannot reach from before or behind"* (41, 42). It is the light-

---

76. In its current and modern use, "Islam" means, at the same time, religion, community, civilization.

During the Meccan period, the term *Islam* was indiscriminately attributed to the great monotheistic religions revealed; and the predicative *muslim* was said of Jews, of Judeo-Christians, and of the properly called Moslems, Mohammad's early followers in that they all abhorred the *shirk* and believed in Allah.

In the Medinian period, to the contrary, *Islam* becomes, a step at a time, the exclusive and proper denomination of the *religion* preached by Mohammad, the code of the new *community*, in the bosom of which a new type of *civilization* was developed.

77. NWY., p. 22 — DR. (p. 18): "Le Koran, c'est la nourriture de l'esprit, la règle de conduite, le texte de prière, l'instrument de prédication; c'est leur [musulmans] hymne et leur histoire; c'est leur foi fondamentale et leur code pour toutes les circonstances de la vie." — ESS. (p. 70): "Le Coran marque jusqu'à ce jour le point culminant atteint par la langue arabe. Pour tous les Arabes comme pour Mohammed lui-même, l'enivrante beauté de sa poésie fait éclater en pleine lumière sa divine origine." — And MARRACCI: "illo utuntur ad iuramenta sua: illum consulunt in graviorem rerum tractatione: illum gestant in bello: illius sententias in vexillis militaribus describunt: illum auro, ac lapidibus pretiosis exornant." MAR. I [De Alcorano], p. 45. — For the "inimitability" of the Koran, see bibliography in BL. VI, p. 236.

giving book, mighty, limpid,[78] of which no one should doubt (2, 2); a mercy from Allah, man's light and sure guide during his individual and social life.[79]

To close, since the Marian elements that we've hitherto analyzed and brought into a synthesis are the Koran's integral part, they also become in practice *light*, a *right path* and *guidance*. Therefore, on a par with any Koranic section, they assume a capital importance and claim an undeniable theological value — because they are *"word of God."*

III. Ecumenical Remark

This other remark is of a practical nature, and therefore integral with the precedent. It can thus be formulated:

---

78. "Their apostles came to them with veritable signs, with psalms, and with the light-giving Book *[munìr]* " (35, 25). Cf. 22, 8; 31, 20. "This is a mighty Book *[azìz]* " (41, 41). — "A light has come to you from Allah, and a light-clear Book *[mubìn]* " (5, 15). Cf. 4, 174.

79. "That which We have revealed in the Koran is a balm and a mercy *[ràhmat]* to the believers" (17, 82). Cf. 6, 157; 27, 77; 28, 86; 29, 51. — "Thus We have inspired you with a spirit of Our will when you knew nothing of faith and the Book, and made it a light *[nùr]* whereby We guide those of Our servants whom We please" (42, 52). — "These signs of the wise Book are a guide *[hùda]* and a mercy for the good-doers" (31, 2-3). Cf. 45, 20. — The Koran is a *code of life*: over and above the Pact with Allah and the severe judgment that shall follow, it prescribes the five "pillars" *[arkàn]* of Islam, and sets the rules for personal, social, and communitarian statutes. Cf. MASSON (*Le Coran considéré comme fondement primordial des lois relatives au culte*), I, p. 449-646;

What utility, or advantage, does the Koranic Message on Mary offer for an eventual *ecumenical*, or *pastoral*, approach?

To avoid misconception, it will be worthwhile to note that the adjective "ecumenical" here is not taken in its proper and rigorous sense, i.e. a wishful effort by separated Christian communities to come into an ecclesiastical communion within the one, true Church of Christ; but in its larger meaning, i.e. the auspicious endeavor by members of different religious confessions to come together into a brotherly understanding of each other, motivated ultimately by their common faith in the one, true God.

That brings us again to another important note: every eventual dialogue that takes place among dissident brothers plays the role of the coin with two opposite sides; it always offers a basic convergence and a basic divergence to start from. Two psychological attitudes are thus born, which in our case can be formulated as follows:

1.) Islam has many a common point with Christianity, even in the Marian sector; basically, however, they are very different.

2.) Though disagreeing with Christianity on account of Mary, Islam offers nonetheless many instances where both converge and agree. In other words, as in any dialectic contrast, so here also one can observe two antithetical attitudes born of the criterion upon which one party prefers to insist — either a criterion advocating obstinately *divisive* factors, or a criterion treasuring preferably *unitive* factors, as a take-off.

Obviously, were we to be in Zakarias' shoes and adopt his Koranic hypothesis and arbitrary evaluation, the all-desired Islamo-Christian dialogue would be jeopardized, if not indeed

---

(*Le Coran considéré comme fondement primordial des lois relatives aux actes humains*), I, p. 647-649; GOT. (IV, *La Legge*), p. 26, 33; (V, *La Morale*), p. 33, 42; (VI, *Il Diritto*), p. 42, 46.

entirely foiled. In fact, how is it psychologically possible to enter into a dialogue and work out some positive approach if the Christian allows himself to confront his Moslem partner with judgments that hurt his feelings, polarize him and turn him off? Zakarias himself agrees on this point (Zk. p. 59).

Truly, the gap of division would widen furthermore when the Moslem hears that his Prophet, Mohammad, was but a poor wild animal that fell miserably in the trap of a shrewd Rabbi (p. 73); that in structuring Islam, he — Mohammad — was not the architect but a mere executive (43); and that historically he was only a "slave to Judaism" — "un serviteur du Judaïsme" (p. 40).

What hope will there remain for a unifying dialogue if the Koran is said to be written by a Jew, and that it contains nothing which is not exclusively and typically Jewish (28)?

How can a Moslem be attracted to openness and feel comfortable to sit down with the Christian in a serene and fruitful conversation if this latter calls his partner's Islam a "myth" (p. 63), a monstrous "bluff" (p. 60), even "the greatest bluff in the Mediterranean history" (p. 58); and actually an "immoral hàrem" (p. 44) and a carrier of lethal germs (p. 46)?

No! The dialogue for an approach must be set upon the basis of mutual respect and esteem, mutual honesty and mutual cooperation in the search of the truth.

First of all, intellectual honesty demands that the truth not be hidden, minimized or disguised.[80] And in terms of an ecumen-

---

80. GARDET notes: two temptations in the matter have to be curbed: one, much older and quite frequent, is to *minimize* the positions of the opponent with the intent of reducing him to error; and the other, to *disguise* the truth in order to please the opponent, despite the risk of being trapped by a levelist syncretism. Cf. GAR., p. 142.

ical dialogue, the genuine and *integral* facet of Christianity and Islam ought to be brought into clearer sight.

None denies that the two monotheistic blocs face each other with a remarkable polarization. That is also true with regard to Mary. For instance, the affirmation or negation by Islam of her Divine Maternity implies for Christianity the affirmation or negation of two basilar dogmas — Christ's divinity subsequent to the incarnation of the Verb, and the Trinity of persons in God.

But neither is it fair to ignore the positive aspects, refusing to take a look at the other side of the coin also. Islam's greatest merit as a whole was, first of all, to have been structured spiritually upon Abraham and the profession of his monotheistic faith. It consequently ought to be acknowledged as a religion basically "*revealed*" — a divine religion on a par with Judaism and Christianity, and not just a mere naturalistic one. Apart from the way with which it was linked to the primitive "revelation," Islam contains objectively the truths come down from God by revelation; it contains as well a complex of truths, rather seeds of truth, which, besides disposing one's mind to the acceptance of the whole truth, contribute efficiently to a positive approach by the two sides.

Secondly, we ought to remember that a marked and decisive influence was exercised initially on the Prophet of Islam by Christianity, though not orthodox.[81] This was "**the main yeast in fermenting Mohammad's religious conscience; a confused but efficient suggestion of dogmas, of catechetical means and of rites; a** *humus* **never entirely denied, upon which rose luxuriant the centuries-old palm tree of Islam.**"[82]

---

81. Mohammad "fut, surtout aux débuts, beaucoup plus près des chrétiens, affirmant la mission de Jésus, Messie, Verbe, et Esprit de Dieu, sa naissance virginale, l'immaculée conception de Marie [?], insistant sur l'Antéchrist, la Résurrection, le Jugement dernier, la vie éternelle." DERM., p. 12. Differently, BL. IV, p. 36.

82. GAB. II, (*La culla dell'Islam*), p. 37.

Mohammad's historic environment was contested by two religious currents: the *shirk*, or polytheist Associationism; and the *nasraniyat*, or Judeo-Christian faction. Ignorance of these twin factors would run one the risk of not understanding adequately the Islamic phenomenon, or of reducing it to an unsolvable dilemma.

True that the Prophet forbids his followers, as a rule, to build ties with the "People of the Book" (5, 51); their only friends must be Allah, His apostles, and the faithful (5, 55). True also that he rails against the Christians for adulterating the Gospel (5, 14, 46); and lays on the Jews God's curse because they broke his Covenant, transgressed the Torah[83] and perverted the words of the Scripture (5, 13, 78). But it is likewise true that the "People of the Book," if believers in Allah and the Last Day and good-doers, and whether Jews or Judeo-Christians [nasàra], will not be doomed to hellfire as the unbelievers (67, 6), the associators and the evil-doers (5, 72) shall; like the God-fearing [muttaqùn] and true Moslems, "they shall be rewarded by their Lord; they have nothing to fear or regret" (2, 62).

There is more than just that. Near the end of his career, the Great Arabian suffered a change of heart toward the Christians, showing them more sympathy than was expected. At that time, while sweeping the past with the synthetical look of his experience, and while simultaneously envisioning, with the eyes of a prophet, the future of his "middlemost" community, he immortalized the "nasàra" (Christians) with a sincere and deferential tribute as "true followers of Christ." Here are his own words as recorded in Sura 5, *The Table* (5, 82-85):

"You will find that the most implacable of men in their en-

---

83. The Koran mentions explicitly the Covenant [mithàq] ratified by Allah through "a true and solemn pledge" (9, 111) with the Prophets, with Mohammad, with Noah, with Abraham, with Moses, with Jesus, son of Mary (33, 7). And while urging the Moslem to faithfully honor it (5, 1, 7; 16, 91, 95; 57, 8), it openly incriminates the nasàra (5, 14) and the children of Israel (2, 40, 63, 83, 93; 4, 154; 5, 12, 70) for breaking it.

mity to the faithful are the Jews [al-yahood] and the Associators [al latheena àshraku], and that the nearest to them in affection are those who say: 'We are Christians' [nasàra]. That is because there are Priests and Monks among them; and because they are free from pride.

"When they listen to that which was revealed to the Apostle, you will see their eyes fill with tears as they recognize in what they hear the truth they already know. And you hear them say: 'Lord, we believe! Count us among your witnesses. Why should we not believe in Allah and in the truth that has come down to us? Why should we not hope for admission among the righteous?'

"And for what they have professed, Allah has rewarded them with gardens watered by running streams, where they shall dwell for ever."[84]

These are the internal, or *subjective*, attitudes that each party should adopt during a dialogue.

As for the *objective* basis, or the doctrinal content, there is for sure no way one can hide the antagonism[85] so alive and operative even today among both religions.

---

84. 5, 82-85. — Elsewhere — perhaps reminiscing with nostalgia over what he had the opportunity to see in Christian monasteries, where he halted over-night during his periodic journeys — Mohammad remembers the flickering lights in "*homes* (temples) *which Allah has sanctioned to be built for the remembrance of His name. In them morning and evening His praise is sung by men (Monks) whom neither trade nor profit can divert from remembering Him, from offering prayers, or from giving alms*" (24, 36-37).

85. Islam's attitude nowadays toward other monotheistic religions is similar to Christianity's attitude toward Judaism: "Il reconnaît sa validité au temps jadis; il affirme qu'il doit le remplacer aujourd'hui; il admet, enfin, que certains de ses institutions dérivent d'institutions juives." BOUSQUET G. H., *Judaisme, Christianisme, Islam, religions apparentées*, in Studia Islamica, 14 (1961), p. 31.

For a personal opinion on Islam's current mentality, even regarding the mystery of the most Holy Trinity (p. 43, 94, 129) and the divinity of Christ (p. 54, 99-100), it is informative to read the conclusions of an Islamo-Christian interview conducted by the Rev. Y. MOUBARAC among seven contemporary

However, the monotheistic faith and other dogmatic truths professed by both parties,[86] though by different formulas,[87] constitute an agreement as precious as ever — an agreement which, by its very nature, would push more toward unity than disunity. Nor should one ignore or under-value the place of privilege the Koran and, after the Koran, Islam reserves to Jesus and Mary.[88] It is an additional stimulus to a broader understanding, to a peaceful living with one another, and to a fruitful cooperation among the two major blocs of the monotheistic creed.

---

personalities and published in the book: *Les Musulmans*, coll. "Verse et Controverse," XIV [Paris, Beauchesne, 1971].

86. Fr. PEIRONE (116) thus compares the *Creed*'s points, which are common to Christianty, rather Catholicism, and Islam, and those which are rejected by Islam, particularly in Christology:

Common Points	*Rejected Points*
- I believe in one God	- Father
- almighty	
- creator of heaven and earth	
- of all that is seen and unseen.	
- And in one Lord, Jesus Christ,	- His only son
- who was conceived by the Holy Spirit	- suffered under Pontius Pilate
- born of the Virgin Mary	- was crucified
- who died [?]	
- ascended into heaven	- was buried
- from thence he shall come	- descended into hell.
- I believe in the Holy Spirit [?]	- the third day he rose from the dead
- the forgiveness of sins	- is seated at the right hand of God
- the resurrection of the dead	the Father.
- and the life to come.	

87. In professing their faith, Christians use a positive formula: "*I believe in One God*"; the Moslems, to the contrary, use a negative one: "*There is no other God but Allah.*"

88. In the Koran, "La place de Maryam est importante, tant du point de vue dogmatique que du point de vue historique." WENS., p. 358. — "La personnalité de Jésus, ainsi que celle de Marie sa Mère, me paraît y avoir plus d'importance que celle des divers Prophètes en particulier dans la conscience du 'Musulman moyen'." BOUSQUET G. H., *loc. cit.*

And in the strictly Marian sector, valuable above all is this fact happily verified in the everyday life. Instead of being motive for a brotherly entente in Protestantism, Mary becomes all too often a tool for disunity, contention and animosity among the different Christian confessions. Quite contrary is the situation, fortunately, in Islam. Mary's sweet image as pictured by Mohammad himself results as a factor for mutual esteem and reciprocal approach. And we have had concrete evidence of that, and in quite recent times.[89]

The average Moslem nurtures for Mary a deep and honest cult of veneration. For him Mary is the *Sàyidat* (our Lady) just as she is for the Christian. To worship her, he too resorts to some devotional practices with a congruent equivalence in Christianity — such as the *tasbìh* (rosary) and the *khìrqa* (scapular). Apart from these popular instances, and if we limit ourselves to the theoretical creeds and dogmas, we find with joy in Islam what we sorrowfully do not find in the various Protestant confessions, i.e. Mary's spotless virginity, her supreme holiness, her sovereign dignity, her intimate unity with Christ; and at the base of these excellent prerogatives, God's preferential, intense and boundless love for her.

The following testimony rendered by the Koran to Mary contains unquestionably a great deal of truth. Far from stalling the investigation for further scriptural enrichment, it favors it. It hastens, at the same time, the acceptance of all that has been divinely revealed about her: **"Allah has chosen you, and made you pure, and exalted you above all women,"** says the Koran (3, 42); on the other side, **"Hail, full of grace, ... blessed are you among women,"** states the Gospel (*Lk*. 1, 28, 42).

---

89. Msgr. MULLA mentions, among other things, the devotion of the Moslems in Bombay while venerating the statue of O. Lady of Mt. Carmel at the church of St. Theresa of the Child Jesus (p. 269); and the national Marian Congress in Beirut, October 1954: "Le comité d'organization comprenait plusieurs musulmans dont le premier ministre du Liban lui-même; l'exposition organisée en marge des séances présentait un stand consacré à 'Marie dans l'Islam'." (p. 270).

Finally, with regard to the substantial *divergences* undeniably existing, we are positively convinced that a "dialogue," more in current vogue today than ever, could smooth over many of their angularities and become a very helpful means for mutual approach.

"Dialogue" with the "People of the Book" was practiced by Mohammad himself during his lifetime. The Koran had once urged it in this manner:

"Say, 'People of the Book, let us come to an agreement: that we will worship none but Allah, that we will associate none with Him, and that none of us shall set up mortals as gods besides Him.' If they refuse, say to them: 'Then at least bear witness, saying, "We have surrendered to Allah as Moslems." ' " (3, 64)

The dialogue we are advocating here should not be reduced to the dimensions of a low-level, cheap and trickling casuistry which provides for a way out of scabrous situations of the moment only. It must be understood as an encounter at a highly intellectual level between competent and authoritative people; people open to sincerity, to mutual esteem, to reciprocal tolerance, and taking as a common ground for confrontation of their respective creeds the authority of their "Book" — Gospel or Koran;[90] people able to free themselves of whims, of proselytic mentality,[91] and of that invisible itch to overcome or "convert" the other party; people with desire burning live in their hearts to mutually enrich each other with the peaceful and joyous acceptance of one another as everyone is, so that the truth — and the

---

90. Cf. HAD. III, p. 7-46.

91. Non-Christians see often in the "dialogue" nothing but a proselytic maneuver. "S'ils le pensent réellement, il est préférable, en ce cas, de suspendre momentanément les dialogues à implications religieuses et de laisser au temps le soin de faire tomber les préjugés et de mûrir les mentalités." *Orientations pour un dialogue entre chrétiens et musulmans,* [Secretariatus pro non-christianis], Roma, Ancora, 1970, p. 23.

truth alone — may emerge established on more solid and lasting foundations.

To set up an *integral dialogue* here is far beyond my limited range in this work. That should include among other topics man's elevation to the supernatural order, the original sin passed on to Adam's descendants, mankind's redemption by Christ's death on the Cross, the Church, the Priesthood, the Sacraments. Since I limit myself to a *partial* one, a dialogue with Marian perspective only, the point above all to clarify will be the *Divine Motherhood* — the compendium of Mary's glories, but also the most serious obstacle for a theological entente between Christians and Moslems. And to clarify the point from the grass roots, one ought to begin with the mystery of the most holy Trinity.

Here are, therefore, the main lines that should regulate an eventual "dialogue" in this respect.

First of all, it is imperative to bring into limelight that the Christian Trinity has nothing in common with the abhorred *shirk,* Associationism, or Arab polytheism. To the contrary, while presupposing the unity in God, our concept of Christian Trinity reconciles itself very well with the most rigid and absolute monotheism. True, several Moslem apologists have in the past gathered up a pile of Koranic quotations to confute the trinitarian dogma. But it is equally true that such quotations, if critically winnowed, do not deal with that which is authentic Christian doctrine, but with heresies that have mushroomed within Christianity itself.

Our Trinity, in fact, involves no division or multiplication in the one and indivisible divine nature, "non-generating and non-generated";[92] but It brings into evidence the fecundity of this

---

92. "Una quaedam summa res est, incomprehensibilis quidem et ineffabilis [...]; et illa res non est generans, neque genita, nec procedens." DENZ.,

nature, or the vital dynamism of Him whom the Koran calls the Living Being, the primary source of life, and the One without whom there can be no sign of life.[93] One only is the nature in God. But it is so dynamic a nature, so rich and exuberant with life, that, independently of any exterior agent, masculine or feminine, it can explicate itself, through the one and only act of knowing *[kàlimat]* and the one and only act of amorous breathing *[rùh ul-qùdus]*, in three Persons. These Persons are no different from God. Nor by nature are they alien to God, as they would be in the rejected *shirk*. But all three are subsisting in the one, indivisible nature of the unique and true God.

After accurately examining the Koran in its entirety and in the texts objecting against the trinitarian dogma, we can state with no fear of contradiction that Islam's sacred Book does not properly know the orthodox Christian doctrine. What the Koran as a whole does consequently assert is the *absence* from it, rather than the *denial* by it, of the authentic Christian creeds.

What I'm saying is evidently true with regard to the trinitarian dogma. The notion of Trinity, as expressed by the Koran (5, 116) and not by the Koranic exegetes,[94] does in no way

---

n. 432. — With BOUBAKEUR we may well agree that the Koran "n'inclut nullement la Sainte Vierge en la Trinité" (BOUB., p. 616). All the more that the Koran abhors any concept of Trinity and multiplicity in God. That, however, does not exclude that the Koran really admits, suggests, and rails against a false notion of the Trinity, which, despite all the good will of Boubakeur, "fait de Marie la troisième personne de la Trinité" (p. 615). It is necessary, therefore, to honestly recognize that the Moslem Holy Book comes to grips with a trinitary doctrine which, in no way, reflects the authentic Christian faith in the mystery of the most Holy Trinity.

93. "Allah is *[al-hàqq]*, the Truth" (22, 6). Cf. note 121, Chap. 1, p. 85. The meaning the term *al-hàqq* involves in the Koranic lexicon, is more realistic than conceptual: in other words, it designates an ontological reality, rather than a logical truth. *Al-hàqq* is *The Reality*. Reality in the fullest and unconditional expression of its term: boundless richness in perfection; fullness of inexhaustible life; life subsisting by itself.

94. "Les musulmans qui voulurent refuter le christianisme comprirent

respond to the Christian faith. No Christian believer could legitimately refuse to subscribe to the following Koranic Text considered anti-trinitarian:

"Say: 'What thing counts most in testimony?'
"Answer: 'Let Allah be our witness. This Koran has been revealed to me that I may thereby warn you and all whom it may reach.'
"Say: 'Will you testify that there are other gods besides Allah?'
"Answer: 'No. I will not testify to such thing.'
"Say: 'No. He is but one God. And I am innocent from the gods you associate with Him.' " (6, 19)

In his ardent zeal and volcanic indignation against any form of Associationism, Mohammad comes to the point of imagining a sort of judicial dialogism, a tribunal. On the day of judgment, Jesus is called by Allah to disprove a charge attributed to him, which is thus formulated by Allah himself:

"*Jesus, son of Mary, did you ever say to mankind, 'Worship me and my mother as gods beside Allah'?* "

---

souvent les formulations chrétiennes comme désignant une pluralité de 'substance' en Dieu. A l'opposé (mais en corrélation) ceux qui s'efforcèrent à une présentation sympatique, et voulurent montrer que les chrétiens étaient bien monothéistes — GHAZZALI, IBN RUSHD, IBN QAYYIM — n'entrevirent guère le dogme de la Trinité qu'à travers une interprétation modaliste." GAR., p. 29. — BAYDAWI, though interpreting the "three" of S. 5, 116 as Allah, Mary, and Jesus, quotes the Christian doctrine of the three persons [aqanìm] in God; but adds immediately that the Father denotes the essence; the Son, the science; the Holy Spirit, the life. BAYD. I, 128. — Cf. HAD. III, p. 290-295.

In the third part of his *Prodromus*, MARRACCI writes at full length against the Moslems on the H. Trinity (p. 16-32) and the divinity of Christ (p. 32-59). And in *Refutata* to S. Four, says: "Notandum est Alcorani verba, iuxta communem Moslemorum sapientum expositionem, nullo modo verum Sanctissimae Trinitatis mysterium oppugnare" MAR. II, p. 178. And sets as an assertion: "Hisce praemissis, dicimus Sanctissimae Trinitatis mysterium non posse a Mahumetanis rationabiliter negari." *Ib.*, p. 179. — Cf. DI MATTEO I., *La divinità di Cristo e la dottrina della Trinità in Maometto e nei polemisti musulmani.* "Biblica e Orientalia," 8, Roma, Istituto Biblico, 1938.

And Christ will not hesitate to answer:

"Glory to you! How could I say that to which I have no right? If I ever said so, you would have surely known it ... I spoke to them of nothing except of what you bade me. That is, *'Serve Allah, my Lord and your Lord.'* And whilst I was in their midst, I watched over them" (5, 116b-117a) to make sure they would comply with it.

Hence Mohammad's anger against whosoever dares ascribe associates to God. Hence his threats of tremendous and inexorable punishments for those who utter such impious blasphemies:

"Unbelievers [kàfara, i.e. guilty of sin for renouncing their faith] are those who say: *'Christ, the son of Mary, is Allah.'* For the Messiah himself said: *'Children of Israel, serve Allah, my Lord and your Lord.'* It is sure that whoever ascribes associates *[yù-shirku]* to God, God will slam in his face the door to paradise and cast him into the fire of hell. None shall help the evil-doers.

"Unbelievers equally are *[kàfara]* who say: *'Allah is a third of three!'* No! There is no other god but Allah. If they don't stop this nonsense talking, a cruel torment shall befall those of them persisting in their unbelief *[kàfaru]*. Christ, the son of Mary, was no more than an apostle *[rasùl]*, like other apostles who passed away before him. His mother was a saintly woman; and both ate earthly food" (5, 73-75), like the rest of all men.

All said, such a concept of the Trinity is erroneous and crassly absurd. It is a caricature; a ridiculous parody. No Christian has ever dreamed of a trinity composed of Allah, Mary, and Jesus.[95]

---

95. Cf. HAD. II, 361-371; 241-297; MASSON (La Trinité), I, p. 84-104;

A question poses itself here: How did Mohammad come up with such a bizarre notion of the Trinity?

A convincing answer is hardly traceable back to foreign sources such as the Colliridians and Marianites;[96] born re-

---

JAL. I, p. 64-71. — In the Moslems' opinion the expression "mother of God" is a horrible challenge to the divine transcendence and man's reason. "C'est le sens ombrageux de la transcendance divine qui amène les musulmans à cette exaspération indignée contre les formules chrétiennes. Et cette exaspération leur place sur les lèvres des invectives très blessantes pour les chrétiens." JAL. I, p. 70.

96. "La question de savoir comment Muhammad en vint à concevoir Maryam comme faisant partie de la Trinité, a été souvent posée. Marracci donne une référence à Épiphanie, adv. Haeres. 78, 23 [...]. Sales, dans son Preliminary Discourse, p. 46, mentionne les Marianites, qui adoraient une Trinité composée de Dieu, du Christ, et de Marie." WENS., p. 358.

From what St. Epiphanius writes of the "Colliridians," one is not allowed to conclude, unless indirectly, that they had recognized Mary as a "Goddess" and, consequently, made her a member of the M. H. Trinity. To this absurd Koranic idea, therefore, no solid "historic" basis has thus far been able to be established. St. Epiphanius' invectives boiled down substantially to these points:

1) — "Since the world is world, the woman was never allowed or permitted to exercise priestly ministry or offer sacrifices, not even Eve herself": Numquam enim, ex quo mundus cònditus est, sacerdotio est functa mulier, ac ne Eva quidem ipsa" (Hear. 79, 2 — MG. 42, 742);

2) — "Mary is to be honored and venerated, not adored. The Father, the Son and the Holy Spirit are to be adored": "Honoretur sane Maria: Pater, vero, Filius et Spiritus Sanctus adorentur: Ἐν τιμῇ ἔστω Μαρία [...] τὴν Μαρίαν μεδεὶς προσκυνείτω (ib., 7 — col. 735);

3) — Unquestionably holy was Mary's person: "But she was no god. She was a virgin, granted. And was never, nonetheless, proposed to us for adoration": "Non tamen deus illa fuit. Eadem et virgo extitit, minime tamen nobis ad adorandum proponitur" (ib., 4 — col. 746);

4) — There are reports of women "who adore the Triumphal Chariot, or Throne; that on major celebrations, they cover it with a cloth, on which they propose the breads of sacrifice for a few days, and then they offer them in Mary's name": "currum sive sellam quadrantem adorantes ac linteo desuper extento, sollemni tempore per aliquot dies panem proponunt et in Mariae nome offerunt: ἀναφέρουσιν εἰς ὄνομα τῆς Μαρίας" (ib., 1 — col. 741);

portedly in Thracia, southeast of the Balkans, the two religious sects would have crossed with their belief in Mary as a goddess over to Arabia where they settled for some time. Nor is it adequate to unearth Mary's "divinization" de facto,[97] the form of Mariolatry reflecting the "Church's cult of Mary by veneration."[98] To be coherent with the historic reality, a satisfactory explanation is to be sought rather in the inner psychological process of Mohammad himself.

In other words: that sort of Trinity composed of masculine and feminine persons must have been a logical consequence of the ideas upon which the Prophet had long mulled on his own, and which came to him mainly from his historic environment.

Taking off from the positive Christian assertion — that Jesus is truly the son of God, Mohammad then reflected upon the basic factor common to every true and proper sonship — the generative act. As we have already mentioned, Mohammad could not grasp that a true and proper generation could take place without carnal copulation, or outside an intimate sexual union between male and female.[99] Therefore in order to explain to himself Christ's divine filiation, he had no choice but to see Mary as a female mated by Allah. And the consequence was as disastrous as grossly erroneous. Rather than blossoming within

---

5) — This "haeresis" of theirs exists in Arabia, but it is of Thracian import (ib., 1 — col. 793). In any case, it can be called more adequately: "a feminine craving for exposure, or better, a fury of a scorned woman": "mulierum fastus, vel muliebris potius furor" (ib., 4 — col. 746).

97. Moslems respond that today 'de facto', "la vera Trinità è quella, data l'enorme importanza del culto di Maria. Gli studiosi europei hanno cercato invano di identificare una setta precisa di cristiani eretici che credesse esplicitamente in quella forma di Trinità." BAUS., p. 538.

98. "Il se peut, cependant, que la conception de Muhammad n'ait subi l'influence d'aucune secte, mais l'influence de la vénération dont Marie était l'objet dans l'Église même." WENS., p. 358.

99. By paternity and generation the Koran understands "qualcosa di molto più materiale a carnale di quello che le interpretazioni più raffinate del dogma centrale del cristianesimo suggeriscono." BAUS., p. 508.

the bosom of the *true Trinity*, as understood and professed by the Christian doctrine, God's generative act ended in a "*tritheism*" (three distinct gods) reproved and condemned by the Christian Dogma. This version of "*tritheism associator*" is made of *Allah* as a father, or virile principle, and of two associates: *Mary* as a wife, "sàhibat," or feminine element; and *Jesus*, as son of Allah and Mary, or fruit of their mutual love union.

Thus only, in tune with Mohammad's conception and his environment's grotesque mentality, could Jesus truly be called a real *son* of God, and Mary a real *mother* of God. And that explains how this typically Moslem-made "trinity" was born; it was gestated by a mentality unable to conceive parental relationship apart from sexual union.

A "trinity" or "triad" of this sort was unquestionably a scandal to the Arabian Prophet, a shock to his convictions. Besides hurting his religious sensitivity, it contrasted sharply with his rigid monotheistic faith. Hence his anger, his volcanic indignation against the "associators." That explains his severest sanctions against them. "**Shirk,**" to ascribe to Allah associates in his divinity, "**is an unforgiveable crime.**"[100] All the more that this sort of Associationism, widely spread among the pre-Islamic polytheist tribes, horrified the Prophet by the formula in which it was expressed; they had already imagined the Godhead shared by female divinities,[101] one of which was Al-Làt. And Mohammad hated to see in Al-Làt the feminine reverse of Al-Làh.

---

100. "Allah will not forgive those who *associate* others with Him; but He will forgive whom He will for other sins. He who *associates* others with Allah is guilty of a heinous sin" (4, 48). — "He that *associates* other gods with Allah has strayed far from the truth" (4, 116). A very sad end waits for the *associators*: "Allah's anger and curse" (48, 6), a "blazing fire" (48, 14), and a "cruel torture" (50, 26).

101. "Have you thought on *Al-Làt* and *Al-Ûzzàh*, and on the third idol, *Manàt*? Is He to have daughters, and you sons? This indeed is an unfair distinction!" (53, 19). — "Auprès du Dieu Hobal ils avaient groupé trois déesses qui avaient ailleurs leurs sanctuaires: elles semblainet ainsi protéger les routes qui, de la Ka'ba, menaient à ceux-ci: al-Lât gardait celle du sud vers at-Tâïf; al-

The absence of a sharp power of abstraction, on one hand, and the panic that the horrendous *shirk* would take roots in his new community, on the other, were responsible for Mohammad's trinitarian conception. Thus directly or indirectly overweighed, he could not rise above flesh and blood and capture from up close the transcending and most limpid reality of the Deity.

All through his religious experience, as we have said, Mohammad kept himself out of the properly divine sphere of life. He could not make up his mind, like Moses, and put off his "shoes" (Ex. 3, 5); nor dared he walk over to the burning bush,[102] thereby barring himself "from reading from within *[ab intra] God's personal life.*"[103]

Even with his extraordinary theopathic experience during the mysterious "night journey,"[104] Mohammad failed to sound

---

Òzzâ, celle de l'Iraq par Hurad; Manât, celle de Yathrib et de la Syrie par Qudaïd." GAUD., p. 24. — "Ce n'est point un hazard de rythme que le Coran a réuni al-Lât et al-Òzzâ, en les isolant de Manât; elles formaient paire: on jurait par al-Lât et al-Òzzâ; et quand même une tradition tardive a tenu à marier les dieux, il a été convenu que Hobal était leur commun époux." GAUD., p. 51.

102. *"Solve calceamentum."* *Ex.* 3, 5. — Mohammad, staying at the margin, "ébloui, ne tenta pas de s'avancer dans l'incendie divin, et par celà même il s'exclut de comprendre *ab intra* la vie personnelle de Dieu." MASSIGNON L., *Les Trois prières d'Abraham*, Tours, 1935, p. 18.

103. "S'il retrouve, gravé dans sa mémoire, la tablette du Dieu créateur qui enjoint à chacun de l'adorer, il ne dégage pas le sens final du précepte, sa volonté n'ose pas adhérer au conséil de la vie parfaite, décline les fiançailles mystiques." *Ibid.*

104. "Glory be to Him who by night raptured His servant from the Sacred Temple [of Mecca] to the Farthest Temple [of Jerusalem] whose surroundings We have blessed, that We might show him some of Our signs" (17, 1). — This refers to the *ascension* to heaven of the Prophet, who, riding a winged horse, *Al-Burqa*, and guided by angel Gabriel, in a wink of an eye, was transferred from Mecca, to Jerusalem, to the Seventh Heaven. "La tradition musulmane en connait tous les détails. Les philosophes et les soufis en ont montré la signification secrète et la valeur mystique." GAUD., p. 92.

the mystery of God's strictly personal life. Hesitant, the great Arabian stopped right at "half the way."[105]

On the other hand, Mohammad could not reap from his Christian instructors but meager and not entirely reliable information. The people he mostly dealt with and learned from were indeed "Christians of ardent faith, but not very versant in the doctrines of their religion; one way or another they were imbued with Judaising heresies."[106] In such whereabouts, Mohammad could not recognize the genuine face of Christianity; he knew only "its mere exterior facet — and this also disfigured by the Christians themselves" of his time.[107]

Two conclusions we draw with certainty from this assumption: that Mohammad's complaints were not with the official and orthodox Christianity, but with a "form of Christianity well defined in time and quite distant in space,"[108] on one hand; and on the other, that the Koran's denial of Christ's divinity, and, in conjunction, of Mary's Divine Maternity, was exclusively motivated by a "tritheistic" concept incompatible with the Christian Dogma.[109] In better words, the Christianity from which Mohammad took his initial inspiration was a peripheral one; one polluted with heresies, torn asunder by logomachies* — some

---

105. "Il n'a pas essayé d'entrer dans la vie personnelle de Dieu; il semble hésitant, s'être arrêté à mi-chemin." MASS. (*Textes Musulmans pouvant concerner la nuit de l'esprit*, 1939), II, p. 399.

106. NAL., p. 194. — Cf. BL. IV, p. 36.

107. HAY., p. 10. — We ought, with Fr. Hayek, to add that this fact continues, unfortunately, to weigh down on the Islamo-Christian relations.

108. HAY., p. 11.

109. "Mais s'agit-il vraiment de la Trinité telle que la proposent, au coeur même du plus rigoureux monothéisme, les Conciles antérieurs du Coran? Tout porte à croire qu'il s'agit plutôt d'une Triade factive composée d'Allah, de Marie, sa parèdre, et de Jésus, leur enfant." HAY., p. 30.

(*). — Fight, or contention about words. (Fares)

philosophical, others theological, and still others exegetical — but all siding each with either of the two most famous and contrasting antiquity "schools," the Alexandrian and the Antiochian.

And from a historic viewpoint, this conclusion is a very important asset for an eventual dialogue between the two doctrinal stands which seem so far apart.

But above all these differences, none ought to ignore a very precious incident which, quoted from the Koran itself, gives a clue to Mohammad's personal feeling and his intimate attitudes.

Despite the severe penalties he invokes against those who dare ascribe to Allah a son,[110] and worse yet a daughter,[111] Mohammad declares himself ready to confess that Allah has a son if that could be proved with certitude. It was near the end of his career that this episode took place, probably in the year 631, on occasion of the controversy with the Christian delegation from Nejran. In these words the Koran records the event: **"If the Merciful had a son, I would be the first to adore him"** *[àwwal al-'àbidìn]* (43, 81).

An open and sincere dialogue aiming solely at finding the truth would bring forth, among others, these following advantages:

---

110. "Surely they lie when they declare: 'Allah has begotten a *son* ' " (37, 152). "They are liars" (5, 70), and "impious" (5, 72). "Never has Allah begotten a son, nor is there any other god besides Him" (23, 91). "Who has begotten no children, and has no partner in His kingdom, He, who has created the universe (25, 2), and all things are obedient to Him" (2, 116).

111. Elsewhere, the Prophet rails against the *female divinities* (53, 19-21). — "What! Has your Lord blessed *you* (the unbelievers) with sons and Himself adopted daughters from among the angels?" (17, 40). — "In their ignorance they ascribe to Him sons and daughters. Far more glorious is He, and exalted above their imputations" (6, 100).

The pre-Islamic Arabs nurtured an invincible contempt for girls, so much that they used to bury them alive soon after they were born. In the wake of that, if ascribing to God sons was a monstrous error, attributing to Him daughters was the most despicable and horrendous audacity.

a.) It would clarify the ideas by intelligently sifting wheat from chaff, thus eliminating doctrinal absurdities and obstacles so far unsurmountable only because they were objectively believed as such.

b.) It would clear off a whole overcast of misunderstandings and prejudices stubbornly rooted in both sides' minds, thus creating a more serene, less tense and less gloomy atmosphere; and then dispose the spirits to accept as logical and valid the Christian teaching on the Trinity, the Incarnation and consequently Mary's Divine Maternity.

c.) It would induce the Moslem — intellectual or common — to a change of attitude vis-à-vis Christianity so far away from, and so close to, Islam, and vis-à-vis the Christians themselves. When he meets one of them, he will not automatically obey his inner impulse and label him vituperatively as a *kàfir* [negator of his faith, polytheist, associator], worthy of all the tremendous consequences the epithet entails in theory and in practice here and in the hereafter.

Once thus freed from all the chronic antagonisms, misunderstandings and prejudices that the Moslem conscience, science and even fantasy[112] had for centuries piled into it, the

---

112. We have called the reader's attention to the brainless inventions proliferated by the fancy of the *Qussàs* (story tellers) and other Moslem authors, not excluding the Koranic exegetes, v.g. MUQATIL. For sheer curiosity only, let me quote here five samples taken from Muqatil, and reported by Fr. NWYIA:

a) The description of Allah's *Throne* ['arsh]: at the Throne's feet, the seven heavens and seven earths lie miserably in the image of a ring lost in the immensity of a desert (p. 69); each of the Throne's feet is as tall as the seven heavens, the seven earths, and the space in between — all summed up together (*ibid.*)

b) The description of the *paradise*: each of the blessed in paradise will own a castle with seventy palaces within, and each palace will include seventy mansions, or living quarters, all built with concave pearls (p. 103). Each dwelling place is furnished with a sofa covered by seventy carpets of different colors, and trimmed with pearls, gold and amethyst. Indwellers will all be dressed in seven-

ecumenical ground becomes the appropriate stage for an Islamo-Christian brotherly entente. Dialogue will be the modality. And Mary will be the unitive factor, the providential **link**. Here it is where she can best offer her mediation. **Here, in the sight of her lovers and admirers — both Christians and Moslems, Mary of the Koran can shake hands with the same Mary of the Gospel.** Rather than widening the gap between the two sides, she will be for them the bridge of conjuction; claimed by both as their own, she will be the **Common Ka'ba** where Moslems and Christians will clasp one another's hand into the worship of the one, true Allah.

At the cost of stirring Zakarias' anger and hearing ourselves charged with temerity, simplicity and silliness (Zk. p. 206), we, along with other respectable and erudite scholars, will persist in retaining **Mary as the point where Islam and Christianity converge.** At the further cost of raising his doubts about our own "psychological sanity" (p. 208), we will never desist from pointing to Mary, as pictured by Mohammad in the Koran, as to an "historic bridge" (p. 188) of approach and a common "crossing

---

ty white silk-brocaded cloaks; each occupant will have his forehead ringed about by a crown adorned with topaz, emeralds, and every other sort of jewels; and each will bear on his head a golden miter built of seventy bezels, a diamond incrusted in each, and worth all the wealth of the East and the West (*ibid.*).

c) *Adam's creation*: Adam was brought out of a handful of tri-colored clay — white, red, and black — taken from the Meccan soil by angel Gabriel, who dug it out from under the sanctuary of Ka'ba; which explains why Adam's children are of white, red, and black skins (p. 80).

d) *Adam's animation*: The spirit [*rùh*], opposed to the matter, was blown into the skull; after circulating for a good while through the whole body, it finally found itself an exit through the nostrils; the moment it burst out, it caused a relieving sneeze which made Adam say, "*Al-hàmdu li-llàh!*" (praise be to God), "and these were the very first words that ever came out from man's mouth" (p. 81).

e) *Moses' stick*: For those who still ignore it, it is called "*Al-Buq'a*"; Adam owned it first, and later he bequeathed it to Gabriel, who, in turn, left it to Moses as a gift (p. 63).

bridge" (p. 144) for both Moslems and Christians. Willingly indeed will we subscribe to Boubakeur's statement in that regard: that today's Islam notices in Mary, the mother of Jesus, "the emblem of an eternal call to reconciliation for all believers" (Boub. p. 612). Above any other woman, Mary was entrusted by Allah with a particular task — to be "un vecteur entre Dieu et l'humanité, un lien entre la spiritualité chrétienne (compte tenu des réticences protestantes) et de la spiritualité musulmane. Pour les musulmans, pour les catholiques et les orthodoxes, elle sera toujours un phare au milieu de la nuit vers lequel se tournent les regards des croyants" (p. 611).*

In either economy of salvation, subjectively valid for one as well as for the other, Mary would fulfill the duty incumbent on her as a mother. Allah wanted her so. By nature she is mother to Christ; but mystically also she is mother to the faithful just as the wives of the Prophet were mothers to the believers[113] [ummahàt ul-mu'minìn]. And a mother unites, not divides.

What turn shall the events take in the future?

I can hardly foretell. But I am optimistic. Based upon the positive results of this present research, indeed encouraged, I think I can from this moment advance the following norm for a practical ecumenism in the Marian sector:

If both Christians and Moslems would take a moment and

(*). "A vehicle shuttling between God and mankind, a link between the Christian spirituality (with awareness of Protestant reservations) and the Moslem spirituality. For the Moslems, for the Catholics, and the Orthodox, she will always be a lighthouse in the middle of the night, toward which turn the eyes of the believers" (p. 611). (Fares)

113. The Prophet's wives are considered as mothers to the faithful [ummàhat ul mu'minìn]. Cf. 33, 6; and note 124, Ch. Two, p. 161.

fix their eyes upon Mary's sweet image, they could repeat to themselves and according to truth, sustained as they are each by the authority of his own revealed Book — Gospel or Koran, this comforting testimony: **Mary is no alien to us; Mary is in the midst of us; Mary is but one of us — a Christian for the Christian, and a Moslem "ante litteram" for the Moslem.**

In other words, Mary cannot be counted among those who incurred Allah's wrath, nor among those who still struggle in the darkness of doubt and error.[114] Mary is found already treading the right path — the path of Allah that Mohammad had come to show,[115] and which leads the believers to life, to God, the fullness of life.[116] Not casually was Mary found on that path. God himself placed her there, and for a reason — that by both her prerogative as an **àyat** and her charming life as a **màthal** she would guide all and support all during their arduous journey to the homeland, the ultimate kingdom of light.

What mostly matters here is that all, Christians and Moslems, recognize the **sign** of the times given them by God and know how to duly evaluate, each within his own communi-

---

114. Cf. 1, 7. — In v. 7 of Sura 1, *The Exordium* [Al-Fatiha], the Moslem exegetes are used to distinguishing three categories of persons: the *Moslems*, to whom Allah has been beneficient; the *Jews*, against whom Allah had expressed His anger; and the *Christians*, who still waggle in error and incertitude.

115. "Our Apostle *[rasùluna]* has come to explain to you much of what you have hidden of the Book with which Allah guides *[yàhdi]* to the path of peace those who seek to please Him; he will lead them by His will from the darkness *[min a-ddhulumàt]* to the light *[il a-nnùr]*; he will guide them *[yàhdi-hem]* to a straight path *[siràt-en mustaqìm]* " (5, 15-16). Cf. note 166, 167, Ch. Two, p. 175.

116. "*Allah!* There is no god but Him, the Living *[Al-Hày]*, the Self-Sub-sisting *[Al- Qaiyùm]* " (3, 2). — "He is the Living *[Al-Hày]*, the Immortal *[La yamùt]* "(25, 58). "He has created *[khàlaqa]* death and life *[wa l-hayàt]* " (67, 2). — "He brings to life *[yùhiy]* and puts to death *[yumìt]* " (7, 158). Cf. 9, 116; 23, 80; 40, 68; 53, 44; 75, 2). — "He brings forth the living from the dead, and the dead from the living" (3, 27; 6, 31). — "He causes to die and make live again" (22, 66).

ty, Mary's exceptional ecumenical position. That from Mary's example they may learn a salutary lesson for a sublimization of self in God. That from the Marian Message, preached by either economy of salvation, they may draw a constant stimulus to a peaceful living with one another under the all-loving, all-vigilant eyes of God.

And if a wish remains in the making it is this: that the day may at last come when, on the heels of repeated brotherly encounters and dialogues, the Moslem, on a par with his twin Christian, may end up with hailing **Mary, mother of God**: mother of the "kàlimat," the Verb Incarnate. Hail her! But also honor her as her sovereign dignity postulates.

As for me, at the closing of this dissertation, I shall consider myself overwhelmingly rewarded if I would one day know that these modest efforts have been instrumental in placing Mary's personality under a better spotlight; that these pages have succeeded in helping someone rediscover the genuine image of Mary as portrayed in the Koran. Apart from Luke, Mary had no warmer and more colorful artist than Mohammad. By his heart he painted her before he could do it by his hand. And no wonder, since he vibrantly admired her as God's prodigious sign [àyat] for salvation, and he honored her as the "Moslem" woman's perfect model [màthal] to imitate. But she was not exclusive in his high regard. On a par with her, and inseparably from her, he also admired and honored her son, Jesus. For Mary and her son, Mohammad's heart and mind seemed to have known no boundaries in terms of love and respect; just as intransigent was his faith in his Creator, and as boundless was his submission to the One, True God — Allah, **Rabb il'alamin!**

BIBLIOGRAPHY

AM.

— AMMAN, EMILE, *Le Protoévangile de Jacques et ses Remaniements Latins.* Introduction, Traduction, et Commentaire. Paris, Letouzey et Amé, 1910.

AMEL.

— AL-'AMELI, 'ABD-ASSAHIB AL-HASANI, *Al-Anbiyā'* (The Prophets). Their lives, and their stories. (Beirut, 1971.)

ANW.

— ANAWATI, GEORGE, O. P., *Islam and the Immaculate Conception,* in *The Dogma of the Immaculate Conception.* History and significance. Edited by Edward Dennis O'Connor, C.S.C. Indiana, University of Notre Dame, 1958, p. [447]-461.

AQQ.

— AL-'AQQAD, 'ABBAS MAHMUD, *Al-mar'at fil-islām* (The Woman in Islam). Cairo, Dār al- Hilāl, s.d.

279

BAQ.   — 'ABD-EL-BAQĪ, MUHAMMAD FUAD, Al-Mu'-gam al-mufahras li-alfāz al-Qur'ān. (Alphabetical Dictionary of the Koran), Beirut, Khayyāt [1945].

BAUS.   — BAUSANI, ALESSANDRO, Il Corano. Introduzione, traduzione e commento. Collez. «Classici della Religione», II. Firenze, Sansoni [1961].

BAYD.   — NASER AD-DĪN ABIL-KHAIR 'ABD-ALLAH, ben 'Omar AL-BAYDAWĪ (+1286), Anwār at-tanzīl wa asrār at-ta'wīl (Commentary on the Koran). 2 vol. Cairo, ed. al-Halabī, 1939.

BEAUME — LA BEAUME, JULES, Le Koran analysé d'après la traduction de M. Kasimirski et les observations de plusieurs autres savants orientalistes. Paris, Maisonneuve, 1878.

BL. I   — BLACHÈRE RÉGIS, Introduction au Coran. II édit. partiellement refondue. (Paris, Besson et Cantemerle, 1959.)

BL. II   — IDEM, Le Coran. Traduction nouvelle. In «Islam d'hier et d'aujourd'hui». Collection publiée sous la direction de E. Lévi-Provençal. (Paris, Librairie Orientale et Américaine. Maisonneuve.) Vol. I, 1949; vol. II, 1950.

BL. III — IDEM, Le Coran (Al Qor'ān) (Paris, G.-P. Maisonneuve et Larose), 1966.

BL. IV   — IDEM, Le Coran. «Que sais-je?» (Paris, Presses Universitaires de France), 1966.

BL. V   — IDEM, Le Problème de Mahomet. Essai de biographie critique du fondateur de l'Islam (Paris, Presse Univ. de France), 1952.

BL. VI — IDEM, *Histoire de la littérature arabe*, des origines à la fin du XV siècle de J.C. (Paris, Librairie d'Amérique et d'Orient, A. Maisonneuve), vol. I, 1952; vol. II, 1964; vol. III, 1966.

BON. — BONELLI, LUIGI. *Il Corano*. Nuova edizione litteraria italiana. Milano, Hoepli [1965].

BOUB. — BOUBAKEUR, HAMZA, *Le Coran*. Traduction nouvelle et commentaires. In «Le trésor spirituel de l'humanité». Collection dirigée par Jean Cavalier. Paris, Fayard/Denoël [1972]. Tome I, Sourate 1-23. Tome II, Sourate 24-64.

DAR. — DAROUZA M., *Al-mar'at fi-l Qur'ān* (The Woman in the Koran). Beirut, 1967.

DERM. — DERMENGHEM, ÉMILE, *Mahomet et la tradition islamique*. Coll. «Maîtres spirituels», L. Paris, édit. du Seuil, [1967].

DIN. — DINET E. et AL HADJ SLIMAN b. IBRAHIM, *La vie de Mohammed* (Paris, Maisonneuve et larose), 1961.

DR. — DRAZ M.A., *Initiation au Koran*. Exposé historique, analytique et comparatif (Paris, Presses Univ. de France), 1951.

EI. — *Encyclopédie de l'Islam*. Dictionnaire géographique, ethnographique et bibliographique des Peuples Musulmans (Leiden-Paris, E. J. Brill), 1936. - 2nd edition, revised, increased, «établie avec le concours des principaux orientalistes» is in the making. Tome I (1960). Tome II (1965). Tome III (1971). The last word in this third volume is *Imran*.

ESS. — ESSAD M. BEY, *Mahomet* (571-632). Translation of JACQUES MARTY and G. LEPAGE (Paris, Payot), 1956.

FAD. — FADL-ALLAH, 'ALĪ, *Al-akhlāq al-islamīyat* (The Moslems, Costumes), Beirut, Dār Maktabat al- Hayāt [1968].

FAKH. — FAKHOURI, GEORGES, *Maryam wal-islām* (Mary and Islam), in «Mary, Mother of God», special issue of *Al-Maçarrat*, 398 (1954), p. [724]-741.

GAB. I — GABRIELI, FRANCESCO, *Aspetti della Civiltà Arabo-Islamica*. Coll. di «Letteratura e Civiltà», VI. Ediz. Radio Italiana [1956].

GAB. II — IDEM, *Saggi Orientali*. Coll. di Letteratura «Aretusa», II (Caltanisetta-Roma, Sciascia), 1960.

GAND. — AL-GANDŪR, AHMAD, *Al-'ibadāt fil-Qur'ān was-sûnnat* (Devotions in the Koran and Tradition). Cairo, Dar al-Ma'arif, 1965.

GAR. — GARDET, LOUIS, *Connaître l'Islam*. «Je sais - Je crois.» Paris, Fayard [1958].

GAR.- AN. — GARDET, LOUIS and ANAWATI, M. M., *Introduction à la Théologie Musulmane*. Essai de Théologie comparée. Paris, Vrin, 1970.

GAUD. — GAUDEFROY-DEMOMBINES, MAURICE, *Mahomet*. Paris, Albin M. [1969].

GEL. — GELAL AD-DĪN MUHAMMAD Ben AHAMAD AL-MAHALLĪ (+1459) and GELAL AD-DIN 'ABD AR-RAHMAN Ben ABI-BAHR as- SUYUTĪ (+1505), *Tafsīr* (Commentary on the Koran with notes on the motives of revelation). Damascus, ed. Hashem al-Katabi [1939].

GOT. — GOTTSCHALK, H., *L'Islam*, in KÖNIG FRANZ, *Christ and Religions in the World*. Marietti, 1967, vol. III, p. [5]-63.

GUID. — GUIDI MICHELANGELO, *Corano, in Enciclop. Ital.* (Treccani), II [1949], p. 348-349.

HAD. I — HADDAD, YŪSUF, *Al-Injeel fil-Qur'ān* (The Gospel in the Koran). Series of Koranic studies.

HAD. II — IDEM, *Al Qur'ān wal'Kitāb* (The Koran and the Book). Series of Koranic studies.

HAD. III — IDEM, *Nazm al-Qur'ān wal-Kitāb* (Composition of the Koran and the Book). Series of Koranic studies.

HAD. IV — IDEM, *Al Qur'ān da'wat nasranīyat* (The Koran, a Judeo-Christian Message). Series of Islamo-Christian dialogues.

HAD. V — IDEM, *Al-Qur'ān wal-Masihīyat* (Koran and Christianity). Series of Islamo-Christian dialogues, Jounieh - Beirut, 1969.

HAY. — HAYEK, MICHEL, *Le Christ de L'Islam*. Ed. du Seuil [Paris, 1959].

HEN. — HENNIG M., *Der Koran*. Aus dem arabischen Übertragen von Max H. Einleitung und Anmerkungen von Annemarie Schimmel. (Stuttgart, Ph. Reclam jun.), 1960.

HENN.
— HENNINGER, JOSEPH. S.V.D., *Mariä Himmelfahrt im Koran*, in *Neue Zeitsher. Miss.*, 10 (1954) p. 288-292.

HIND.
— HINDIÉ, GRÉGOIRE, *Le culte de la très Sainte Vierge chez les Mahométans de Syrie*, in «Alma Socia Christi» 9 (Roma, accademia Mariana Internaz., 1953), p. [268]-275.

JAL. I
— ABD-EL-JALIL, J. M., *Marie et l'Islam*. Études sur l'histoire des religions», 8. Paris, Beauchesne, 1950. - It is the amplification of the article already published in H. DU MANOIR, *Maria* (Paris, Beauchesne, 1949), I, p. [183]-211, with the title: *La vie de Marie selon le Coran et l'Islam*.

JAL. II
— IDEM, *Brève Histoire de la Littérature Arabe* (Paris, 1946).

JEF.
— JEFFREY, ARTHUR, *The Foreign Vocabulary of the Qur'án*. Baroda, Oriental Institute. Geakwad's Oriental Series, 79. 1938.

KAS.
— KASIMIRSKI M., *Le Coran*. Chronologie et préface par Mohammed Arkoun. Paris, Garnier - Flammarion [1970].

KEL.
— KELLERHALS E., *Der Islam*. Seine Geschichte. Seine Lehre. Sein Wesen. Zweite durchgesehe Auslage [Basel-Stuttgart, Evang. Miss. Gm. b. H.], 1956.

MAR.
— MARRACCI L., *Alcorani Textus Universus* (The Koran's Complete Text) (Patavii, ex typ. Seminarii), 1698.

MAR. I — MARRACCI L., *Prodromus ad Refutationem Corani* (Refutation of the Koran). Ibid. 1698.

MAR. II — MARRACCI L., *Refutatio Alcorani* (Refutation of the Koran). Ibid. 1698.

MAS. — MASSON D., *Le Coran*. Préface by J. Grosjean. Introduction, version and notes by Denise Masson, in «Bibliothèque de la Pléiade» Gallimard [1967].

MASS. — MASSIGNON, LOUIS, *Opera Minora*. Textes recuellis, classés et presentés avec une bibliographie par Y. MOBARAC. Coll. «Recherches et documents». Beirut. Dar al-Maaref, 1963, vol. I, II, III.

MASSON — MASSON, D., *Le Coran et la révélation Judéo-Chrétienne*. Etudes comparées. Paris, Adrien-Maisonneuve, 1958, 2 vol.

MONT. — MONTET, EDOUARD, *Le Coran*. Traduction intégrale. Petite Bibliothèque 40, 41. Payot. Paris, 1958.
T. I, Sourates 1-21
T. II, Sourates 22-114

MOUB. I — MOUBARAC Y., *Abraham dans le Coran*. Paris, Vrin, 1958.

MOUB. II — IDEM, *Pentalogie Islamo-Chrétienne* (Beyrouth, ed. du Cénacle Libanais) 1972-73.
T. 1, L'oeuvre de Louis Massignon
T. 2, Le Coran et la critique occidentale

T. 3, L'Islam et le dialogue Islamo-Chrétien
T. 4, Les Chrétiens et le monde Arabe
T. 5, Palestine et Arabité

MUL.   — MULLA, PAUL M. A., *Comment certains milieux islamiques on réagi au stimulant de quelques manifestations récentes de la doctrine et de la piété catholique concernant la personne privilégiée de Marie mère de Jésus*, in «Virgo Immaculata» 17 (Roma, Accademia Mariana Internaz. 1957), p. [268]-281.

NAD.   — AN-NADWI ABULL-HASAN ALĪ AL-HASANI, *Al-arkān al-ārba-'at*: Islam's four pillars: prayer, zakat (alms), fasting, hajj (Visit to Mecca). Beirut, Dar al-Fan, 1968.

NAG.   — NAGGAR, ABD-EL-WAHHAB, *Qisas al- anbiyā'* (Stories of the Prophets), Cairo-Beirut, 1966.

NAL. I   — NALLINO, CARLO ALFONSO, *Maometto*, in *Enciclop. Ital.* (Treccani), 22 (1949), p. 193-197.

NAL. II   — IDEM, *Islamismo*, in *Enciclop. Ital.* (Treccani), 19 (1949) p. 603-614.

NOL. I   — NÖLDEKE THEODOR, *Geschichte des Qorāns*. Bearbeitet von Friedrich Schwally. Erster Teil: *Über den Ursprung des Qorāns.*

NOL. II   — IDEM, *Geschichte des Qorāns*, völlig umgearbeitet von FRIEDERICH SCHWALLY. Zweiter Teil: *Die Sammlung des Qorāns* mit einem literar-historischen Anhang über die muhammedanischen Quellen und die neuere christliche Forschung.

NOL. III — IDEM, *Geschichte des Qorāns*. Dritter Teil:
Die Geschichte des Korantexts von G.
BERGSTRÄSSER und O. PRETZL. Mit 8
Tafeln. Hildesheim, G. Olms, 1961.
[Fotomechanisher Nachdruck der 2. Auflage,
Leipzig 1909.]

NWY. — NWYIA, Paul, *Exégèse Coranique et Langage
mystique*. Nouvel essai sur le lexique technique
des mystiques musulmans. Beyrouth, Imprim.
Catholique, 1970.

PAR. — PAREJA, J. M., *Islamologie*. En collaboration
avec L. HERTLING (Munich) A. BAUSANI
(Rome) TH. BOIS (Beyrouth). Imprim.
Catholique, 1957-63.

PEIR. — PEIRONE, FEDERICO, I.M.C., *Cristo
nell'Islam*. «Quaderni Missionari», 7, Torino,
ediz. Missioni Consolata, 1964.

PES. — PESLE, OCTAVE et TIDJANI AHMED, *Le
Coran*, traduit de l'arabe (4me ed.). Paris,
G.-P. Maisonneuve et Larose, 1967.

QER. — AL-QERDAWI, YŪSUF, Al-'ibādat fil-islām
(devotion in Islam). Beirut, Dar al-Irshad,
1971.

QUAD. — QUADRI GOFFREDO, *Maometto*, in «En-
ciclopedia Filosofica» (Centro di Studi
filosofici di Gallarate), ed. Sansoni, 19 IV
(1937), p. 277-281.

SAB. — AS-SABŪNĪ, MUHAMMAD 'ALĪ,
An-nubūwat wal-anbiyā' (Prophecy and Prophets), Beirut, Dar al-Irshād, 1970.

SAL. — EL-SALEH, SOUBHI, *Mabāhis fi 'ulūm al-Qur'ān* (Research about the Koran's teachings), Beirut, Dar al-Malāīyn, 1969.

SAUV. — SAUVAGET J., *Introduction à l'histoire de l'Orient Musulman*. Eléments de Bibliographie, Edition refondue et complétée par Cl. Cahen (Paris, Librairie d'Amérique et d'Orient, A.- Maisonneuve), 1961.

SAV. — SAVARY, CLAUDE, *Le Koran*. Traduction, précédée d'un abrégé de la vie de Mahomet et accompagnée de notes. Paris, Garnier, 1960.

SH. — BINT ASH-SHATI' ['Aishah Abd-ar-Rahmān], *Nisā' an-Nabī* (The Wives of the Prophet). Cairo, Dar al-Hilal, 1967.

SHAR. — BEN ASH-SHARĪF, MAHMŪD, *Al-adiyān fil- Qur'ān* (Religions in the Koran). Cairo, Dar al-Maarif, 1970.

SID. — SIDERSKY, D., *Les origines des Légendes Musulmanes dans le Coran et dans les vies des Prophètes*. Paris, Geuthner, 1933.

STR. — DE STRYCKER E., S. J., *La forme la plus ancienne du Protoévangile de Jacques*. Recherches sur le Papyrus Bodmer 5 avec une édition critique du texte grec et une traduction annotée [...] En appendice les versions arméniennes traduites en latin par HANS QUECQUE, S. J. (Bruxelles, Société des Bollandistes), 1961.

TAB. — BEN GA'FAR MUHAMMAD BEN GARĪR AT-TABARĪ (+922), *Gāmi' al-Bayān* (Commentary on the Koran). Cairo, ed. Shāker 1960.

TABB. — TABBARAH, 'ABD-AL-FATTAH, Rūh as-salāt fil-islām (The spirit of prayer in Islam). Beirut, Dar al-Malāīyn, 1968.

TOD. — TODDE, MAURO MARIA, La "Saida" Maria nella dottrina e pietà islamiche, in «La Madonna nel culto della Chiesa». Coll. «Lumen et fons», 9. Brescia. Queriniana 1966, p. [208]-218.

ULL. — WINTER L. M., Der Koran. Das heilige Buch des Islam. Nach der Übertragung von LUDWIG ULLMAN neu bearbeitet und erklärtet (München, W. Goldmann), 1962.

WAT. I — WATT W. MONTGOMERY, Mahomet à la Mecque. Traduction de F. Dourveil (Paris, Payot), 1958.

WAT. II — IDEM, Mahomet à Médine. Traduction par S. M. Guillemin et F. Vaudou (Paris, Payot), 1959.

WENS. — WENSINCK, A. J., Maryam, in Enc. de l'Islam, III, p. 357-360. Article reproduced in Turkish in Islām Ansiklopedisi. Istanbul, Maarif Basimevi, 19 VII (1957), p. 781-785; — and also abridged in Shorter Encyclopedia of Islam, Edition on behalf of the Netherlands Academy by H. A. R. GIBB and J. M. KRAMERS (Leiden, Brill, 1953), p. 327-330.

ZAK. — ZAKARIAS H., L'Islam, Entreprise Juive. De Moise à Mohammed.

T. I — 1. Conversion de Mohammed au Judaisme.
2. Les enseignements à Mohammed du Rabbin de la Mecque.
T. II — 3. Composition et disparition du Coran arabe original et primitif.
4. Lutte du rabbin de la Mecque contre les idolatres et les Chrétiens.
(Cahors), 1955.

ZAM. — GAD-ALLAH MAHMŪD Ben OMAR AZ-ZAMAKHSHARĪ (+1144), *Al-Kasshāf* (Commentary on the Koran). Beirut, Dār al-kitāb al- arabī, 1947.

ZK. — ZAKARIAS, HANNA, *Voici le vrai Mohammed et le faux Coran*. Paris, Nouvelle éditions Latines, 1960.

Index of Authors Mainly Quoted

AM. — 87, 121, 141, 143, 248.

AMEL. — 61, 66, 67, 71, 73, 87, 90, 204.

ANW. — 26, 27, 44, 62, 113, 117, 122, 136, 138, 143.

AQQ. — 207, 209.

BAQ. — 116, 117, 122, 129, 145, 147.

BAUS. — 39, 44, 49, 50, 62, 69, 70, 80, 100, 102, 122, 123, 129, 155, 156, 175, 177 178, 185, 188, 201, 214, 215, 236, 269.

BAYD. — 58, 61, 62, 65, 66, 67, 69, 70, 71, 72, 73, 81, 87, 88, 90, 92, 95, 126, 131, 135, 141, 144, 175, 265.

BEAUME — 39.

BL. I — 27, 32, 33, 34, 37, 38, 40, 42, 46.

BL. II — 39, 81, 92.

BL. III — 34, 52, 57, 58, 62, 92.

291

BL. IV   — 32, 38, 57, 70, 156, 157, 175, 188, 214, 231, 236, 258, 272.

BL. V   — 237.

BL. VI   — 31, 32, 81, 171, 215, 236, 251.

BON.   — 62, 286.

BOUB.   — 7, 45, 61, 62, 64, 67, 71, 81, 111, 160, 175, 188, 202, 264.

DAR.   — 114.

DERM.   — 181, 214, 251, 258.

DIN.   — 55, 73, 205, 230.

DR.   — 30, 32, 176, 205, 236, 254.

EI.   — 173, 186, 193, 196, 201, 236.

ESS.   — 54, 159, 193, 205, 254.

FAD.   — 158, 207, 209.

FAKH.   — 26, 29, 136.

GAB. I   — 100, 117, 171.

GAB. II   — 118, 209, 258.

GAND.   — 30, 38, 46, 127, 128, 131, 203, 215.

GAR.   — 29, 45, 114, 117, 136, 141, 164, 176, 193, 212, 257, 265.

GAR.-AN. — 162, 193.

GAUD.   — 31, 48, 62, 77, 83, 158, 159, 160, 167, 168, 171, 172, 173, 181, 182, 186, 209, 270, 271.

GEL.   — 61, 67, 69, 71, 73, 81, 90, 92, 95, 131, 141, 144, 157, 175.

GOT.   — 55, 167, 255.

GUID. — 32, 37, 40.

HAD. I — 29, 67, 69, 126, 132, 135, 136, 144, 229, 230, 232, 234.

HAD. II — 30, 41, 42, 43, 46, 47, 48, 49, 50, 52, 55, 92, 117, 147, 170, 171, 188, 213, 214, 215, 231, 237, 267.

HAD. III — 31, 79, 92, 103, 155, 174, 184, 263, 265.

HAD. IV — 235.

HAD. V — 42, 45.

HAY. — 26, 29, 31, 61, 65, 67, 70, 71, 72, 73, 84, 86, 87, 88, 90, 96, 104, 105, 114, 125, 135, 140, 141, 143, 158, 195, 200, 272.

HEN. — 26, 70, 71, 86, 157, 175, 188.

HENN. — 106.

HIND. — 26, 135, 140, 158.

JAL. I — 26, 27, 28, 29, 44, 62, 136, 196, 267.

JAL. II — 29, 34, 40.

F. — 31, 50, 62, 103, 122, 145, 147, 155, 171.

KAS. — 39, 71, 175, 188.

KEL. — 55, 156, 214.

MAR. — 92, 205, 220.

MAR. I — 51, 113, 204, 251, 254.

MAR. II — 55, 58, 62, 70, 71, 98, 113, 129, 135, 142, 157, 177, 188, 198, 265.

MAS. — 70, 86, 120, 155, 175, 188, 213.

MASS. — 29, 45, 58, 122, 136, 149, 151, 157, 158, 164, 166, 193, 204, 205, 271, 272.

MASSON — 77, 99, 126, 145, 151, 173, 213, 255, 267.

MONT. — 57, 62, 71, 92, 157, 175, 188.

MOUB. I — 171, 172, 173, 176, 196, 201, 216, 236, 260.

MOUB. II — 147, 170, 175, 176, 216, 236.

MUL. — 26, 98, 111, 160, 262.

NAD. — 201, 203.

NAG. — 90, 204.

NAL. I — 62, 170, 182, 251, 272.

NAL. II — 54, 137, 147, 162, 167, 174, 213.

NOL. I — 38, 42, 43, 50, 52, 147, 216, 236.

NOL. II — 39.

NWY. — 27, 65, 66, 73, 78, 79, 81, 87, 120, 162, 168, 254, 274.

PAR. — 32, 37, 39, 170, 196, 212, 236, 237.

PEIR. — 26, 27, 44, 93, 160, 223, 237, 261.

PES. — 157, 175, 188.

QER. — 166, 171, 203.

QUAD. — 117, 236.

SAB. — 61, 66, 67, 69, 70, 73, 87, 88, 90, 105, 144, 171, 172, 208.

SAL. — 30, 46, 51, 214.

SAUV. — 31, 218, 220.

SAV. — 71, 175, 188.

Index of the Main Arabic Words

Arabic Word	Definition	Page
a'adda	: He (Allah) has prepared	101
abb	: father	64
àbd	: servant	96
Abdallah	: servant of Allah	96
Adn (Eden)	: vineyard (garden of -)	104
ahbàr	: Levites	61
ahl el bait	: household (Mohammad's)	160
"Ahl il-Kitàb"	: "People of the Book", i.e. Jews and Christians	55
'alam-in	: worlds, visible and invisible; universe	156
al-bìrr	: the good deed	198
al fauz ul'adhìm	: the supreme triumph (entry into the garden of paradise)	104

297

al-hàqq : the Truth (Allah) 85

al-Hày ul Qayùm: the Living Being, the Subsisting One 117

Allah : the Supreme Name of God 22

al malà'ykat : the angels 76

al Masìh : the Messiah 81

al mutahharùn : the purified 212

al-yahood : the Jews 260

a'màl isshaytàn : Satan's deeds 130

amm : paternal uncle 64

àmran farì-yan : strange, shameful thing 95

àmran maqdìyan : it is a decreed thing 86

ansàr : helpers of Allah or Mohammad's 180

arda'l
  muqàddasat : the holy land 133

arkàn : pillars of Islam 202

ar-Rahìm : the Clement; Allah's Majestic name 50

ar-Rahmàn : the Merciful; Allah's Majestic name 47

ar-rùh ul-qudus : the Holy Spirit 78

asbàb un-nuzùl : motives of revelation 39

assùhuf ul ùla : the former revelations (Torah, Gospel) 170

a'ùzu bil'lah : I take refuge in Allah 83

awaynà-huma : We (Allah) gave them (Mary and her son) a shelter 99

àwliya	: patrons, saints, Allah's friends	163
àyat	: sign, miracle	120
ayàt	: signs; Koranic Verses	38
ayàt ul'lah	: Signs of Allah	123
bàdi	: the Maker (Allah)	119
bashìr	: bearer of good news	47
Bàsmala	: doxology, as "In the Name of the Father, etc."... is for the Christian	39
bid'	: innovation (new religion)	170
bint	: daughter	64
bi rùh il-qùdus	: with the Holy Spirit	133
dalàl	: error, ignorance	85
dàr	: abode, home	102
dar al-'àkhirat	: abode of the other life	102
dàr al-muqàmat	: abode of the perpetual stay	102
dàr al-muttaqìn	: abode of the Allah fearing people	103
dar-al qaràr	: home of the peaceful sojourn	101
dàr as-salàm	: abode of peace	102
dhalimùn	: iniquitous	130
dhìkr	: remembrance: "Remember in the Book"	53
Dhu'l Jalàl	: the Venerable, the Majestic One	117
dhurriyàt	: generations	64

fàhishat	: sexual crime	128
Farg	: genitalia (female's)	142
fasiqùn	: impious	130
Fàtiha	: Exordium of the Sura	39
fàtir	: the Modeller	119
fi na'ìm	: in state of bliss; in paradise	101
firdàus	: paradise	104
gazà	: reward	101
ghàdab	: wrath (Allah's)	130
ghàyb	: the world of arcane realities known to Allah alone	71
ghùsul	: bath	128
Gibrìl	: Gabriel, the angel	80
hàdath	: minor impurity, or sin	128
hadith	: oral tradition	51
hàjj	: pilgrimage	203
halìm	: benign; clement	145
hanif	: who is not a Jew nor a Christian, but a free and non-conformist person as was Abraham	171
haràm	: evil deed, illicit	83
hawàriyun	: the Twelve Apostles	180
Hegira	: migration from Mecca; beginning of the Moslem Year	54
hijàb	: veil, curtain	70

hùda	: guide, guidance	184
hudud Allah	: bounds set by Allah	55
Hùwa	: He (Allah)	117
Iblìs	: Satan	77
Ibn Maryam	: Son of Mary	140
Idris	: Enoch	49
ijmà	: general consensus among Moslem Scholars or Leaders on religious or non-religious issues	162
iktàsaba	: to earn (a sin)	129
imàm	: Leader during public prayer or worship hour	195
Injeel	: Gospel	150
ìrka-i	: Bend your knees (to Mary)	202
ìsmu-hu	: His name is (Jesus)	81
Ismu'llah al A'zam	: the Supreme Name of Allah	117
'Issa	: Jesus	49
'Issa b'nu Maryam	: Jesus the Son of Mary	81
istàfa	: to choose, select, predestine	125
istafà-ki	: He (Allah) has chosen you (Mary)	132
istinbàt	: Mystical interpretation of the Koranic Text	33
ìthm	: sin	129
ittaqàu'llah	: those who feared Allah	101
ittaqu'llàh	: Fear ye Allah	198

janàbat	: major impurity, or sin	128
jànnat	: garden, or paradise	72
jannàt 'àden	: gardens of Eden (paradise)	103
jànnat 'aliyat	: elevated garden	101
jànnat al mà'wa	: garden of refuge	101
jànnat an-na'ìm	: garden of pleasure, paradise	103
jannàt el-firdàus	: gardens of paradise	103
jànnat na'ìm	: garden of bliss	103
juthùwu	: genuflection, bending of the knees	45
kafìrùn	: unbelievers, infidel	47
kàlimat	: word; mental concept	81
kàlimat min-hu	: a Word from Him (Allah)	81
kàna	: he was	96
kàsaba	: to earn (the guilt)	129
khàliq	: the Creator	119
khàtam	: seal; crowning; the last in a series	173
khatì'at	: sin, wrongdoing	129
khìrqa	: scapular	262
Kìbla	: point toward which the faithful turn to pray; Mecca	69
kitàb	: book	185
kùfr	: infidelity; idolatry	195

là'nat	: curse (Allah's)	130
li-'l-alamìn	: for the universe	187
ma'ìn	: fountain, spring (idea of fresh water)	100
makànan sharqìyan	: a place to the east	69
maknùn	: mysterious; arcane; known only to God	212
man Kàna sabìyan	: Who was a child (Jesus)	96
masihiyùn	: Christians	229
màthal	: example, model	120
mà'wa	: refuge, shelter	101
màysir	: gambling	129
mihràb	: shrine, battlefield, niche in the Temple	69
mikhàd	: throes, pains of labor	143
mìllat	: faith; religion	171
min as-siddiqìn	: of the righteous	134
min rùhi	: of My Spirit (Allah's)	78
min rùh il'lah	: of Allah's Spirit	78
min rùhi-na	: of Our Spirit	77
mi'ràj	: mystical night; journey (Mohammad's)	149
mithaq	: a covenant	259
mubàhala	: ordeal to prove the truth	45
mubàsshir	: proclaimer of good news	41

muhàrrar	: free, totally vowed to Allah's service	65
muhàrra-rat	: free and totally devoted to Allah's service. (Mary)	198
mujrimùn	: wrongdoers	130
munafiqùn	: hypocrites	47
mùndhir	: warner	41
mùnkar	: prohibited action	129
muqàddas	: Holy	133
musàddeq	: confirmer of the earlier revelations (Torah, Gospel)	81
musàlaha	: agreement or compromise	45
mushrikùn	: Associators, who ascribe associates to Allah in His divinity	41
muslimùn	: Moslems; surrendered to Allah	175
mutàhhar	: pure, purified	131
nabì	: a prophet	47
nadhìr	: a warner	47
nasàra	: Judeo-Christians	41
nasranìyat	: Judeo-Christian sect	259
Nisà	: Women (Sura 4)	115
nisà'l'alam-ìn	: the women of the universe	157
nuqàddisu làka	: We sanctify Your (Allah's) Name	133
nùr	: light	131
nùrithu	: We (Allah) shall give in inheritance.	101

Qàdr	: the blessed and fateful night during which Allah decrees or communicates things	215
qànit	: devout; fearing Allah	184
qaràr	: stable, peaceful sojourn	100
qìsas il àmbiya	: stories of the prophets	27
quddùs	: Holy	133
qussàs	: storytellers, or writers	27
rabb	: Lord	147
rabb al-almìn	: Lord of the Universe	147
ràbwat	: mound, hillside (idea of elevation)	100
Ramadan	: the fasting month in Islam	21
rasùl	: messenger of Allah	21
ra'uf	: compassionate	145
rìh	: wind	78
rìjs	: abominable thing	128
rùh	: spirit; breath; soul	78
rùh-una	: Our Spirit	77
Sabil Allah	: Allah's religion (Islam)	162
sab' samawàt	: Seven Heavens	119
sàhibat	: lady companion (lover, wife)	149
Sàyidat	: Our Lady (Mary)	262
salàt	: prayer, petition	201

sàlih	: holy, goodly	134
sàlih-at	: a holy (woman)	134
salihùn	: the goodly, the holy	133
sallu alàihi	: pray on him (Mohammad)	77
Sayidna Issa	: Our Lord Jesus	24
Settena	: Our Lady	24
shafà'at	: intercession	165
shafì	: Intercessor	164
shahàdat	: profession of faith: "There is no other God but Allah"	203
shirk	: associationism: ascribing to Allah associates (like Mary and Jesus, mere creatures) in His divinity	259
siddìq	: righteous (man)	133
siddìqat	: righteous (woman)	133
siddiqùn	: the righteous	133
siràti mustaqìman	: My (Allah's) religion is a straight path	175
siyàm or sàum	: fasting	202
sùbha	: Moslem rosary	148
Suras	: Koranic Chapters	38
taawìl	: allegorical interpretation of the Koranic Text	33
tafsìr	: literal interpretation of the Koranic Text	33
tàhhara	: to purify, make holy	127
tahhàra-ki	: He purified you (Mary).	127

tahùr	: pure, purified	131
ta'ifatàin	: two Communities: Jewish and Judeo-Christians	170
tanzìl	: the "downing" of the revelations	213
tasbìh	: to say the Moslem rosary	148
tashbìk	: raising of hands	45
tawàkkul	: abandon of self; trust in God	209
tawfìqi	: conventionally adjusted, accommodative, text	38
tawqìfi	: text set, established, unchangeable	38
tayàmmum	: total bath of body	128
ukht	: sister, by blood or otherwise	64
umm	: mother, by blood or otherwise	64
ummahàt ul-mu'minin	: mothers of the faithful (Wives of the Prophet)	276
ùmmat mùslimat	: A Moslem Nation	179
ùmmi	: illiterate; national	236
Umm'ul Kitàb	: The Matrix of the Book; the prototype of Koran kept by Allah in heaven	212
ùqnut-i	: Be devout (to Mary)	202
ùsjud-i	: Prostrate yourself (to Mary)	202
usùwat hàsanat	: good example	196
wa'àdakom	: He (Allah) promised you	101
wa'àdana	: He (Allah) promised us	101
wahi	: reflectional knowledge; revelation	80

wàlad	: a child	149
walì	: patron, saint, friend	164
wàlid-at	: mother, parent	140
wa sàllimu	: wish peace	77
wàsm	: brand, stamp	182
wudù	: ablution (partial bath)	128
Yahia	: John	49
yu-basshìru-ki	: announces to you (Mary)	81
zakàt	: alms-tax	203

INDEX

Aaron

Amran's son, 61
head of the priestly class, 64
Moses' brother, 61
Maryam's brother, 94, 95

Abraham

Allah's chosen one, 61
most exalted of Allah, 60, 125
descendants of, 60, 64
remembered in the Book, 53
righteous, 134, 185
channel of revelation, 170, 172
father of the faithful, 171
Allah's dearest friend, 171
a *hànif*, 171
a Moslem *"ante litteram"*, 176
father of *muslimin*, 176, 185

Abyssinia

Christians of, were Monophysites,
46
migration to, 48
origin of *ar-Rahmàn*, 50

Adam

most exalted of Allah, 60, 61, 64, 125
creation, animation, 275

"Aggiornamento"

updating, 28

Aisha

Prophet's youngest wife, 158, 159,
181, 204, 215
her love affair, 186, 188

Allah

the Supreme Name, 117
Arabic grammarial root, 117
Most Excellent Names of, 124, 145,
146, 147
One, Creator, Remunerator, 7, 148
frequent recurrence of —'s name,
117, 118
Numinous Being, 146, 147
Despotic Lord, 147
Absolute Umpire, 74, 75, 85

His will, 74, 75, 85
decree, 74, 75, 86
a "slave owner" dealing with men,
   145, 146, 147
dearest people of, 60, 116, 117, 162
chosen ones of, 61
blessings of, on Christians, 46
ordained Jesus a Prophet, 94
gave him the Gospel, 94
has no son, 149
no consort, 149
no daughters, 231, 270, 271, 273
dictates, when revealing, 213

Alms

pure, and purifying, 131

Amran

Moses' and Aaron's father, 61, 62
most exalted of Allah, 60, 125
confused with Imran, Mary's father,
   61, 62, 63

Angels

nature, 76, 77
tasks, 77
rebellion, 77
tend to Mary's spiritual needs, 72
Angel, (see "Gabriel")

Anna

Mary's mother, 65, 239
sterile, old, 65
names her child, "Mary", 67, 239, 241
vows her to the Lords' service, 60, 65
a totally "free" gift (muhàrrar), 60,
   65, 66
disappointment, frustration, 61, 66,
   67
Joachim and, 65, 239, 241

Annex

of the Temple, 69
is it the "mihràb?", 68, 69
or the "place to the east?", 68, 69
or the "holy of holies?", 69, 70

Annunciation

to Mary, 74, 75, 76
the Announcer, 76, 77, 78
place of the, 74, 75, 76, 87, 88
Mary's age at the time of the, 88
to Zachariah, 76
where, 87

Apocrypha

Proto-evangelium of James, 70, 237,
   238, 239, 240, 241, 242, 243, 244,
   245, 246, 247, 248, 249, 250, 251,
   252
Mary and Jesus' birth met large
   response in early Chrstian literature,
   mainly the —, 110, 111, 221, 234,
   235, 238, 240, 247, 250
Gospel of the Nativity (Ps. Matthew),
   88, 121, 141, 234, 243, 247
Infancy Gospel, 221, 235, 247, 250

Arabia

Statue of Our Lady of, 23
Allah's name in the south of, 50
Allah's name in the north of, 50

Ar-Rahìm

"The Merciful", 49, 50
origin, 50

Ar-Rahmàn

"The Clement", 49, 50
origin, 50

Associates

Allah has no, 266, 267, 270, 273, 274

Associationism

"shirk", ascribing associates to Allah
   in His divinity, 118, 264

Associators

"mushrikùn", 41, 47, 52, 54, 55, 110,
   118, 119, 129, 130, 259, 267, 270,
   274

Attributes

Allah's, 124, 145, 146, 147

Augustine's

sentence on the moment of Mary's birth, 137

Àyat

(see "sign")

Badr

incursion at, 58

Basics

elemental, for peaceful co-existence of Christians and Moslems, 23

Vatican II urges return to, 23, 28

Bàsmala

Fàtiha, 38, 39, 277

Exordium, 39, 277

Biblical Personalities

most favorite of Allah, 116, 117

Bibliography

Marian, 25, 26, 279

Blachère, Régis

opinion of, regarding Sura 3, 57, 58, 63

Boubakeur, Hamza

statement on Mary, 7, 160

objective outlook on her role, 208, 209, 276

on her exclusion from the Trinity, 265

Breathing

Gabriel's, into Mary to conceive Jesus, 77, 86, 116, 183, 187, 192, 248

Allah's, into the clay to create Adam, 86, 275

"breath" of Jesus to animate the birds, 247

Cairo

Koran's Typical Edition of, 51

Calumny

of the Jews against Mary, 59, 94, 95, 96

Chastity

the woman who kept her chastity, 7, 94, 95, 116, 117, 183, 186, 187, 192, 206, 208

— as virginity, 74, 75, 83, 84, 116, 117, 121, 141, 142, 143, 144, 145

— as purity, 73, 131, 132, 133, 262

Child (Jesus)

promised to Mary by Gabriel, 74, 75

how shall Mary have a, 74, 75, 84

identified as a "Word" from Allah, 81, 82, 83

Mary carried her — in her arms, 94

— as a baby, 95, 96

— , baby, talking as an adult, 94, 96

Childbirth

place of, 89, 91

throes of, physical or moral, 89, 91

Children

Allah has no, 145, 149

Christianity

impact of, on Mohammad's mind, 45, 48

which Christianity, 230, 236, 258, 259, 272

Colliridians

and Marianites, 268

Community

Islam, a theocratic, 55, 178

Islam, a middlemost, 41, 43, 55, 177, 232, 259

Companion
female, (sahibat); Allah has no, 149, 266, 267

Conception
Immaculate — in Islam, 135, 136, 138, 139

Controversy
Christological, 45, 57, 59

Cradle
Jesus speaks from the, 94, 96
Jesus preaches from the, 75
as an adult, 94, 96

Critique
internal, 46, 55

Crucifixion
of Jesus, denied by the Koran, 107, 261

Cult
(see "worship")

Daughters
pagan Arabs disposed of their, 114
practice mitigated by the Koran, 114
Allah's daughters (?), 270, 271, 273

Dependence
Koran's, on the Ps.-Matthew, 68
textual (?), 234
oral, not literal, 235, 236, 237, 238

Descendant
Mary and her — , protected from Satan, 61

Descendants
Abraham's, 60

Imran's, 60
kinship, 64

Dialogue
definition, limitations, 256
"ecumenical", 257, 258
difficulties: (Kelly-Olson), 10, 263
obstacles: (R. Hassan), 11, 263
a "way of life", necessity, 9
advantages for each party, 274

rules for a good dialogue:
1st rule, 257
2nd rule, 257
3rd rule, 263

psychological attitudes for —:
a) intellectual honesty, 256, 257
b) Mohammad knew the wrong Christianity, 251, 252, 258

objective issues of dialogue:
a) recognition of common points, 260, 261, 262
b) recognition of substantial divergences, 263

role of the "two sides of a coin" in dialogue:
a) divisive factors, 256
b) unitive factors, 256

main lines that should regulate a dialogue, 264, 265, 266
who should engage in dialogue, 263
Mohammad was first to call for dialogue, 263

practical advices:
a) admitting Islam a revealed religion on a par with Judaism and Christianity, 258
b) understanding Mohammad's anger against the "associators", 259, 267
c) understanding his bizarre notion of the Trinity, 268
d) avoiding Zakarias' prejudiced, abrasive attitude, 256, 257

Mary's role for a happy dialogue, 275, 276

Mohammad's change of heart toward the Christians, 259, 260
Boubakeur's vision of Mary's efficiency in dialogue, 276

East

"place to the —", where, 69

Elizabeth

Mary's relation to, 62

Embroideries, around:

Mary's parentage, 61
Mary's life in the *mihràb* of the Temple, 70
the Levites' debate in choosing a tutor, 71
Baby Mary's tenderest years, 72
Gabriel's tasks and performance, 73
the Annunciation, 87, 88
Christ's birth, 90, 91, 92
Mary and her son by the palm tree, 105
Allah's Throne, 274
the Paradise, 274
Adam's creation, animation, 275
Moses' stick, 275

Emigration (s)

(see "Hegira")

Emir

Abdullah, 22
faith of the, 23

Eschatological

piety, 41, 47, 198, 199, 225, 226
(see "parousia")

Events

Mary's social, 60
Mary's social — in the N.T., 97
Mary's eschatological, 97, 105

- refuge, 98, 99
- whereabouts of refuge, 105

- "hillside", an allusion to flight into Egypt?, 98
- paradise, 99
- real paradise, 101, 102, 103, 274
- components of paradise, 100

Mary's last things, 97, 98, 105
- Mary's death, annihilation (?), 97, 106, 107
- Mary's assumption, 97, 106
- Mary and her son's survival in paradise, 107, 108

Example

Allah set in Mohammad an, 168
Allah set an — in Mary, 186
(see "mathal")

Exclamation

Sura Three's — in addressing crowds, 56

Exordium

Fàtiha, 38, 39, 277
(see "*Bàsmala*")

Faith

Abraham's, 23
Islam structured upon Abraham's Monotheistic, 258
profession of, Islam's first pillar, 203
a fool's, 193

Fall

Adam's collective, denied by the Koran, 138

Falsehood

monstrous, 59, 118, 227
Koran immune of, 254
slanderous, 140, 227

Fasting

Mary vows a — to the Merciful, 89, 93, 201, 202, 203, 204
the mute — , 204

Mohammad decreed — , 203, 204
one of Islam's pillars, 203

Father

Allah is no, 141, 145, 148, 149, 261, 266, 267, 270, 273

Fatherhood

Mohammad's understanding of, 149

Fatima

Mohammad's beloved daughter, 113, 158, 159, 182, 204
inferiority of, to Mary, 113

Feelings

the Moslem's, on hearing Mary criticized, 7
on hearing talks about "sources" for the Koran, 211

"Fiat"

Allah's categorical imperative bringing Jesus into being, 82
"*Be, and it is!*", 75, 85, 243

Gabriel (Gibrìl)

Angel, 73
Spirit from Allah, 74, 77, 80
Messenger of Allah, 74, 76, 84
announces to Mary her selection, 73
and the birth of her son, 74, 75, 76, 80, 81, 82

Ghàyb

domain of arcane things known only to Allah, 71, 106

Gospels

apocryphal, 110, 143, 234, 238, 240, 250, 252
canonical, 93, 111, 246, 250
(see "apocrypha")

Growth

the child Mary's — in the Temple, 67, 68, 69

Hegira

a) First (small) — to Abyssinia (615 A.D.), 48, 54
successive — s to Abyssinia, 48, 50
b) Big — (4th?) from Mecca to Medina (622 A.D.), 41, 42, 54, 57
Big — marks beginning of Moslem Era, 54
and separation of Meccan and Medinian periods, 41
its repercussion for Islam and Mankind's history, 54

Heresies

Christian — in Arabia, 45, 46, 48, 253, 268, 269, 272
Islam, a Christian heresy, 228, 253

Hillside

(see "events")

Histories

of Yahia's (John's) birth, 51
of Issa's (Jesus') birth, 52

Hobal

pagan god, worshipped by pre-Islamic Arabs, 231, 270, 271

Holiness

definition, 133, 134, 198
Koranic expressions for,
    - *siddìq* (righteous), 133, 134
    - *sàlih* (saintly), 133, 134
    - *qànit* (devout), 184, 185
    - *tahùr* (pure), 131
Who are holy, righteous, 134
Mary's, (see "sanctity")

Holy Spirit

of the Christian doctrine, 77, 121, 248
Koranic "Holy Spirit", 78, 79
equivocation and accuracy, 78
identification with Gabriel, 74, 75, 76, 78, 79, 80

Hostilities

bet. Christians and Moslems, 10, 11, 13, 256, 263, 267

Household

(see "wives")

Hypocrites

the —, 47, 55, 129, 130, 165, 178, 186, 189, 194

Ideologies

Judeo-Christian — in the Hijaz, 218, 251

Immortality

the Koran professes, 110
grants — to Idris, Jesus, 110
ignores — to Mary, 110
(see "survival")

Impurity

Satan's deed, 130
(see "purity")

Imran

mention of name only, 60, 61
who is he?, 95
—'s wife, principal actor, 60, 61, 65, 66, 67
—'s wife's vow, 60, 65, 66, 67
—'s family, 64
—'s descendants, 60, 61, 125
identified with Joachim, Mary's father, 65
confused with Amran, Moses' father, 61

Imrans, The: Sura 3

origin, 54
chronology (Medinian), 54
structure, 57
characteristics, 54, 56, 57
Christological details, 59
polemic with the Jews, 55, 58, 59

Infancy

Mary and Jesus' — (see "apocrypha")
The Arabic — Gospel, (see "apocrypha")

Intercession

(see "prayer")

Intervention

Allah's — in choosing Mary's tutor, 175

Islam (surrender to Allah)

a) concept, definition, 172, 173, 174, 175, 177
Allah chose — a religion, 175, 178
Allah imposed —, 185
Allah is pleased with —, 185

b) Islam is "good news", 173
"guide", 174
"right path", 175
"religion of Allah", 174

c) Characteristics of —, 138, 205, 206
— is a religion flat, formalistic, 137
the God of Abraham is the God of —, 176
the faith of Abraham is the faith of —, 176
— is to belong to Moses, Jesus and Allah's messengers, 176
the five fundamental pillars of —, 137
(see "Moslem(s)")

d) Issues — does not stand for, 138, 205, 206

a) Adam's collective downfall, 138
b) Christ's divinity, 118, 138, 145, 154, 266, 277
c) Christ's divine sonship, 118, 119, 154, 265, 266
d) Christ's human paternity, 118
e) Christ's crucifixion, 107, 261
f) Man's divinization by Grace, 138, 139
g) Mary's Immaculate Conception, 135, 136, 138, 139
h) Mary's Divine Motherhood, 145, 150
i) Original Sin, 136, 138
j) Trinity in God, 78, 138, 265, 266
k) Trinitarian life, 138, 139, 149
e) Islam is silent on Mary's Assumption, 97, 106
surprisingly, — admires Mary's virginity, 84, 118, 206

Ismael

the Protoparent of all Arabs, 92, 231

Jacobites

(see "heresies")

Jesus (Issa)

name of — , 75, 81, 151
The Messiah, — , son of Mary, 75, 81, 82, 151
noble, 75
the most favored of Allah, 75, 110
one of the righteous, 75
friend of Allah, 79
a Spirit from Allah, 79
a Word from Allah, 75, 76, 82, 83, 246
Allah endowed — with charismatic powers, 75
preached from the cradle, 75, 94
a Baby, talks like an adult, 94, 96
is a mere creature, 75, 85

not son of Allah, 118, 119, 145, 149, 265, 266, 273
Servant of Allah, 94, 96, 153
Allah made — a sign to mankind, 75, 76, 85
Allah made — a mercy to mankind, 75, 86
recipient of Allah's favor, 197, 198
"Ibn Maryam", 81, 151
the *"raison d'être"* of — , 154
died? annihilated?, 106, 107, 108
not crucified, 107, 261
survives with Mary, his mother, in paradise, 107, 108

Jesus and Mary

reasons for pairing their names, 109, 110, 118, 150, 151, 154
are Allah's creatures, 107
not divinities, 266, 267
ate and drank as the messengers of the past did, 109
annihilated (?), 106, 107
both enjoy real, physical, survival in paradise, 106, 107
"in body and soul", 108

Jews

occupy a predominant portion of Sura, 3, 58
polemic with the — , 55, 58
Mohammad's charges against the — , 59
two major crimes of the — , 59
their calumny of Mary, 94, 95, 96
opposition of the Jewish clans at Medina, 55

Joachim

Mary's father, 65, 239, 241
(see "Imran")

Joseph, the Chaste

story of, 186
righteous, 184

saintly, 134

Judeo-Christians

polemic with the — , 41
(see "nasàra", "People of the Book")

Kaaba

Judeo-Christian Church of Mecca, 230
Waraka, Bishop of — , 63, 230, 231
pagan Temple in Mecca, 231

Kafirùn (infidel, unbelievers)

polemic with the — , 47, 129, 130, 267, 274
(see "associators", "hypocrites")

Koran, The

—definition, 22
copy of the "Matrix", kept in heaven, 212
Allah's words transmitted in Arabic, 212
"straight", He "downed" it to Mohammad, 212, 213, 215
   -a "guide", 174
   -a "good news", 173
   -a "right path", 175
   -a "correction" for Gospel and Torah, 174
   -as the "only infallible guide", 175
—revelation of the — , 212, 213
first hearers, readers, of the — , 34
transcription of the — , 38
linguistic perfection, 31
chronological criterion, 38
text, 38
authenticity, integrity, 32
obscurity, 32
interpretation, 32
division, 29
—the compilation of the — in use today, 30, 38

not Mohammad's own work, 37, 38
Ali's — , 30
Cairo's Official Version of the — , 30
the only scripture in present research, 28, 29, 31
—the — , code of religion flat and formalistic, 137
sources, 216, 217, 218
the — , a "creative irruption", 217
embroideries on the — , 27

Koranic

issues, 31
exegetes, 34
Mariology, 28
Message on Mary, 210
embroideries, 27

Kuwait (Persian Gulf)

Emir Abdullah of — , 22
Carmelite Mission in — , 21
acceptance of Christianity and Islam in —, 23

Lebanon

situation of — in the 30's, 19
the Cedar of — , 23
the Virgin's mute fasting in — , 204

Lot

the — fell to Zachariah to tutor Mary, 72

Marian Facts

which, 35
historic, 253
prophetic, 254
dependence on the Apocrypha, 234, 235, 251
theological value, 252
are indivisible portion of the Koranic Message, 255

Marian, Koranic Material

sources, 45

not theological, nor Mariological, 44

interpolated, 42, 44

why, 42

scanty, 43

still relevant, conspicuous, 44

and is "Word of God", 255

Haddad's criterion, 42, 49

Marian Suras

which, 40, 41

Mary

a) **name**: Maryam

Anna calls her child, — , 40, 41, 61, 67, 118

meaning of — , 67

occurrence of — in the Koran, 41, 115, 116

the only female called by her — in the Koran, 115, 116, 118

Allah ordered remember her — in the Book, 116

b) **identity**: 115

daughter of Imran (Joachim), 113

and of Anna, 65, 239

paternal home of — , 69

sister of Aaron (?), 64

mistaken for Myriam, Moses' sister, 61

Anna offered — a "free gift" (*muhàrrar*) to God, 60, 66

had — and her descendant protected from Satan, 6, 67

Allah accepted — and grew her a goodly child, 61, 67

Mary fulfills her mother's wish, 70, 71

c) **a model**: (see "mathal")

d) **a "Moslem"**: (see "Moslem")

Mary of the Koran: Book

perspective, 12

aim by Author, 9, 276, 278

call for an ecumenical entente, 24

Mary's Dignity

eminent, unparalleled, 7, 155

not absolutely, but relatively, superlative, 156

outranks all women of the universe, 7, 157

including the Household of the Prophet, 158, 159

Mary's Faith

(see "mathal")

Mary's Image

in the Islamic Tradition, 208

sweet, sympathetic, virginal, 113, 117

impact of — on Mohammad's mind, 117, 278

Mary's Obedience

unconditional, 74, 75, 85, 86, 183, 185

Mary's Position

privileged, 113

singular, 114

eminent, 119

Mary's Role

in Allah's plan, 119, 120

in an eventual dialogue, 275, 276

Mary's Sanctity

a. definition (see "holiness")

b. Allah nurtured a preferential love for Mary:

- she is His beloved , 125

- of His dearest friends, 125, 134, 184

- His favorite, 197, 198

c. Allah predestined Mary, 124, 125

chose her, 73, 125, 127, 132, 134

welcomed her to serve Him in His house, 61, 67, 126

d. Allah made her:
- righteous (siddìqat), 134, 184, 185
- goodly (sàlihat), 134
- devout (qànitat), 183, 185
- on a par with Abraham, 134

e. Mary's —
as purity, (see "purity"), 127, 132, 133
as virginity, (see "virginity"), 84, 116, 206
as religiousness, (see "mathal"), 198

Mathal (example, model)

definition, 188, 189, 190, 191, 192
dimensions of — 's meaning, 192
to the believers Allah set a — in Mary, 186
a shining —, 20
of faith, 193, 194, 195, 196
of religiosity, 198
of self-restraint, 205, 207, 208

Mecca

Birthplace of the Prophet, 173
Rabbi of —, 221, 224, 225
Synagogue of —, 224, 254
Bishop of —, 63, 230, 231, 235

Meccan

period (612-622), 40, 41, 47, 48, 49
Suras (S. 19, 21, 23, 43), 40

Mediation

Mary's, 167, 168
Mohammad's, 167

Medina

Yathrib, the City (of the Prophet), 54
hegira to —, 34, 41, 43, 45, 54, 55, 57
Christological Controversy at —, 45

rupture with the "People of the Book", at —, 171

Medinian

period (622-632), 40, 41, 47
Suras (S. 2, 3, 4, 5, 9, 33, 57, 61, 66), 41

Men

a "*step higher*" than women, 114

Mihràb (shrine, niche)

nature, 69, 70
(see "annex")

Mohammad

A) background, 33
illiterate (?), 237
baptized by Bishop Waraka, 21, 230, 231
married Bishop's niece, Khadija, 230
adhered to the Hanafite sect, 232
knew Christians and Clergy of his time, 235
recognized revelations to Abraham, Moses and Jesus, 170

B) mission, task, 120
a) in the Meccan period:
- a warner (nadhìr), 47
- a bearer of good news (bashìr), 47
- his opponents, 118, 119
b) in the Medinian period:
- a prophet (nabì), 41
- a messenger (rasùl), 41
- his opponents, 45, 47

C) genial strategy, 170
clash with the "People of the Book", 55, 118, 119
charges, 171
rupture, 172, 173
declares himself Allah's Prophet and Messenger, 172

more: the "sealing" of all the Prophets, 173
Mary's virginal character obsessed him, 117, 206
as did Allah's memory, 117
his courteous gesture while purifying the Kaaba, 231

D) unfulfilled wish of — , 181
turns affection to Fatima, a woman, 182
affiliates female believers into his household, 182
wanted Mary a perfect "Moslem", 182, 183, 184, 185, 207, 208
near end suffered change of heart toward Christians, 259, 260
died, 42, 181

Monophysites

(see "heresies"), 55, 253

Moslem (muslim)

definition, 175, 176, 178, 179, 180
meaning of — , 175, 176, 177, 178
who is the — , 175, 176
Moslems *"ante litteram"*, 169, 172, 178, 179, 180
Mohammad, the first — , 178
Mary, a — *"ante litteram"*, 183, 184, 185

Motherhood

Mary's — , real and physical, 140
virginal: *ante partum*, 141, 142
    in partu, 143
    post partum, 144
not divine, 145
stated by Mohammad since his early career, 139, 140
Mary's — of Jesus is her ultimate *"raison d'être"*, 154

Mubàhala (ordeal)

description, 45, 57

Muhàrrar (totally free)

description, 45

Musàlaha (compromise)

description, 45

Myriam

Aaron's sister, 62
confused with Maryam, the mother of Jesus, 61, 62, 63

Nasàra

Judeo-Christian sect, 41, 232, 233
Church of the — in Mecca, 221, 224, 226, 227, 230
Bishop of the — , 230, 231

Nativity

Mary's, 60, 110, 111, 238
Gospel of the — , 88, 121, 234, 243, 247

Nejràn

Delegation of, 45, 52, 59, 63

Nestorians

(see "heresies")

Noah

Allah exalted — , 60, 61, 64
chosen — , 60, 61
descendants of — , 60, 61, 64

Othman, ben Affan

destroyed current copies of Koran, 30
imposed his own, 31

Parousia

preaching of — , 226
(see "eschatological piety")

Peace

Christians and Moslems living together in, 7

Vatican II's plea for, 13
a *"way of life"*, 19

People of the Book

definition, 41, 47, 55, 56, 117, 118, 150, 170, 259, 263
polemic with, 55, 56, 170

Piety

(see "parousia")

Poles

opposite — of the Immaculate Conception Dogma, 139

Prayer

ascending, descending, 163
examples of, 164
as intercession, 165, 166
requisites, 165, 166
why to pray, 201
Allah's prayer on the Prophet, 163
Mohammad's, 165
Mary's, 199, 200, 201, 202

Priesthood

literary output on, 25
No — in Islam, Sacraments or Church, 162, 166

Prophetess

Mary, the — , sister of Aaron, 64

Prophets

stories of the, 27, 168, 236

Purity

definition, 127
correlate to "stain", "impurity", 127, 128, 129, 130
kinds of, 131, 132,
as holiness, 133, 134, 135
Mary's, 127, 131, 132, 133
(see "stain", "impurity")

Reaction

Mary's — to Gabriel, 73, 74, 83, 84

Reader

word to the, 19

Readings

seven — , dictions, of the Koran, 30

Remarks

preliminary, 25-40
dogmatic, 252
ecumenical, 255

Retreat

Mary's, into the Temple, 60, 68

Revelation

Koranic concept of, 212, 213, 215, 217
motives of, 39, 217
(see "Koran")

Righteousness

essential elements of, 185

Rosary

the Moslem, 148, 262

Rùh (Spirit)

plurality of meanings, 79
reference to God, 79
distinct from God, 79
is Gabriel, 80
confused with *rìh* (wind), 78
Allah's power, 80
reflexions of, 80
parallelisms with Sura 3, 80

Saints

cult of — in Islam, 167

Sin

Islam denies Original — , 136, 137, 138, 139

Solidarity

psychological — bet. Jesus and his mother, 96
(see "unity")

Son

Christ is not — of Allah, 145, 149, 273

Sources

Vatican II stresses return to — , 28
Jewish — for the Koran: 219
   a) patrons, 220
   b) Zakarias' opinion, 220
   c) absurdity of his opinion, 223, 225, 226
Christian — for the Koran: 228
   a) patrons, 228, 229
   b) Haddad's opinion, 229, 230, 231
   c) acceptability of his opinion, 233

Stain

definition, 127
kinds of, 127, 128, 129, 130
   - legal, ritual, 127
   - physical, physiological, 127, 128
   - religious, 128
   - moral, 127, 128, 129, 130
—s as evils, sins, 129, 130
—s nestling in the heart, 129, 130
—s, the cleansing from which belongs to Allah alone, 130, 131
(see "purity", "impurity")

Stone

Black — of the Kaaba, 231
Type of Christ, 230

Survival

of Jesus and Mary in the Islamic Paradise, 98, 99, 100-106

physical, 107, 108
in body and soul, 108, 109, 110

Syncretism

Christianity is a hybrid—in the opinion of recent Moslem authors, 111, 171

Theology

Koranic, Marian, 44

Thing

Mary is charged with a strange — , 94, 95

Things

last — , 47
(see "events")

Throes

Mary's pain from — , 143, 144

Titles

of Suras, origin, 50, 51, 57
disagreement of — with text, 51, 58

Triad

Moslem, 110, 270

Tribes

Jewish — at Medina, 58

Trinitarian

life — is unknown to Mohammad, 139, 149

Trinity

Moslem, 78, 265, 266, 267, 270
where Mohammad got it from, 268, 269, 270
why had Mohammad failed the right notion, 271, 272
Mohammad's readiness to believe in the — , if, 23, 273

Tutor

miraculous selection of Mary's — , 71, 72

Uhud

defeat at — , 58

Unity

Mary's — to Christ, 151, 152, 153
metronymic, 150

Values

basic — Christians and Moslems share together, 7, 256, 261, 262

Vatican II

declaration of — , 13
— 's plea for peace, 7, 13
for return to basics, 23
and sources, 28

Veil

Mary took a, 68
meaning of taking a, 70, 71
source and history, 207

Veneration

(see "worship")

Verdict

of the Merciful, 53, 54

Verses

Marian, how many, 44
quality, 44

Virginity

(see "Mary's sanctity")
(see "Motherhood")

Voice

mysterious, comforts Mary by the palm tree, 89, 92

source of the, 92
same, heard Hagar in the desert, 92
invites Mary to eat and drink, 89, 92, 93

Vulgate

Koran's Official Version in use today, 32

Waraka, ben Nawfal

Bishop of Mecca, 63, 117, 230, 231, 235
Khadija's uncle, 117, 230
noted erudite, 63, 117
translated the Gospel in Arabic, 117, 230

Wives (household)

of the Prophet, 115, 158, 160, 161, 162, 207
number of the, 206
jealousies, quarrels, 204
mothers of the faithful, 161
must show dignity in public, 161
be talked to from behind the curtain, 161
demand respect, civility, 162
not to be touched after death of the Prophet, 162

Women

Sura 4, the — , 115
biblical women, 115, 116
four are the — of the universe, 158
humiliating situation of pre-Islamic —, 114, 209
inferiority of — to men, 114
except for Mary, none is called by her name, 115, 116
Mohammad rehabilitated the — , 209
and made — a requisite for Islamic paradise, 206

Worries

Mohammad apologetic — , 109, 110, 115, 118

Worship

  bounds set by Allah for — , 159
  Mary's — follows her dignity, 159,
    160
  Islam underrates Mary in terms of
    worship, 159
  forms of — , 160
    - veneration, 160
    - invocation, 163
    - imitation, 168

Mary worshipped like a Moslem:
  - showing devotion, 202
  - genuflecting, 202
  - prostrating, 202, 203

Zachariah

  Mary's tutor, 61
  miraculously selected, 71
  Imran's relative, 62
  senile, 84
  reaction to Gabriel, 83, 84